THE ART OF COARSE FISHING

SPECIMEN HUNTING

THE ART OF COARSE FISHING

SPECIMEN HUNTING

Introduction by John Bailey

CollinsWillow
An Imprint of HarperCollins*Publishers*

First published in 1993 by
Collins Willow
an imprint of HarperCollins Publishers
London

Based on The Art of Fishing

A CIP catalogue record for this book is
available from the British Library

ISBN 0 00 218512 1

Printed and bound in Hong Kong

Contents

Introduction

Ever since the monks sat and fished for their Friday lunch, anglers have longed to catch specimens. However, it is only since the last war that big fish began to be specifically targeted. Better tackle, greater mobility and increased leisure time all helped the emergence of specimen hunters, but the greatest impetus of all was the work of one man, Richard Walker.

Walker gathered a group of friends around him and between them they caught more huge fish than any angler would have believed possible. Walker himself caught a record carp and went on to design big-fish rods, hooks, landing nets, bite alarms and even leger weights as well as introducing new methods and baits.

Coarse fishing would never be the same again and for many of us anglers brought up in the 1950s and '60s, Walker became our hero. We bought his books, read his articles in *Angling Times* and even wore Walker-type floppy bush hats. Many of the contributors to this book learned their fishing during this exciting period. Like Graham Marsden, Neville Fickling, Chris Yates, Gord Burton and Andy Little, I can remember when Walker was God and his friends were kings. Happily, one of those men, Peter Stone, is still angling and writing as much as ever and in this book you will find his advice on catching Cherwell chub.

Though he never neglected the basics of understanding the fish and its habits, Walker launched the first hi-tech tackle on to the angling scene. Since the 1950s, the advances that ➧

he pioneered have taken off dramatically. In this new book, you will find examples of rods, reels, rigs and baits that would have defied belief just 20 years ago. Big fish are now hunted by more anglers using more highly sophisticated methods than ever before. You will learn all about these advances in this book. In fact without them you would find fishing very much harder, for the fish have had to learn too, in response to anglers' increasing expertise, to avoid being repeatedly caught.

Specimen hunting will continue to flourish and grow because big fish are beautiful, exciting and in every way a worthwhile quarry. Tens of thousands of modern anglers are following in the footsteps of Walker in finding specimen hunting the sport's ultimate challenge. This book covers every important species, from the little dace to the mighty carp and pike and many famous waters are explored in the process. Whether you want to fish Loch Lomond, the River Wensum or Hollowell Reservoir, it will give you the information you need to get stuck into the big ones that we all so badly want to catch.

Finally, please remember that specimen fish are old fish and irreplaceable and that catching them is a privilege. It is a lesson to us all to see how men like John Wilson, Andy Little and John Watson treat every fish, big or small, with respect.

John Bailey

Guide to carp fishing

Carp are cunning, they grow big and fight furiously – it's not surprising they are so popular with anglers. But how do you catch a specimen? The successful specimen hunting family, Bryan, Jon and Stephen Culley, tells you how.

Mirrors and leathers are varieties of the common carp *(Cyprinus carpio).* The crucian carp *(Carassius carassius)* is a separate species which is related to the carp family (as are roach, bream and tench) but does not reach the same enormous size as the common carp – which can often grow in excess of 50lb (23kg). Whatever the size, carp provide excellent sport.

Where to go

The beginner should try a water with a large head of carp – where bites (or 'runs') are not too scarce. This will increase the chance of getting to grips with a fish before patience wears out. You will find that tackle dealers and anglers are only too happy to tell you about the carp waters you can fish in your area.

The more experienced angler may prefer the challenge of a water with fewer carp but of a higher average weight. These fish will be wary and more difficult to hook. If you are to get one on the bank you must be prepared to put in the hours.

Lakes are generally best for really big fish. Canals and rivers are neglected and can be worth a try; few of the carp in these waters have been caught before so they often fall to less sophisticated baits and methods.

Locating the fish

Finding the fish is the secret to catching them. Walk around the water looking for tell-tale signs. Small clusters of bubbles or dark patches of muddy water indicate feeding carp. Look out for fish capering about – leaping clear of the water, for example.

During daylight carp retreat to the cover of islands, lily beds, weedbeds and overhanging or sunken trees. A bait cast tight up to these fish-holding areas will often produce runs.

On gravel pits it is worth trying a bait along the bottom of gravel bars. You can precisely pin down the location of these by careful plumbing with a float or by casting a lead and timing the drop.

The Culleys suggest the following waters:

- **A1 Pit,** nr Newark, Nottinghamshire. A 40 acre (16ha) gravel pit. Carp to 20lb (9kg) plus. Not difficult. Day tickets on bank.
- **Angler's Paradise,** Beaworthy, Devon. Eight lakes. Largest lake 4 acres (1.6ha). Some fish over 20lb (9kg). Lakes vary in difficulty. Ring 0409-221559.
- **Broadlands Lake,** Ower, nr Romsey, Southampton, Hants. Carp to 20lb (9kg). Fairly easy. Tickets from the Fishery Manager, 0703-733167 or 0703-869881.
- **Cuttle Mill,** Wilshaw, North Warwickshire. Two waters approximately 9 acres (3.6ha). Good head of carp to 10lb (4.5kg) plus, with some over 20lb (9kg). Day tickets from site. For details, ring 0827-872253.
- **Yateley,** Sandhurst Road, Yateley, nr Camberley, Surrey. Four Lakes. 13 acre (5.3ha) North Lake has produced a 45¾lb (20.75kg) specimen. Difficult. Apply: Leisure Sport Angling 093-2864872.

◀ Many carp-holding lakes are picturesque and tranquil – until a powerful fish grabs your bait and the action starts. Carp like the cover of heavy weed so look for them by features such as lily beds and reeds.

Choosing the tackle

Before selecting your gear you should ask yourself a few questions. For instance, are you going to fish the margins or at long range, and is the water snaggy? And what size fish are you after? If in doubt, get advice from a tackle dealer or an experienced carp angler – especially one who knows the water you want to fish.

Rods You don't have to buy a special carp rod if you already have a through-action, 11 or 12ft (3.3 or 3.6m) rod with a 2lb (0.9kg) test curve. This is a good bet for most carp on most waters, especially at short to medium range. However, if you want, you can select a rod with a fast taper, tip action for fishing at longer range. Also, the further out you fish the heavier the weight needed to cast. So use a powerful rod, such as one with a 2½lb (1.1kg) test curve, when the weight is over 2oz (57g). Below that a 2lb (0.9kg) test curve rod will do and for close-in fishing with lighter weights use a rod with a 1¾lb (0.8kg) test curve.

Reels The reel should be of a sturdy, open-face design and have a spool with a line-holding capacity of at least 140m (153yd) of 8lb (3.6kg) line. It should lay the line evenly on the spool, so that a running fish is able to take line easily. A baitrunning feature is useful – it allows the fish to run without your needing to take the bail arm off.

Line Choose your line strength to suit the water – 8lb (3.6kg) is suitable for open waters but step up to 10 or 12lb (4.5 or 5.4kg) if there is heavy weed or snags.

Hooks A variety of carp hooks is available and choice is very much a personal matter. In any case hooks should be strong and sharp. Useful sizes range from 4s to 10s. Obviously, the bigger the fish, the bigger the hook.

▲ ***Effective carp baits include: dog biscuits (1) which you must soak before use or they swell inside the carp; cooked peanuts (2); flavoured boilies such as strawberry oil (3), oceanic oils (4) and tropicana oil (5); milk concentrate (6); sweetcorn (7); chick peas (8). Breadcrust (9), breadflake (10) and luncheon meat (11) can work on waters not often fished for carp.***

◀ ***Whatever their size, carp are hard fighters and good fish for getting beginners interested. This fine specimen was caught in the margins on floating breadcrust bait.***

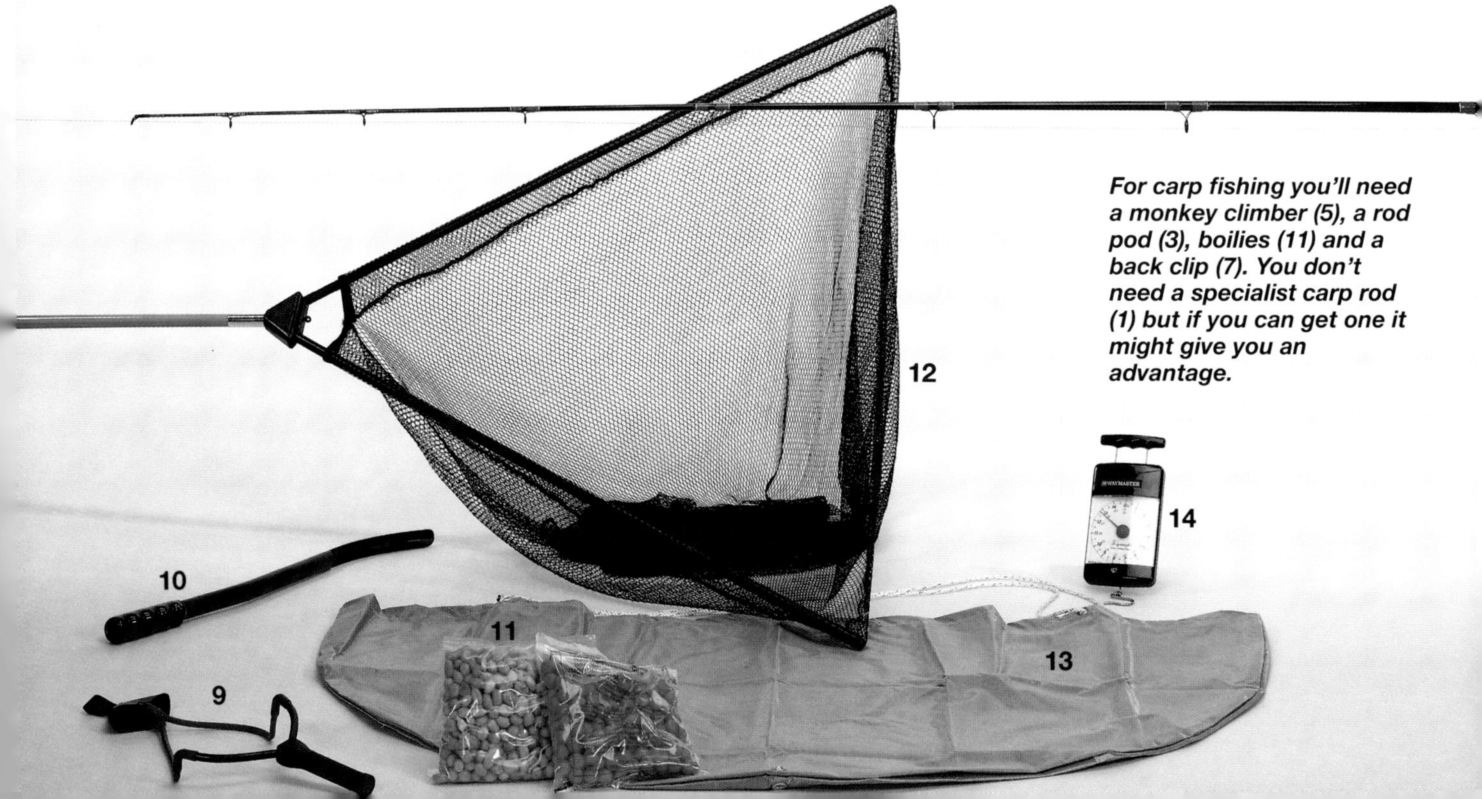

9 10 11 12 13 14

For carp fishing you'll need a monkey climber (5), a rod pod (3), boilies (11) and a back clip (7). You don't need a specialist carp rod (1) but if you can get one it might give you an advantage.

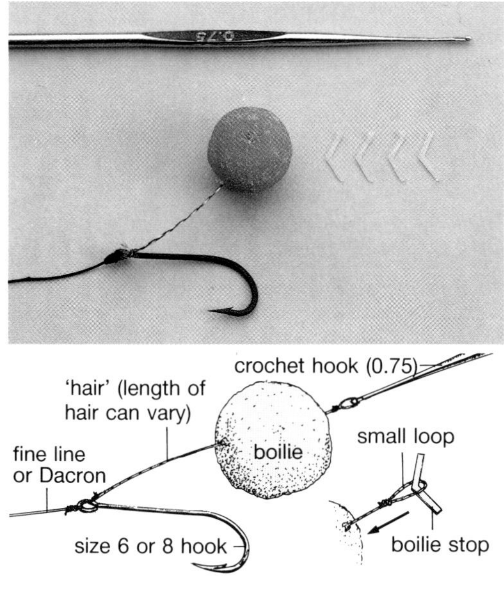

▲ To make a boilie hair rig push a size 0.75mm crochet hook through the boilie. Tie a loop in the hair and draw it through the boilie. Put a stop in the loop and pull hair to tighten stop against boilie.

Carp baits

Boilies have an advantage over other baits in that smaller fish, such as bream and tench, are less likely to take them. You can buy boilies or make them at home. The range of flavours and colours is so wide that it is impossible to say which are best. You must experiment to find out which ones the carp on your water prefer.

Other good baits include breadflake and crust, luncheon meat, lobworms and sweetcorn (although the carp may be wary of these baits on hard-fished waters).

Dog and cat biscuits are good floating baits but soak them well before use.

Bite indication

The monkey climber works on a simple principle: that of the old-fashioned dough bobbin. The 'monkey' is a plastic cylinder free to slide up and down a vertical metal needle. The top of the needle is usually enlarged to stop the monkey flying off. The line passes between the climber and the needle. On a run the monkey climbs the needle as the fish takes line. It drops if the fish runs at you. When you strike, the line is freed from the indicator. Monkeys can be fitted with glowing isotopes for night fishing, and fished together with electronic alarms.

Carp rigs

Rigs for carp divide into two categories: those for bottom-feeding fish and those for surface feeders.

Hair rigs Most carp are caught on the bottom, with the bait on the hook or on a 'hair' (a length of fine line). A hair rig is effective because it leaves the hook entirely free – so there is a much greater chance of it catching in the fish's mouth.

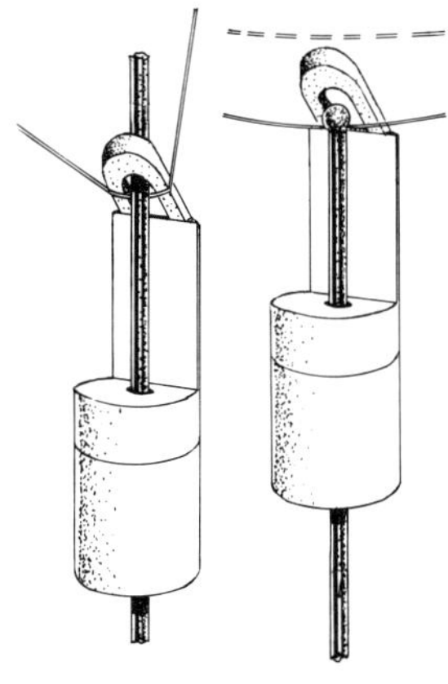

To set up your monkey climber, pass line between the loop and the needle. Leave the bail arm disengaged so that a running fish is free to take line. A run causes the monkey either to rise and hover on the needle or, if the fish runs towards you, to drop back.

▲ With a bolt rig it's important to back clip the line. This keeps tension in the line which helps set the hook. The line is wedged behind the clip (7).

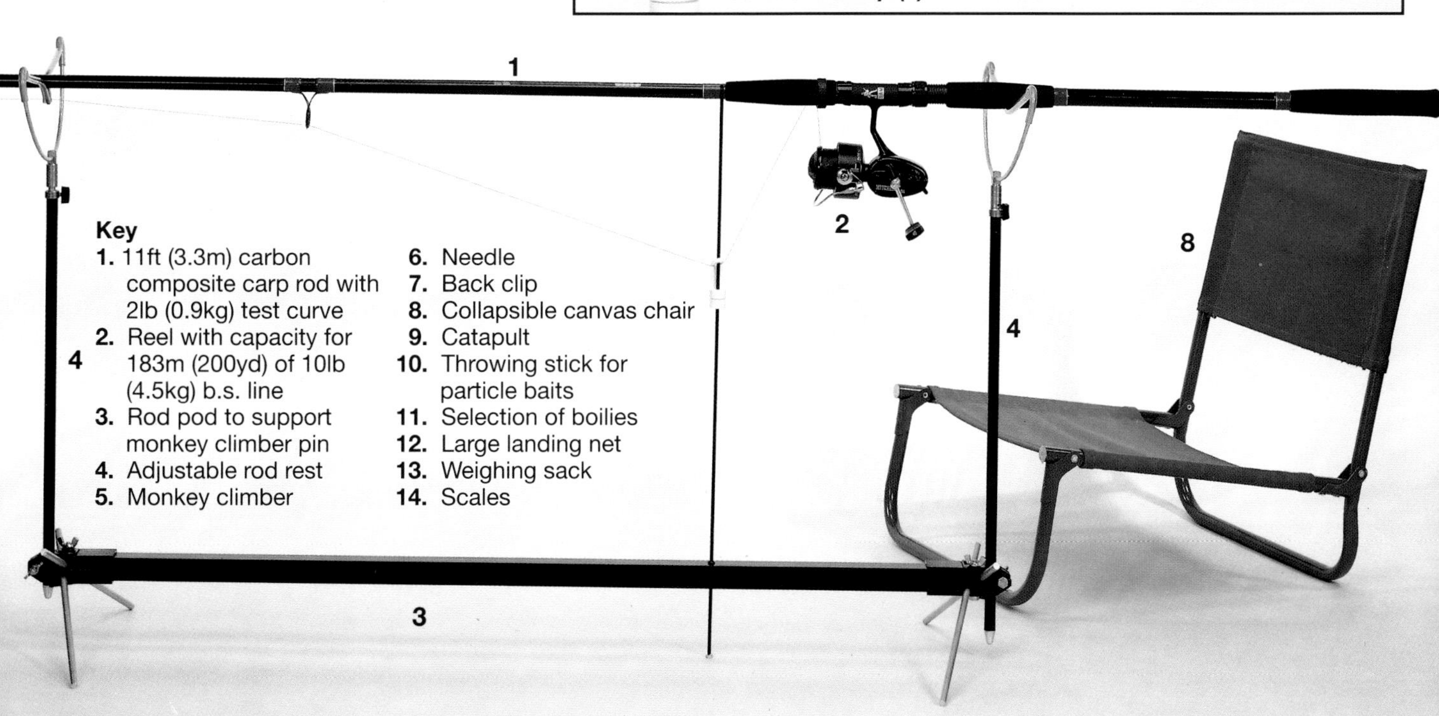

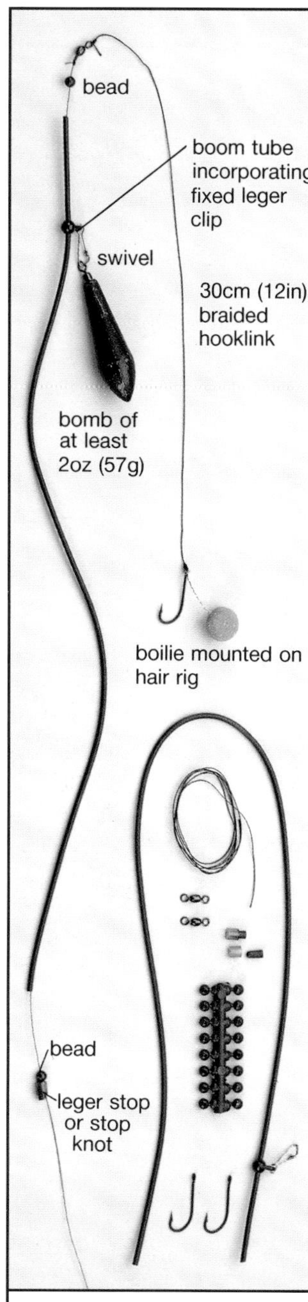

Anti-tangle rig

Anti-tangle booms let you cast long distances without the line tangling and they help to keep the line off the fish's back as it is brought in. To prevent tangles, make sure that the length of the hooklink is shorter than the length of the boom. The boom can be either stiff or flexible.

Rigs for surface feeders

The **running bomb rig** (right above) works on waters up to 1.8m (6ft) deep. The bomb anchors the rig. Use binoculars to watch the bait. A different coloured hookbait helps you to pick out your floater from the loose feed. On waters deeper than 1.8m (6ft) use the **controller rig** (right below). This acts as a casting aid rather than as a bite indicator. So, when spotting bites, watch your hookbait rather than the controller.

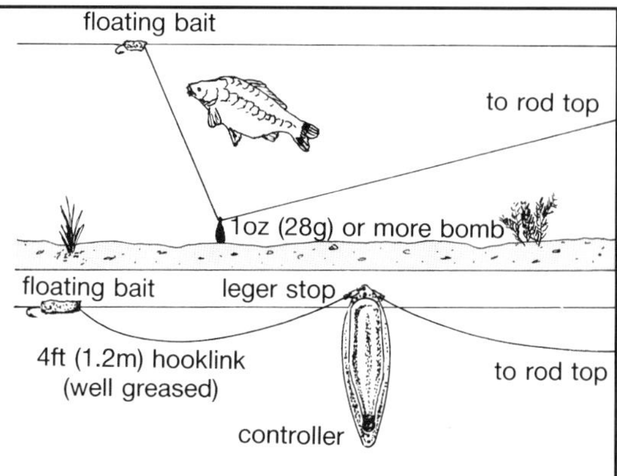

Bolt rigs A hair rig is normally used together with an anti-tangle bolt rig. Plastic booms with a fixed wire clip are available from tackle shops. A heavy bomb of about 2oz (57g) is clipped to the boom and the boom is free to slide on the line over a short distance.

It is in the nature of carp to suck in morsels of food and blow them out again before finally swallowing them. With the hair rig, a carp sucks in the bait along with the hook and as it blows it out again the hook pricks the inside of the fish's mouth, causing it to bolt. Line is pulled through the boom as the fish runs. The stop knot comes up hard against the boom and the fish hooks itself against the weight of the bomb. This self-hooking principle depends upon the hook being free from bait.

Running leger rigs Some baits have to be fished on the hook because it is not practical to put them on a hair. (For example, lobworms won't go on a hair and bread will go on but won't stay on.) These baits are normally fished on a running leger.

Surface rigs Fishing on the surface is one of the most exciting ways of taking carp and it always pays to throw in a few floating baits during the day to see if the fish are interested in feeding on the top.

Fishing for carp

Accurate casting and feeding is always important. Find a likely fish-holding spot and cast close to it. Encourage the fish to feed by using a catapult, throwing stick or bait dropper to present free offerings around your hookbait. Sometimes it is possible to intercept margin-feeding fish by dropping a bait right in the fish's path.

When carp fishing, patience is a virtue but if you are not getting results and you can see signs of fish in another part of the water, don't hang about – move on.

Caring for carp

It is important to use a large landing net with a soft mesh to protect the fish. Always unhook your carp on grass or an unhooking mat, weigh them in a net sling and then photograph them and get them back into the water as soon as possible.

► Bryan Culley's patience was rewarded with this double-figure common that fell to a simple hair rig. He took it from a river – an often neglected water for carp but worth a try if you are prepared to wait.

The supreme challenge of specimen bream

Graham Marsden has caught hundreds of big slabs over the years and rates them as the specimen hunter's supreme challenge. Double figure fish are now a realistic target if you use the right tactics, says Graham.

Fishing for big bream has a flavour all its own which compels committed anglers to try again and again for an elusive prize.

Big bream may not be the fiercest fighters but they are wily customers, rarely caught by casual anglers.

Moderately sized fish under 8lb (3.6kg) often come in large shoals and are easy enough to catch in decent numbers. On the other hand, you get bronze giants, usually in small shoals, which are often extremely difficult to catch. But if you make the effort first to find them and then to hold them in your swim, you could savour one of coarse angling's most deeply satisfying moments – as your net yields to the bulk of a dark bronze colossus.

Choosing a water

Although there are one or two rivers that hold specimen bream, stillwaters are the best places to find them. Large lakes, meres, reservoirs and gravel pits are typical bream havens.

As a rule of thumb, any water with a reputation for producing big nets of bream, made up of individual fish weighing less than 6lb (2.7kg), is very unlikely to hold bream of more than 8lb (3.6kg). So if you want to target the big fellers, look for a water known to hold specimens. If only the odd fish of size has been taken don't be put off – big bream are rarely caught by accident. Such a water may be waiting for someone like you to come along and set out your stall for the big fish.

Choosing a swim

Once you have found a water that holds specimen bream, the best way of selecting a swim is to visit the water at first light and watch for bream rolling at the surface. Take note of each rolling spot, join the dots together like a child's puzzle, and a pattern normally forms. You'll see the surface is being broken in a clear line or arc. This route reflects the path the bream are taking

▼ ***Blickling Lake, Norfolk – big bream country. Focus your efforts at least 25m (27yd) out. You don't usually catch big bream any closer to the margins.***

▶ ***A caster and redworm cocktail. Such a juicy titbit just might be the downfall of a bronze behemoth. On the other hand, maggots, bread and lobworms are all good choices of hookbait to woo the mighty specimens.***

Tip *Regular habits*

Big bream have a habit of feeding at about the same time each night (if they feel like feeding at all). Always note the time when you catch one. Eventually you can learn their feeding times and know when to be specially alert.

▶ ***Breadflake on the hook. You might need a bigger hook such as a size 10 or 12 for this bait.***

along the bottom – anywhere along this route is the swim to fish.

On some waters you hardly ever see the bream. In this case the best way to select a swim is to plumb the depths, preferably from a boat, or as best you can from the bank. Look for features that are attractive to bream – such as ledges, bars and basins – and start there. If there is one, choose a feature that lies closest to the downwind bank. The vast majority of big bream are caught at least 25m (27yd) from the margins.

In summer and early autumn big bream tend to adopt nocturnal habits, feeding some time between dusk and dawn. From late autumn onwards they begin to feed more during daylight hours. Early morning to around mid day is usually the most productive period at this time of the year.

Baits and prebaiting

The most successful baits for big bream are maggots, casters, lobworms, redworms, bread and sweetcorn – but not necessarily in that order since bream in different waters have different preferences.

Fixed paternoster rig for specimen bream

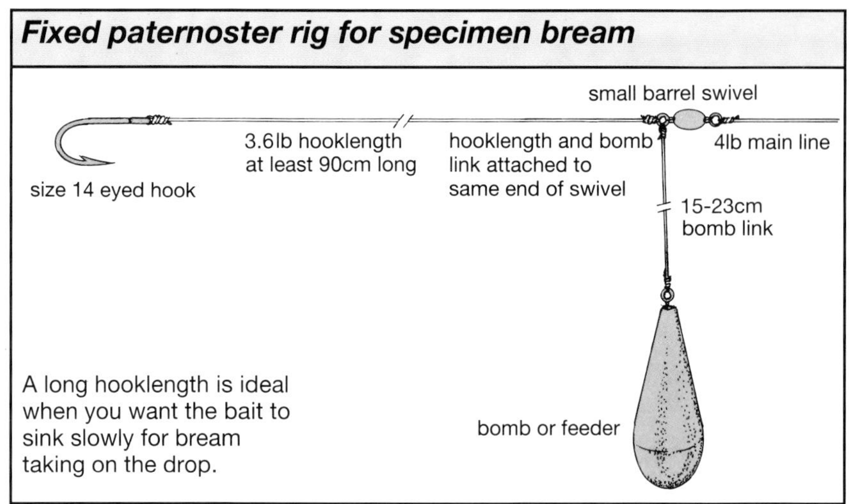

A long hooklength is ideal when you want the bait to sink slowly for bream taking on the drop.

Tip ***Brief nosebag***

When you catch a bream, get your bait back into the swim as quickly as you can for more of the same. Bream enter a swim, feed for a short spell and then move out pretty fast.

Before you wet a line, bait your swim with hookbait samples for several days or for as long before as you can manage. Two baits is the norm – a holding bait and the main hookbait. For instance, a bed of casters may act as the holding bait, and a handful or two of maggots as the main hookbait. Other combinations include: sweetcorn/lob-

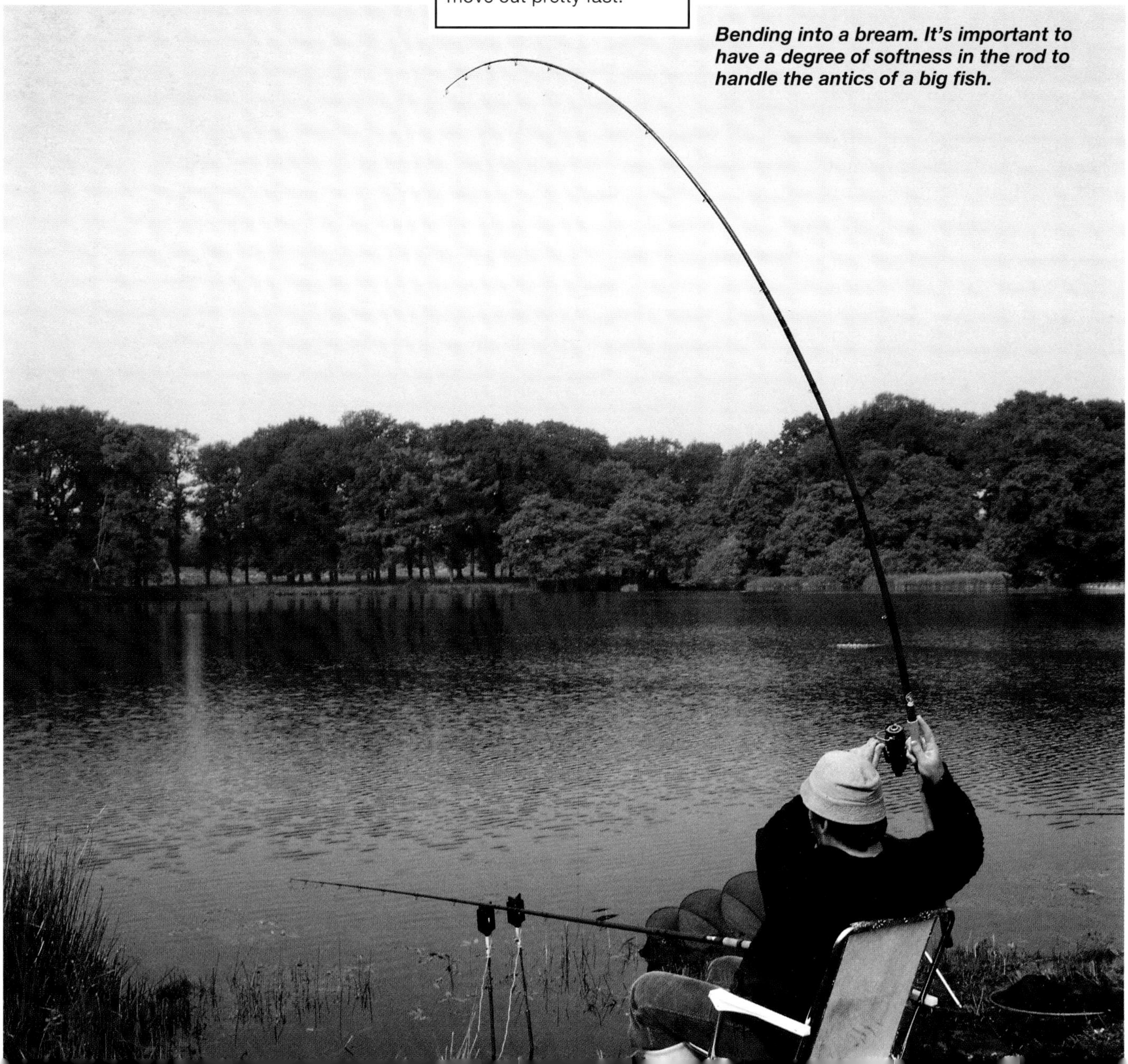

Bending into a bream. It's important to have a degree of softness in the rod to handle the antics of a big fish.

worm; groundbait/bread; squatts/maggots (or casters); casters/redworm. Quite a few permutations of these baits are worth a try. Many anglers often add another holding bait to the main one. Hempseed, rice and stewed wheat are the most popular.

It's difficult to judge how much bait to put in when prebaiting, since this varies from one water to another. A pint of maggots, two tins of corn, 3-4lb (1.4-1.8kg) of dry weight groundbait, and similar amounts with other baits, should be regarded as about the minimum. The maximum is about twice as much. These amounts serve as a rough guideline until you learn from experience what is the right amount for your water.

Try to prebait at the same time each day, preferably at the time you intend to introduce bait on the night you fish. Place the bait in exactly the same spot each time.

Tackle and technique

Rods are largely a matter of personal preference. However, for big bream it's a good idea to combine stiffness in the rod with a supple tip. The stiffness enables you to cast accurately at a distance and gives you the power to pick up a long line on the strike. The supple tip is the shock absorber you need to play big fish on light line, and gives a safety margin on the strike.

Graham Marsden favours a 12ft (3.6m) rod with a 1.25lb (0.57kg) test curve. It has a supple action for the top third, while the rest is fairly stiff – a fair choice for the job.

Fill a fixed spool reel with 4lb (1.8kg) line

▲ Twilight in puce – two rods, looking like lightweight machine guns waiting to ambush an enemy patrol boat, are primed for evening bream action on a Cheshire mere.

▼ The Elder Statesman of fish – a big bream with broad shoulders and Winston Churchill expression. Many anglers consider specimen bream to be the ultimate target.

Super slab

Any bream over 8lb (3.6kg) is a specimen. But the record stands at 16lb 9oz (7.29kg), for a fish taken from a gravel pit in southern England.

Greenhouse bream – bigger fish

According to Graham Marsden, the phenomenal increase in the size of bream in recent years is largely due to a succession of mild winters which have provided the right conditions for bream to feed for more months of the year, and for their food sources to multiply. With more food, who knows how big a bream may grow?

► ***A mature gravel pit in full summer splendour. At this time of the year night fishing is generally more productive. It helps to get an idea of the lake's layout in daylight.***

and use hooklengths of 3½lb (1.6kg) when fishing open water (almost always the case for big bream).

A 14 is a good hook size when using maggot, caster and redworm. But be prepared to go smaller when the bream are being fussy. A size 12 upwards is better for bread, sweetcorn and lobworm.

A fixed paternoster rig serves well as a big bream rig. You can attach a swimfeeder in place of a bomb.

You don't want to miss a bite, so set up some audible and visual bite indications. Try a bite alarm at the front of your rod or rods and any type of bobbin indicator which hangs on a loop of line between the butt ring and the reel. Don't use a monkey climber as it creates too much friction, making a wary bream drop the bait.

Big bream bites tend to lift the bobbin steadily and you should strike after it moves 13-15cm (5-6in). If you use a bolt rig or a short hooklength you can expect drop back bites.

Keep your landing net, bait and torch within easy reach and have a keepsack ready in case you wish to hold on to a fish for photographing in the daylight.

Plan to arrive at the water at least an hour before darkness so that you have plenty of time to bait up, tackle up and settle in. Make sure you cast to the swim several times before it gets dark, so you get a feel for it. Take note of tall trees, telegraph poles or similar objects on the far bank. Their silhouettes can be very useful in giving you something to aim for when trying to cast accurately in the dark.

◄ ***The author with an 11½lb (5.2kg) bream captured from a Cheshire mere. You have to put in some preparation and thought if you want the thrill of this stamp of fish.***

Gravel pit pike with Neville Fickling

Gravel pits are great places to get to grips with big pike. Late in the year, Neville Fickling showed how he does it on the syndicate pits he runs.

The two 12-year-old gravel pits run by a syndicate are right next to each other in the Nottinghamshire countryside. One is for carp and the other for pike. Both are typical deep, clear pits, except that fewer anglers fish them. This doesn't mean that they see less angling hours – syndicate anglers tend to be a bit fanatical.

8:30AM Carp pit

Neville decided to start on the carp pit – an odd decision on the face of it, but he'd been planning this expedition for days and his reasoning was faultless. Both pits contained pike, though there had been a steady transfer from one water to the other since the syndicate had taken over.

There may have been fewer pike in the water Neville had chosen, but no-one fished for them – after all, there was a specimen pike water just a cast away. With the lack of angling pressure, the fish ought to be less wary. On top of that, Neville had pre-baited a swim with a load of old mackerel and herring bits. The plan wasn't looking so far-fetched, after all.

The pit consists of two arms, with a thin neck joining them. This is further narrowed by two gravel bars. Any fish moving from

▶ One of Britain's best known specimen hunters, Neville Fickling has held the British record for both zander and pike and is secretary of the Pike Anglers Club. He runs four syndicate fisheries (where anglers club together to gain the exclusive rights to a water) for pike and carp.

▼ Neville checks for a run after the line had fallen, or been pulled, out of the bait clip. You can sometimes provoke a lazy pike into attack by taking the bait away – making it think it's losing an easy meal.

Freeze 'em, choose 'em, use 'em

◀ *A selection of deadbaits ready for use when the pike are being choosy. Here Neville has a rudd, two smelts and two herrings. He keeps them cold at the bankside with a frozen cool pack and an insulated box.*

▶ *This defrosted smelt is correctly hooked up and ready for casting. A small fish, it has become a very popular pike bait and is one of Neville's favourites. He has used it with great success over the years.*

one arm to the other would have to pass through this area. It was here that Neville had pre-baited, and where he cast his hook-baits – a float-legered mackerel and a float-paternostered smelt.

He used two 12ft (3.7m) pike rods with a test curve of 3lb (1.4kg). You need a hefty rod to cast half a mackerel 60m (66yd) and to handle big fish. The margins were still weedy after the summer so Neville's reels held 15lb (6.8kg) line. Bite detection was from two butt-end electronic indicators.

9:30AM Furious inaction

"I'd have thought we'd have had a run by now." The remark of a seasoned specimen hunter, that. Neville poured some coffee from his thermos, settled down in the boot of his hatchback and looked at his rods as if to suggest he was disappointed with their performance. The rods did not react.

A hatchback for shelter was a real boon on a day when the sun took one look at the frost on the ground and retreated behind a cover of thick mist for the rest of the day. The wind wasn't as retiring, however, and gusted icily round the corners of the car, blowing away the mist from time to time to reveal the thick grey clouds skulking above.

Tip Double treble trouble

You often need to change traces down at the water. Something like this wraparound hook-holder with its protective sleeve is very useful for keeping your spares tidy, with the trebles safely out of the way.

Pike from mature gravel pits

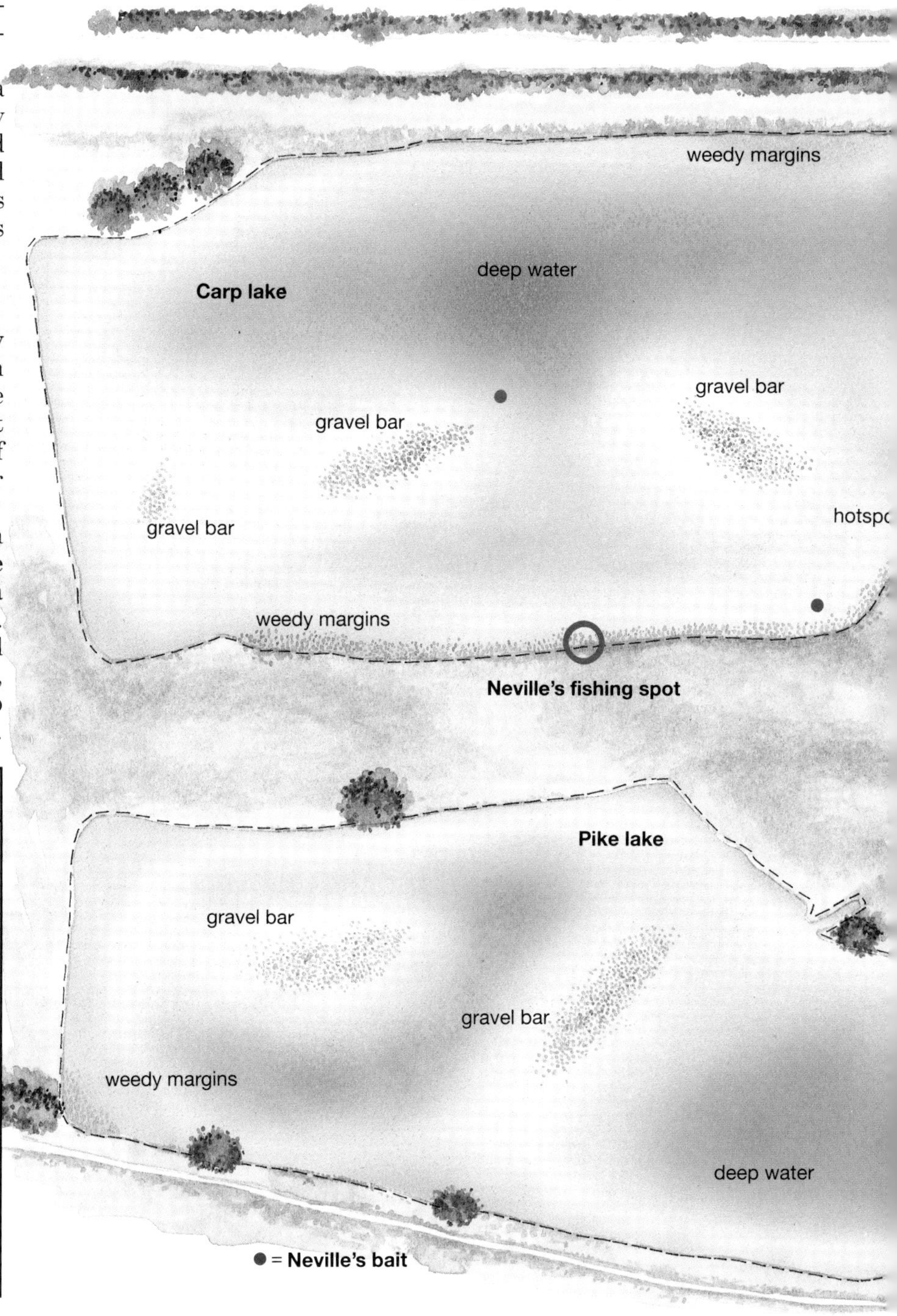

weedy margins
Carp lake
deep water
gravel bar
gravel bar
gravel bar
hotspc
weedy margins
Neville's fishing spot
Pike lake
gravel bar
gravel bar
weedy margins
deep water
● = Neville's bait

A nice enough day for penguins, but what about pike?

Sitting some distance away from the rods is good for two reasons. There's no point clumping around on the bank after you've cast out the baits, especially if you're fishing the margins. It also allows the right amount of time between registering a bite and striking. For Neville, the timing is right when he walks to the rod, winds down and strikes. Not that there was much of that going on this particular morning.

10:00AM Whose idea was it?

"Well, it doesn't look as though my infallible plan to catch us a pike is going to work after all," said a disconsolate Neville. "I'll have to try the other pit, but I don't think that'll work if this one hasn't." Ah well, no plan is absolutely foolproof – pike are too unpredictable.

▲ What's going on out there? Neville tries to will the pike into feeding during the long blank period after he moved to the second pit. Complaining a fish on to the hook is a well-tested and often used technique.

"Try to work to some sort of pattern with your baits. Don't just cover a lot of ground – look for an obvious feature."

gravel bar

weedy margins

deep water

weedy margins

pre-baited area

gravel bar

gravel bar

weedy margins

Neville's fishing spot

Pike logic

There will be days when the conditions seem to be perfect, your baits are in the right place, and yet the pike resolutely fail to bite. On other days when everything's wrong, they can still be queueing up to get at your bait.

There are many factors which determine how a venue fishes on any one day. Some are to do with the weather, the colour of the water and so on. However, other factors are unique to predators.

A healthy pike eats three times its weight every year. So a 20lb (9.1kg) specimen eats 120 fish of ½lb (220g) in a year. Eating one of these per day leaves 245 days when the pike won't feed. So for a venue with only a few fish, chances will be limited. In well stocked waters, there are always some pike feeding.

In any case, you can usually tempt a pike that's not very hungry by offering it an easy meal. On some days all the pike may happen to be hungry at once – making for a day you won't quickly forget.

Once set up on the pike pit, Neville pointed out the obvious features. It was another deep pit with weedy margins, with the remains of the summer rushes in the shallows. There were several features you couldn't see, in the form of gravel bars making obvious drop-offs for patrolling pike. Neville knew where these were from long experience of this pit.

There were several noted catching areas and Neville set up at the number two hotspot because the number one area had had too much fishing pressure recently, making the pike much more wary of feeding there. With a float-legered half mackerel in the weedy/reedy margins, it was back to the car boot to avoid bankside noise. The other bait – a rudd deadbait suspended from Neville's own tangle-free invention, the Pikesafe paternoster boom – was 60m (66yd) out over a gravel bar.

11:30AM Thumb twiddling

The change of venue did not bring the pike crawling up the bank, much as Neville had gloomily supposed. Ah well, it's been a good day to look at the *principles* of gravel pit piking, if not the fish themselves. The wind howled over the bleak landscape and Neville shivered. Even a cup of spectacularly strong coffee couldn't dispel the gathering pessimism.

11:45AM Slack time

Who was being pessimistic? Neville stood up rather suddenly, though there was no sound from his bite indicator. A glance at the line showed the reason. Fishermen have always been able to spot bites – long before the shriek of a buzzer was even dreamed of – and Neville had just spotted one. The line had gone slack – indicating a pike bringing the bait towards the bank. The float hadn't darted off, however, so Neville began to play with the bait, trying to tease the fish into a full-blooded take.

You can't wait too long for pike to make up their minds. When a pike doesn't move off with the bait but swallows it instead, you might not get all the signs of a typical bite. If you sit and wait for a run to develop, there's a good chance your trebles will end up at the back of it's throat, or worse – in its gut. Fish don't deserve to die like that.

Neville finally provoked some sort of reaction from the pike, so he struck. For a second there was a deep curve in the rod and then it sprung straight. After a morning without a run, it was disappointing to say the least. Neville wound in the deadbait to see the damage. Sure enough, there were deep tooth marks scoring the sides of the rudd. "Most likely a jack which didn't really feel like it," said an unhappy Neville, "but we might as well make sure." He cast out a smaller bait to the same spot, in case the pike wanted a snack rather than a full meal.

Gravel pit pike rigs

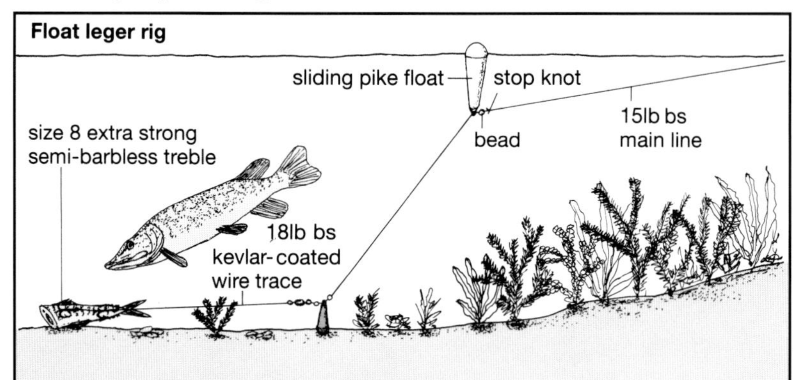

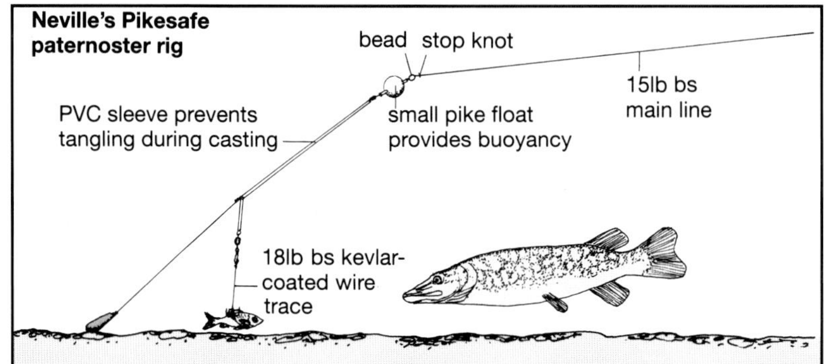

Neville uses more than two rigs for pike, but these two are particularly effective for gravel pits.
The float leger keeps the line above any weeds which would hamper the retrieve.
The Pikesafe paternoster rig helps prevent tangles on casting and keeps the bait off the bottom (left).

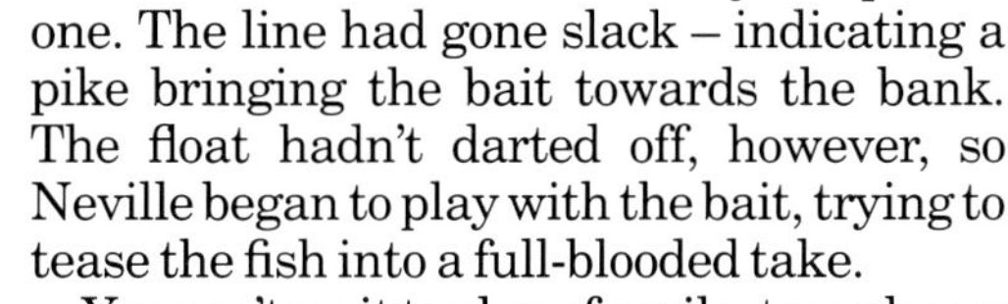

► ***One of the hazards of fishing the margins – weed. Still, it's put the biggest bend of the day so far in Neville's rod. His hope was that it was not the only bend of the day.***

The pits

Neville recommends these pits close to the syndicate waters.

- **A1 Pits,** near Newark – day tickets available on the bank.
- **Leisure Sport,** by North Hykeham near Lincoln – permits available.
- **Manor Farm,** by North Muskham near Newark – day ticket.
- **Richmond Lake,** near Lincoln – day ticket.
- **Winthorpe Lake,** near Newark – Sheffield and District AA controlled.

▲ *The pike Neville had waited for all day struggles at the surface, trying to dive for the shelter of the weeds in the margins.*

12:05PM Splashdown

The new bait landed in the water, right by the place the last one had been attacked. Neville tightened the line and set up the indicator. Still looking glum, he walked back to the car boot and was about to speak when the buzzer let rip. A smile crossed his face. There was no messing this time as he struck, and the arc of the rod seemed to suggest that this was no jack.

The fish set off on a run, and Neville gave it line, backwinding. At a water like this, with heavily weeded margins, the trick is to tire them out in deep water, where there are no snags, and then hurry them through the weeds. The pike ran again, but it wasn't going to have much joy against 15lb (6.8kg) line. The important thing is always landing the fish – losing one might leave it trailing trebles and trace around, which could be fatal.

Neville manoeuvred the pike to the surface in the shallows and it looked to be all

▲ *A large landing net is essential when fishing for any species which can grow big. Pike not only grow to heavy weights but can be very long, so don't stint on size.*

► *For an expert, unhooking a 15lb (6.8kg) pike is easy, and is most quickly done standing up. If you're not that proficient, lay the fish down on an unhooking mat and kneel over it to do the job safely.*

over. The pike had other ideas however, and it dived as soon as it saw the weeds. Neville applied as much pressure as he dared at such close range and got it back to the surface again. That didn't appeal to the pike and once more it made for the weeds. Once more it was turned away as it attempted to reach safety, and this time on the surface it looked tired. Tired, but not defeated as with a flick of the tail, it dived one last time. At this stage, Neville was not going to let this one get away, and he steered the fish towards ever shallower water.

After the struggles had subsided the pike surrendered to the wide arms of the 1.1m (42in) landing net. A 90cm (36in) net will do at a pinch, especially on waters where there aren't any big specimens, but Neville recommmends you get the bigger size if you're serious about pike.

12:13PM Unhooking

Neville estimated a 14-15 pounder (6.4-6.8kg) as he was unhooking it. The priority was to remove the hooks from the fish and put it back in the water as quickly as possible. The experienced hands of the big pike hunter had the trebles free in seconds, without even pausing to put it down. The scales were already set up and the fish weighed in at 15lb (6.8kg) exactly. Almost before the pike knew it had been landed it was back in the water and finning its way into the depths.

A new bait was hooked up and cast to the same area the fish had come from. Pike are sometimes found in small groups and recasting to the area which has just produced a fish can often bring more of the same. This time however, it was not to be and there was no more action. At 2.00pm Neville wound in and grinned. "Well, I reckon we've done it then." Even the wind howled its approval – time to get back into the warm.

▲ A perfect gravel pit pike which Neville is keeping very calm. The more gently you handle them, the less they struggle.

▼ Back into the cold winter waters of the pit with this pike. You should always return fish carefully – hold them until they swim off.

Tactics for barbel

The barbel is often regarded with something approaching awe – as a tremendous fighter caught by the lucky few. But catching one may be easier than you think. Martin Hooper tells you how.

▼ *Chris Yates plays a big barbel among the thistle-down. A centrepin reel is favoured by many anglers because it enables them to give line immediately.*

To catch barbel you have to be familiar with their nature and feeding habits. They are a specialized fish – streamlined and with an underslung mouth. The torpedo-shaped body enables them to swim with ease in the fastest currents. The four mouth barbels on the upper jaw – two at the leading edge and two at the trailing edge – are used to detect food lodged among stones and gravel on the river bed. It makes sense, then, to fish for them on the bottom of the river.

Feeding the swim

It may sound obvious but you can only catch barbel if they are in the swim. It is no use fishing blindly in the hope that one may eventually turn up – you might have to wait forever! By feeding a swim you greatly increase the chances of an encounter.

Shallow clear rivers make it easier to spot your quarry but you can still use the same tactics on deep, coloured waters.

To get the the fish interested, feed free offerings within a tight area on to the bed of the river.

The simplest way – if the flow and depth are not too great – is to throw in a few samples. If the flow is such that the bait is washed out of the swim before it reaches the bottom, it's best to try a baitdropper or swimfeeder.

Load the dropper with samples of the hookbait and swing it out into the feed area. When it reaches the bottom a plunger releases the bait. Droppers have a limitation, though. If you try to cast too far they have a nasty habit of opening in mid-air –

◀ *The business end of an eight-pounder (3.6kg). The fish's sensitive barbels are used to detect particles of food.*

dispersing both the loosefeed and the fish. This is the time you should start using a swimfeeder.

By baiting regularly on each visit to a water, you can 'brainwash' barbel so their appetites are tuned into your attractor. Hempseed is one of the cheapest and most effective. Liberally laced with a few choice hookbaits – such as sweetcorn or luncheon meat – it forms an enticing patch on the river bed. If there are any barbel around in feeding mood then it won't be long before they move into your swim.

If the stretch you have chosen sees a lot of a certain bait, then the barbel become accustomed to eating it. If not, then prebaiting is essential. It can take a considerable time to introduce the fish to a new bait.

The hardware

Barbel are one of the most fickle of biters and the most powerful of fighters. So you need to get your tackle right.

A rod of around 1¼lb (0.56kg) TC with a through-action is fine. There's no need to break the bank – any mass-produced rod will do, provided it meets the basic requirements.

The reel A barbel specialist would probably choose a centrepin reel. This type enables you to respond immediately to the demands of an accelerating fish. Giving line with a fixed-spool reel is done through the gears and is therefore less direct – you have to anticipate what a barbel is going to do next, and that isn't easy!

Line of around 6lb (2.7kg) b.s. is about right. Use forged heavy wire hooks.

▲ Where the current is strong a baitdropper like this is the answer. It is ideal for introducing samples of your hookbait directly on to the river bed – where the barbel are!

To complete the set-up you need a big landing net. One of about 1m (3ft) across with big mesh – so that it doesn't get caught by the current – is ideal.

End rigs and tactics

There are all kinds of leger rigs but one of the most versatile is a three-in-one rig which incorporates sliding stops.

With the stops pushed well up the line it's a free running rig; hard against the boom it becomes a bolt rig; just pushed away from the boom it is a variable-length confidence rig. Within a matter of seconds you can change the rig to suit the mood the barbel are in on the day – giving you a much

Tip The edge

On heavily fished stretches, prebaiting with a less common bait can often give you the edge – helping you to catch more and bigger barbel.

The lazy man's rig

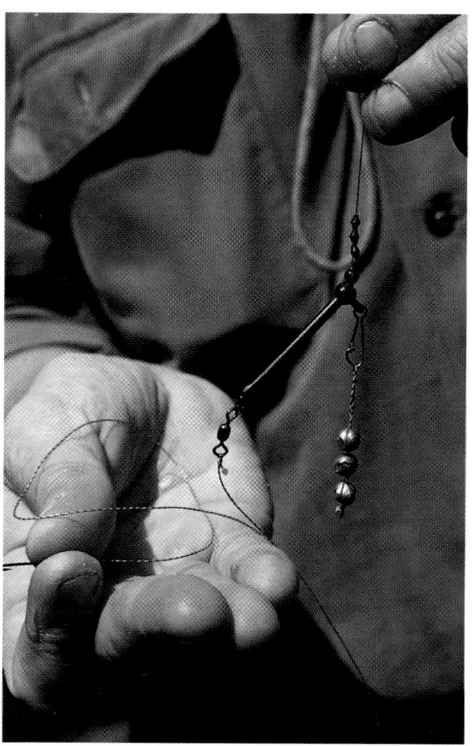

Martin says: "I use a somewhat different end rig from other anglers I have met – the 'lazy man's rig'. At one time if I wanted to change tactics from, say, link leger to a bolt rig, it meant tackling up again. But this rig is three rigs in one."

To convert the free-running rig to a bolt rig replace the swan shot by a 2oz (56g) lead and push down the stops on to the boom. The confidence rig is just the same, but the stops are pushed between 10cm and 60cm (4in-2ft) away from the boom.

Martin recommends a size 8 hook for sweetcorn. The device for putting the leger stops on the line is shown (right).

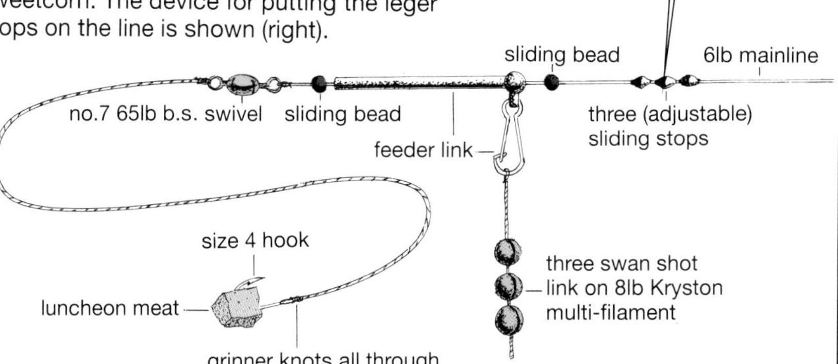

Hooking luncheon meat

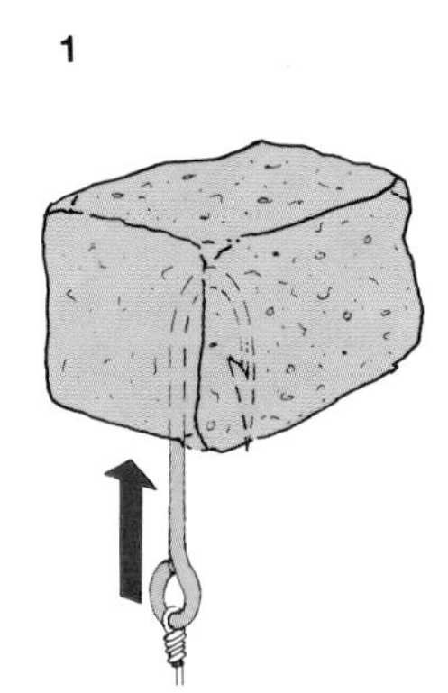

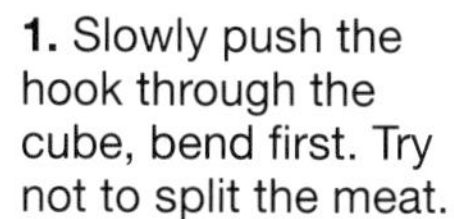

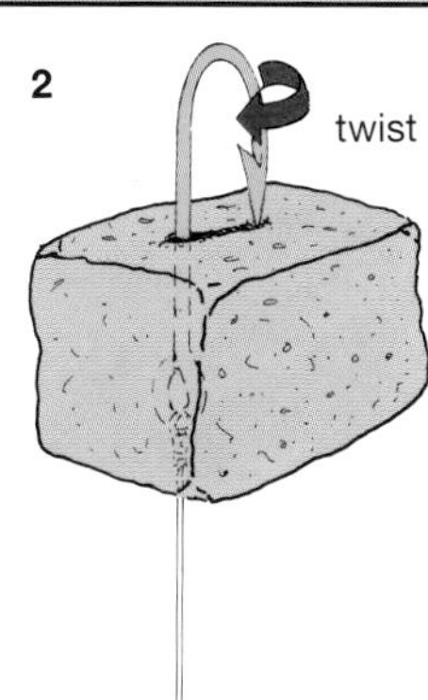

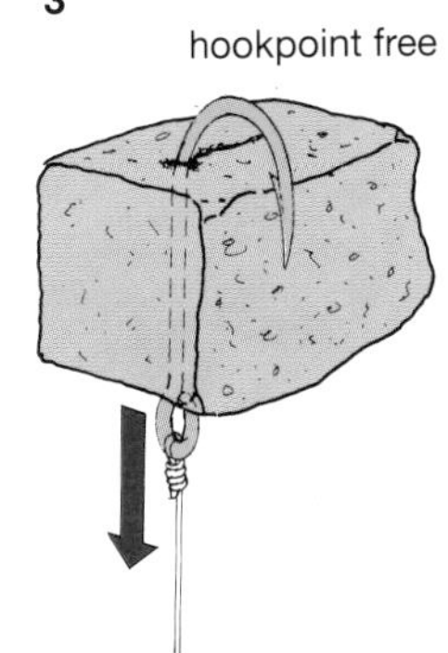

1. Slowly push the hook through the cube, bend first. Try not to split the meat.

2. When the point is clear, twist the shank of the hook through 90°.

3. Some anglers bury the point in the meat. Martin prefers to leave it free.

Tip A happy ending

Your end tackle is extremely important. Check your hook each time before you cast out. If there is any sign of damage then replace it. Hooklengths should be checked and dealt with just as ruthlessly. It's a horrible feeling when a fish is lost – even more so if the reason is through neglect.

greater chance of hitting bites.

A free running rig is the commonest choice when the barbel are their usual shy selves and you are fishing with one rod.

It's essential to hold the rod, feeling for bites with the line held between your finger and thumb. Bites are rarely savage, rod-wrenching affairs. This is particularly so with larger fish and on heavily fished waters. The bites are often tiny plucks – more akin to dace bites than anything else.

The bolt rig comes into play when fishing with two rods. Obviously, quick biting barbel are likely to be missed if you are trying to watch the ends of two rods at the same time. What's needed is a method where the fish can take care of hooking itself. This is what a bolt rig does.

The bait is fished on a hair rig. When a fish picks it up it does one of two things. It either moves on to take the next piece of food, pricks itself then panics and bolts (hence the name of the rig) and, by doing so, hooks itself. Or it realizes its mistake and attempts to eject the bait – with the same result. This usually produces a fairly posi-

◄*A simple, sturdy free-running centrepin such as this is ideal. Unlike fixed-spool reels, centrepins have no gears – making the contact between angler and fighting fish more direct.*

▼*Martin Hooper stalking barbel on the Dorset Stour. Fish spotting in clear waters is made much simpler if you wear a pair of polarizing glasses and a hat to shade your eyes. It is easier to catch a barbel if you can see where it is.*

tive indication and gives you a chance to pull the hook home.

The confidence rig works on much the same principle as the bolt rig. The difference is that you should leave slack line to allow the fish to move away with the bait until it suddenly hits the stop. As its name suggests, this rig works best when the fish are feeding without a sense of caution. In clear water this is indicated by fish moving all over the swim trying to get as much food as possible before the others get it all. In coloured water if a lot of line bites are occurring without any fish being hooked, the chances are that they are feeding confidently too.

The advantage of this rig is that by the time a fish feels the hook it probably has it well inside its mouth. There is little chance of it ejecting the bait. With this method you should make no attempt to strike – if you do the likelihood of foul hooking is very high.

Picking swims

The more time you spend on the bank looking for fish, learning their habits, feeding patterns and preferred swims in times of low waters through to flood conditions, the greater are your chances of hooking up with a really big barbel. This is a much better general approach than feeding what merely looks like a good swim. If it looks good it was probably fished yesterday and may well be fished again tomorrow. The fish will be hard to catch – if they are there at all.

The farther you get from the car park, and all the other anglers, the better are your prospects of a good day's fishing – and possibly of connecting with that elusive double-figure specimen.

Tip Be prepared

When touch-legering a rod rest should be used only for the purpose its name suggests – to rest the rod on while it is not in use.

Often barbel bites are extremely fast and shy. The angler who puts the rod on a rest misses nearly every bite before he has even cleared the rod rest.

Always hold on to the rod and be ready at any moment to respond to the slightest twitch.

► An angler plays a barbel on the Royalty fishery on the Hampshire Avon. Barbel exhaust themselves during a fight. Return them to the water as soon as they have recovered.

▼ John Watson cradles a big Wensum barbel. With its bronze, streamlined body and large fins it is easy to see why the barbel is such a powerful and handsome adversary.

Andy Little goes for winter carp

On a bitterly cold day carp expert Andy Little tackles Rocla Lake in Buckinghamshire. Twenty years ago anglers believed carp didn't feed in the winter – could Andy beat the elements and tempt them to bite?

It is common knowledge among anglers that carp fishermen are slightly obsessed. While most of nearby Milton Keynes sleeps through a bitterly cold late November dawn, Andy Little is sitting happily by a former gravel pit.

Today he is ignoring his own frequently repeated advice – in the winter carp are reluctant feeders so stick to the waters you know. The plummeting winter temperatures had halted carp fishing completely at his normal venues, so Andy looked for a change of water.

He chose Rocla Lake at Linear Fisheries, Linford, Buckinghamshire – not much more than a decent cast away from Milton Keynes and a venue known for its hungry winter carp.

► Andy Little is one of those anglers who have brought about the current popularity of carp fishing. He is a well known angling writer and always ready to try new ideas. Andy has caught more 30lb (13.6kg) carp in England than any other angler.

6:50AM *It's cold and dark*

As we walk down to the bank a small island is dimly visible in the pre-dawn light. Andy likes the look of it: "There will be a carp or two round there," he judges. But he had been advised to fish a bit further on, at a swim which had been producing some good

▼ Setting up before sunrise on a freezing morning... Andy arrived with rods and rigs ready prepared. It saves valuable fishing time and he prefers to tie knots in front of the fire at home rather than on a cold bank.

What to fish for in Rocla Lake

Rocla, a large lake of around 35 acres, is very well stocked. Over 2500 carp have been introduced since 1986. Roach, bream, perch, tench and pike over 30lb (13.6kg) can also be caught at the gravel pit. It is around 8ft (2.4m) deep and prolific in the summer. In recent years specimen fish included bream to nearly 8lb (3.6kg), tench to 6¾lb (3.1kg), roach to 2¼lb (1.2kg) and carp to 18lb (8.1kg).

◄Andy reels in to try a change of bait. This swim has been producing carp with some consistency – until today. He is fishing 75yd (68m) out from the bank.

carp regularly – despite the nip in the air.

Setting up, Andy gives some advice that ought to be heeded by beginners and experienced anglers alike: "Go home if the weather's horrible! Some anglers lose their instinct for self-preservation. They will be cold, luckless and have a bad time, and then go off fishing for weeks." We have an idea he is going to ignore this advice too – it certainly seems a morning well up on any scale of uncomfortableness. Andy, however, doesn't seem to notice the cold.

Andy Little fishes Rocla Lake

"Carp don't like any dramatic temperature variations... but I've not yet found any conditions where they will not feed at all."

Fishery facts

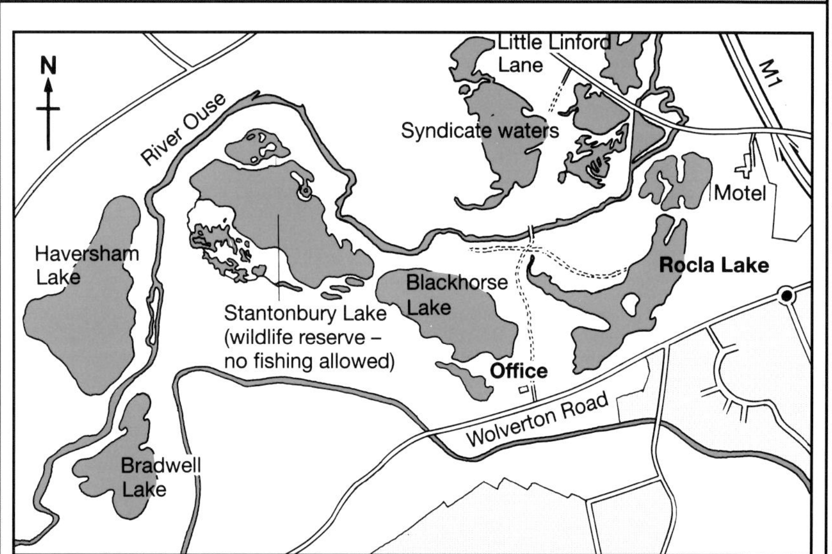

Linear Fisheries, Linford, has 250 acres of well stocked matured gravel pits and three miles of bank on the River Ouse. There are 10 lakes including syndicate waters. Day tickets £3.00 per rod. Day Season £30.00. Ask for jnr, OAP & disabled rates.

For tickets write to Len Gurd, The Secretary, 2 Northcroft, Shenley Lodge, Milton Keynes, Bucks. MK5 7BE. Telephone (0908) 607577.

How to get there

● **By car** From junction 14 on the M1, turn on to the A509 towards Newport Pagnell. At the first roundabout turn left (A422) then right at the next roundabout. At the T-junction turn left, under the motorway, and keep straight on over a roundabout. You will see Rocla lake on the right. The entrance is on the right after the lake.

● **By train** Services stop at Wolverton Station – on Inter-City services use Milton Keynes Station.

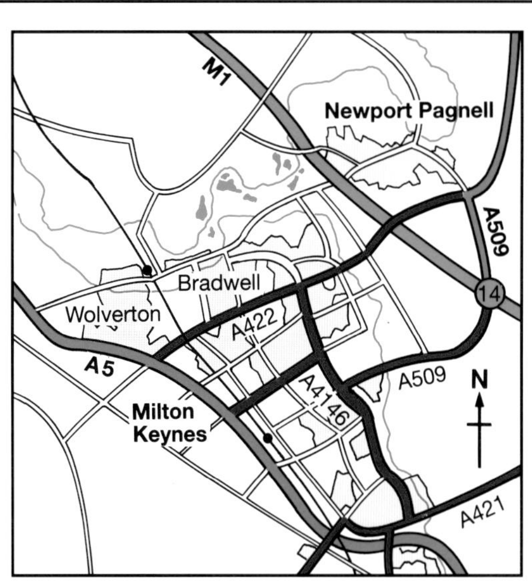

▲Boilies galore: 18mm strawberry yoghurt and kiwi fruit, 14mm peanut and some cheese flavour midis. He also has some pop-up micro baits dipped in a sweet flavour enhancer. Some anglers taste every flavour!

7:00AM *Tackling up*

Andy acts on a tip that carp have been feeding regularly at one particular spot – 75yd (70m) out. He sets up his kit very quickly – it is worth a close look...

Equipment Andy looks very much at home with his rods – which is not surprising since he designed them himself! He's fishing with two $2^{1}/_{4}$lb TC DAM Andy Little Carp rods. Andy was formerly a chief engineer so knew exactly what he wanted in terms of design and materials.

He's fishing with 8lb (3.6kg) line using optonic audible indicators and visual indicators. He decides on a helicopter rig using the mini-swivel held in place with float

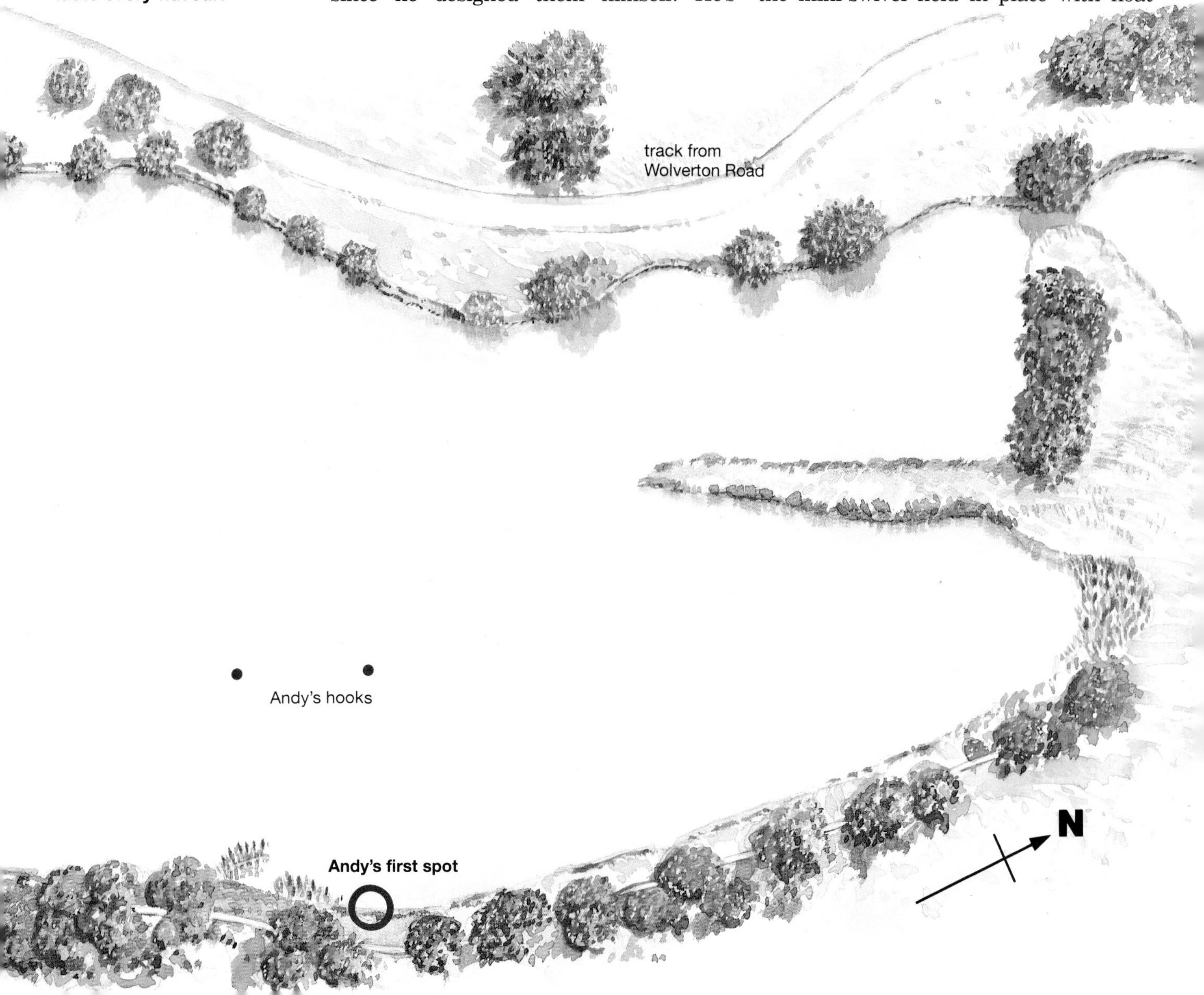

track from Wolverton Road

Andy's hooks

Andy's first spot

N

▲ ***Boilies strung through PVA water-soluble string make an effective groundbait. After you have cast the string dissolves and the boilies lie in a tight area around the hookbait.***

Carp tackle

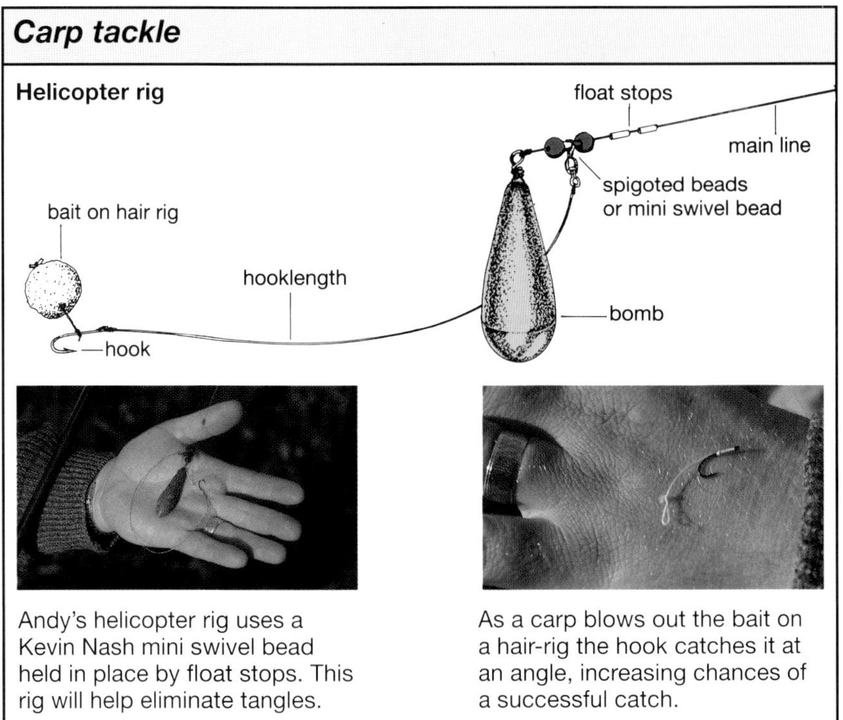

Andy's helicopter rig uses a Kevin Nash mini swivel bead held in place by float stops. This rig will help eliminate tangles.

As a carp blows out the bait on a hair-rig the hook catches it at an angle, increasing chances of a successful catch.

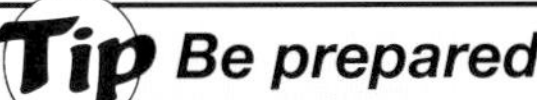

Tip Be prepared

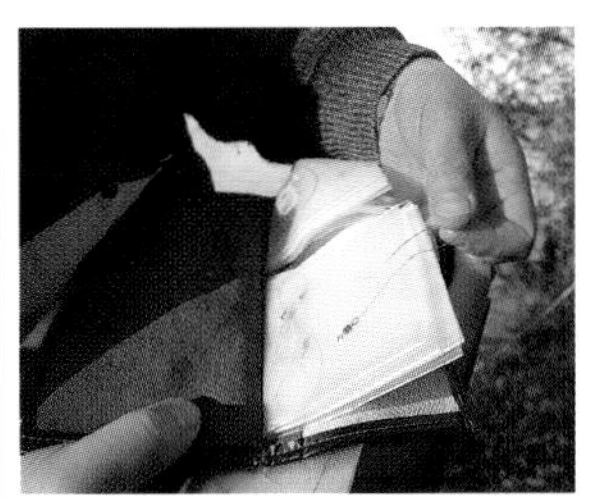

Andy keeps a variety of rigs in handy plastic sleeves. All he needs to do is attach them with a swivel. They eliminate tackle box tangles.

stops. It's a set-up that avoids tangles and one which Andy uses frequently. He has a 7lb (3.2kg) hooklength, and attaches a hair-rig to his size 10 hook with dental floss.

This may sound quite a complicated rig to set up in the chilly dark – our hands were too cold to make notes – but Andy is as cunning as the carp he hunts: "Cold hands on a bleak bank don't make it easy to tie a rig. I come with my rod set up and my rigs already prepared in plastic sleeves. It means I can spend more time fishing instead of setting up." In 10 to 15 minutes he's all ready to start the business of the day.

7:10 AM Fruity baits

Andy groundbaits with a Cobra throwing stick. He can send boilies winging 80-100yd (75-90m) out with more accuracy than a catapult.

After casting far into the dawn he settles down by his rods. He has various boilies with him: 18mm strawberry yoghurt and kiwi fruit, 14mm peanut and some cheese flavour midis. He also has some pop-up micro baits dipped in a flavour enhancer. Andy starts with the strawberry yoghurt.

"Sweet bait flavours disperse easier in cold weather – glucose-based particles travel a long way. In a sense, the sweet particles dissolving in the water amount to five times the number there would be if we were using savoury baits. Meatbaits and catfood probably work brilliantly here in summer, but they won't work as well in winter."

7:40AM A fishless dawn

The sunrise is spectacularly orange, but the cold has entered our bones – except for Andy, who is intent on the fishing. Experience tells him that his left rod is over a silty bed and his right rod over harder ground. Despite the complete lack of twitches he is convinced he will catch in spite of the cold.

"Carp don't like any dramatic temperature variations, but I have a feeling they are more likely to feed following a drop in temperature rather than a rise. I've not yet found any conditions where they will not feed at all," says Andy.

"This is a prolific fishery. In summer we would have had a couple by now, but in winter we may have just one bite all day." We all concentrate harder on the bite indicators.

Because carp eat less in the winter, Andy is economical with the loose feed. He attaches a short string of boilies to his hook on PVA water-soluble string. It means his loose feed is in exactly the same position as his hookbait.

Fixing the boilie

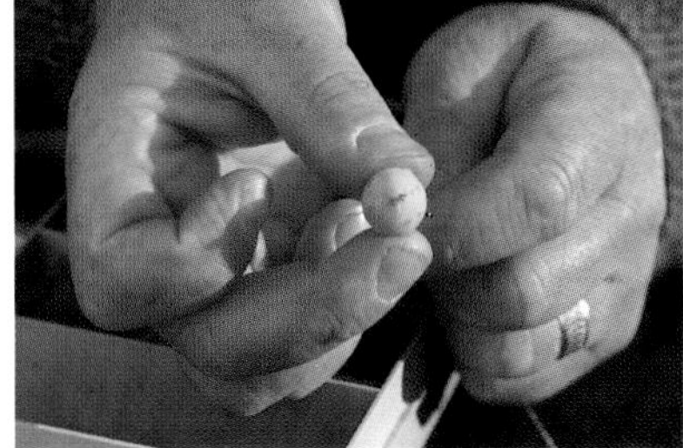

Ordinary household items can become handy weapons in the armoury of any carp angler. A crochet hook (left) is invaluable for threading boilies on to a hair-rig – in this case of unwaxed dental floss. The floss (above) is looped round a freezer bag tie that's been cut and dyed. This will hold the boilie in place when being cast.

◀ ***Andy's second swim is opposite an island – where his instincts tell him carp are feeding. The cloud and increasing cold shouldn't affect fishing.***

Tip Cool tips for the winter

Andy gives the following advice for winter fishing:
● Smear glycerol around your rod rings to stop the line from freezing against the rings.
● Don't overbait. Carp do not feed much in winter – if they eat too much loose feed they won't take your hookbait.
● Winter is not a time for experimenting. Stick to known baits on regularly fished, stocked waters.

9:00AM Time to talk

Fisheries manager Len Gurd joins us for a while. He is full of encouraging tales of winter carp caught on the lake.

What has been Andy's best fishing moment? "My sons are aged five and seven. When one landed two twenties I was more chuffed than with any fish I've ever caught. But no matter how many I've caught, I enjoy every fish I get."

Andy is not happy with the present trend in carp fishing that makes size all important. Some anglers scorn smaller carp today, but before the era of boilies catching *any* carp was a triumph.

1:00PM The move

With scarcely a bump on the line all morning, Andy has tried every bait and most tricks. He decides to follow his earlier instinct and fish around that island we spotted in the pre-dawn gloom.

Unbelievably it is even colder at the new spot. Andy sets up lighter tackle with a number 8 hook. He will be fishing 80yd (75m) out at a depth of 7ft (2.1m) The weather conditions have changed, the sun gives up the struggle against the cold and it gets darker and windier. A gloomy despondency has set in for everyone except Andy, who is fishing with renewed optimism.

The lure of a pub with warm food and a fire becomes too much to stand. We pull out, promising Andy we'll bring him back some fish and chips.

2:15PM The fish

OK, so we missed it. There are no photographs of Andy struggling with his carp because we were still returning from enjoying local hospitality. A fair size carp took Andy's strawberry yoghurt boilie and

▶ ***When fishing near the island Andy changes to a simpler legering set-up – to avoid tangling in the reeds. This rig uses a 2oz (56g) weight and a hair-rig.***

▼ ***Jackpot! Andy landed a handsome carp after a struggle in which it headed determinedly for the reeds around the island. Andy dunks his hands in the water before handling his fish.***

◀ *At 7lb 14oz (3.5kg) it may not be a massive carp, but in such conditions Andy is very pleased to have made the catch.*

▼ *This is Andy Little's own design inflatable mat. The carp cannot slip off the mat and damage itself, as it could with normal mats.*

Mix carefully

The introduction of new carp into established carp waters can be disastrous. A well known carp water near Farnham was first stocked in 1951. Forty years later new carp were added. Even though the fish carried health certificates they suffered from a parasite that killed the original carp.

▼ *No carp fisherman worthy of the name ever puts a carp in a keepnet. It damages the carp's scales and leads to infections. As soon as he can Andy carefully releases his fish.*

headed for the weeds round the island. Andy played it for seven or eight minutes before landing it.

We arrive back in time to see Andy placing it on an inflatable fish mat of his own design. He has put his hands in the water before handling the fish: "In the winter your hands will be a lot warmer than the carp. You should cool them down in the water before handling them. It is better that you are uncomfortable rather than distressing the fish."

The carp weighs 7lb 14oz (3.5kg) and is carefully returned to the water. The fish is in good condition and swims away apparently none the worse for its adventure. You can tell Andy is pleased to have caught in such bad weather.

A winter whopper

At 7lb 14oz (3.5kg) Andy's carp was pleasing enough, but he has caught fish such as this specimen of over 30lb (13.6kg) (left) during the winter.

Fish like this are not impossible to catch in the cold season, although this carp was caught in a private water.

Just twenty years ago it was widely thought that carp were too difficult to catch in the winter. With the arrival of boilies on the scene – and year-round fishing at some waters – carp seem to have gained the habit of winter feeding and are regularly caught.

2:30PM The escapee

On his next cast Andy strikes again. This time the carp makes determinedly for the island and is lost among the weeds – even Andy doesn't land every fish. But he is happy to have had two bites.

When the light fades and frostbite begins to attack us a little later we are happy to pack up and get back to a warm car. Catching his carp in such cold conditions was quite an achievement – particularly when we heard later that this carp was the last to be landed for some time as the cold November became an even colder December.

It has been a fascinating day, revealing many of the secret wonders of the carp fisherman's world. True, there is a lot of technology involved in winter carping, but it is that basic instinct for finding the fish that really won the day.

Bite indicators

If you could look under the water you would be able to see a fish taking the bait and know exactly when to strike. This is impossible unless the water is shallow and clear, but with the right type of bite indicator you can get a good idea of what's going on in any water.

Apart from the float there are a great many other methods of bite indication. They are all designed with the same purpose in mind – to tell you when a fish has your bait in its mouth.

Choosing the right one

It's not just a matter of knowing when you've got a bite – you also need time to strike. If a fish feels resistance it lets go of the bait and you end up striking at nothing. This is why it is important to suit the indicator to the species you're after and the water you're fishing.

Touch legering involves the simplest form of bite indication – holding the line between forefinger and thumb and feeling for little plucks. It allows you to work a legered or free-lined bait delicately through a flowing swim, paying out line and detecting bites at the same time. (Rolling a bait along the bottom does not work with static forms of indication – like a quivertip, for example – because they require constant tension in the line.)

Touch legering works well when a mobile approach is required – when fishing for big chub and barbel on small streams and rivers, for example. Watch the bow in the line at the same time as holding the line. When the line goes tight it means that a fish has grabbed the bait.

Tip *Rod top*

Don't underestimate the rod top as an indicator for legering on running waters. These days float rods have extremely fine tips which are perfectly sensitive enough to register bites from bold biting species like chub and barbel.

Set up the rod as you would a quivertip – with the tip pointing up at an angle of about 45° and slightly upstream. Float rods are longer than leger rods but this is often useful for controlling fish in weedy or snaggy swims.

▼ Touch legering – an angler uses his fingers to feel for bites on this small, overgrown river. It's a good method when you are adopting a roving approach – moving from one swim to another.

The dough bobbin is a simple but effective still-water indicator. Take a piece of bread about 5cm (2in) in diameter from a fresh slice and squeeze it on to the line between the reel and butt ring. (Stale bread won't stay on.) Pull the line down so that the bobbin hangs about 30-45cm (12-18in) below the rod. The line between the bomb and bobbin is kept taut by the bobbin's weight.

The kind of bites you get depend on the species and just how the fish takes the bait. A fish moving away from you causes the bobbin to rise. One that swims towards you causes it to drop back. Because the bite has to be transmitted through the rod rings before reaching the indicator, the fish feels more resistance than with rod top indicators. For this reason it is best used for bold takers like tench, carp, big bream, perch and eels.

The fact that the dough bobbin usually flies off the line each time you strike is an advantage – the bobbin gets stuck in the butt ring if it doesn't come off. But this also means that you have to put a new bobbin on the line after each cast. Wind causes the bobbin to swing about, making bites harder to spot. You can reduce the effects by letting the bobbin dangle inside a jam jar but the technique really works best in still conditions.

Washing-up liquid bottle tops make good indicators. You simply fasten the top to the line by means of the little plastic link and cap after casting. They have an advantage over the dough bobbin in that they can remain on the line when you strike – the line is able to run smoothly through the plastic link, and if you wish you can leave the bail arm of the reel off so that the fish continues to take line. Plastic bottle tops are lighter than the average sized dough bobbin but you can make them heavier by glueing some shot or a leger weight inside them.

▲ The dough bobbin may look crude but it works, and on a tranquil summer's morning there are few sights as exciting as that of a bobbin rising steadily towards the rod butt.

▼ Washing-up liquid bottle tops make cheap and cheerful indicators. Unlike dough bobbins, they allow line to flow freely from the reel spool when a fish runs with the bait.

Rod-end indicators

These present fish with less resistance than other indicators but they are designed for fish that don't move far with a bait – species like roach and small skimmer bream. Tench and carp tend to pull these indicators to their extremity and even bend the rod before you have time to strike. So if you're after these fish it is wise to use a different type of indicator.

The swingtip works well on still and slow-moving waters such as land drains. They are made from a length of stiff, fairly dense material such as cane, glass-fibre or carbon. This is fixed to a flexible link – usually silicone rubber tubing or nylon – and the link is attached to the end of the rod by means of either a screw and threaded end eye, or a peg, glued into the end of the rod, over which the rubber fits. The tip itself has one or more rings through which the line is threaded.

The rod is set horizontally, and at an angle of about 45° to the bank so that the swingtip hangs almost vertically with its tip just off the water and leaning slightly forward. A bite is signalled when the tip pulls forward or drops back.

Swingtipping is a good method for roach which often produce fast, snatchy bites on other types of indicator. Its main disadvantages are its susceptibility to the wind – which causes it to bounce about – and to increased flow which causes it to straighten out and lose sensitivity.

The quivertip is the most versatile form of rod-end indicator and can be used to catch just about all species – though it is particularly suited to bream, chub and barbel. It is simply a fine extension of the rod itself – either permanently built into the end of the rod, pushed on to a spigot or, like the swingtip, attached by means of a screw. Quivertips vary in length from 20-60cm (8-24in). The finest – most flexible – tips are for still waters and the stiffest for medium to fast-flowing rivers.

The knack is getting just the right amount of tension in the tip. Too little and the tip won't register bites soon enough, too much tension and the fish feels resistance and drops the bait before you have a chance to strike.

Bites vary: there's the persistent tapping or knocking of a roach or perch, the slow, delicate pull of a skimmer bream, the rattle of an eel and the bold yanking round of chub and barbel. Choosing the tip, setting it up correctly and reading the bites is very much a matter of experience.

The springtip is similar to the quivertip in that it is an extension of the rod but differs in that it is connected to the rod by a spring. Unlike a quivertip – where tension gradually increases as a fish pulls it round – a bite causes the springtip to 'collapse'. This makes it extremely sensitive and a good choice for shy biters like roach and skimmers on still or very slow-flowing venues. Avoid the designs that double up as either a springtip or quivertip.

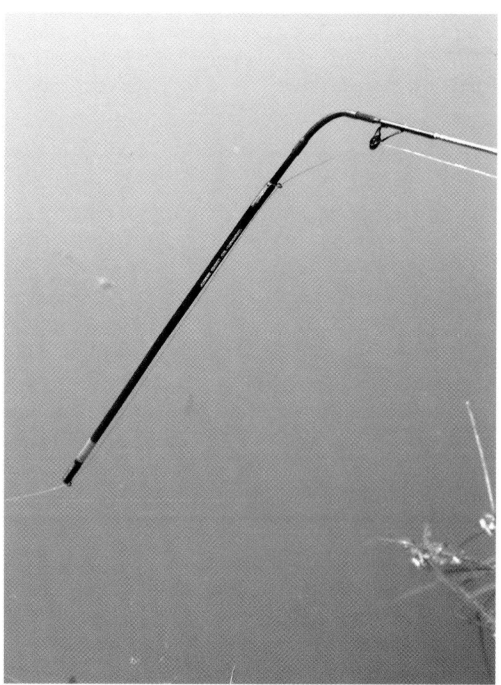

► Swingtips – by tradition a favourite choice with the bream angler – had lost some popularity to the quivertip but they are currently enjoying a revival with matchmen for shy biting stillwater roach as well as bream. Their advantage over the quivertip is that they allow quick snatches to develop into hittable bites.

▼ A range of quivertips of different stiffnesses allows you to cope with still and running waters. The secret to good quivertipping is in tensioning the tip. You need a bit of tension so that you can see the bites but if there's too much a fish will drop the bait before you have time to strike.

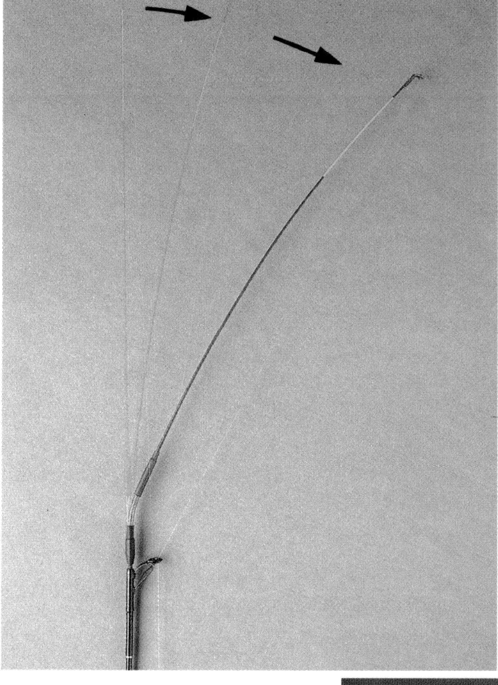

▲ Springtips work on a similar principle to quivertips but differ in one important respect: tension does not gradually increase as a fish pulls the tip – it collapses instead.

Butt indicators

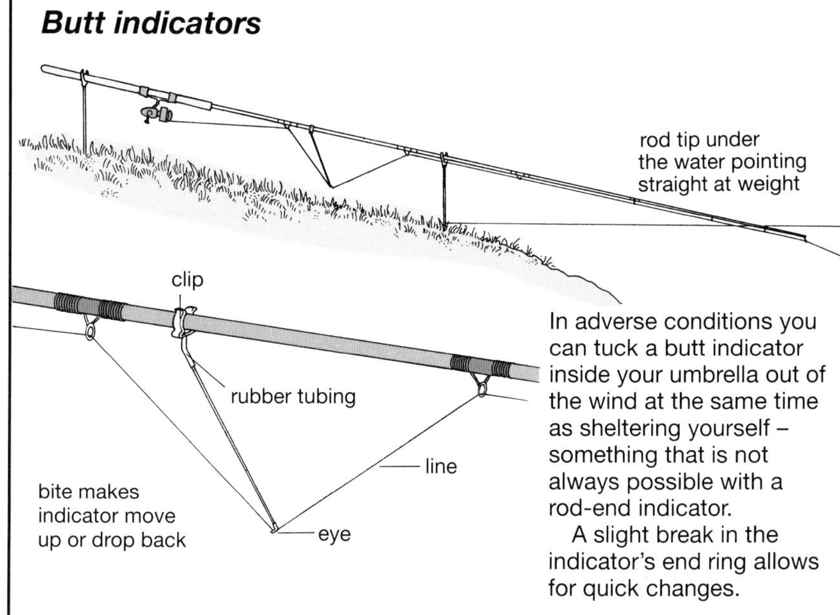

In adverse conditions you can tuck a butt indicator inside your umbrella out of the wind at the same time as sheltering yourself – something that is not always possible with a rod-end indicator.

A slight break in the indicator's end ring allows for quick changes.

Tip: Night sight

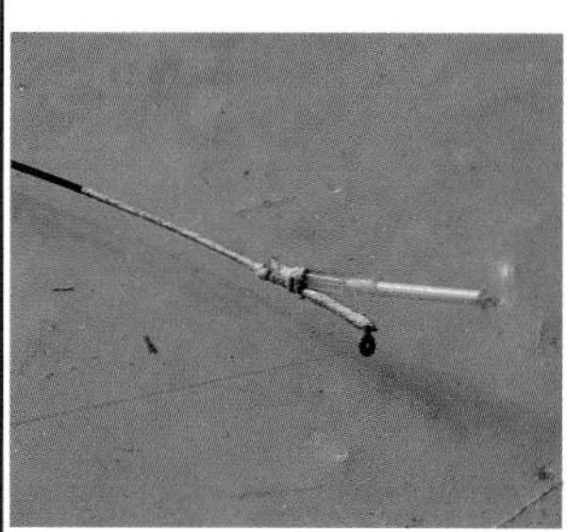

Night legering is often the most productive means of catching specimens but how do you see the bites? One answer is to fit your indicator with a light of some sort. Little plastic phials containing glowing isotopes are available from tackle shops. Tape or whip one to the end of your indicator.

▼ Monkey climbers work on the dough bobbin principle but because the monkey is constrained by a 'needle' it is not as susceptible to windy conditions.

It is important to make sure the pin is spotless or else the monkey won't slide properly.

Running line indicators

Two popular, sophisticated forms of running line indicator are the monkey climber and the electronic alarm. They can be used separately or together for species that run with a bait – fish like carp, eels and pike, for example.

The monkey climber is based on the dough bobbin principle. It consists of a solid PTFE body – the monkey – which slides freely on a thin stainless steel rod – the needle. The needle is 45-90cm (18-36in) long and is clamped so that it stands vertically between the reel and butt ring. The line passes through a loop on the monkey and this is pulled down until suspended about 45cm (18in) below the rod. The reel's bail arm is left off.

A fish that runs away from the angler with the bait causes the monkey to climb the needle and hover as line runs through the loop. A fish that runs towards the angler causes the monkey to drop.

On the strike, the monkey flies to the top of the needle and the line is instantly released from the loop. (The monkey itself is prevented from flying off the end of the needle by a metal pommel.)

Electronic indicators can be used with monkey climbers so that an audible as well as a visual indication is given. The line passes over a wheel or behind a wire arm on the head of the indicator – depending on the type – and a run causes the alarm to sound.

▲ If you are going to use two alarms on two different rods at the same time, get ones with a 'tone' control. By setting the two alarms at a different pitch and keeping the relative positions of the alarms the same, you know immediately which rod has a run.

Going after perch with Nigel Witham

The quarry is specimen perch and nothing less than a two pounder (0.9kg) will do. Who better to lead the assault on Haversham Lake than Nigel Witham of the Perchfishers?

◀ Nigel Witham has been fishing since he was big enough to hold a tiddler net. He has concentrated mainly on roach and perch – which for him typify English coarse fishing.

He has taken many perch over 2lb (0.9kg) with a best of 3lb 9oz (1.6kg). He has also caught three roach over 3lb (1.4kg) – the biggest being 3lb 14oz (1.8kg).

▼ The margins are shallow at Nigel's spot, but there's a deep hole about 30m (33yd) out – perfect for perch on an overcast March day.

What do you do when you want big perch? Well, you pick the right time of year, the right venue, get the right conditions, fish the right swim, with the right tackle, and then you probably give up and go and fish for something easier.

Bearing this in mind, Nigel Witham is only quietly optimistic about his chances. He's chosen Haversham Lake at Linear Fisheries – a day-ticket water with unexplored potential – in early March, but now comes the hard part.

11:00AM Plumb spot

So, it's a blustery Friday a week before the end of the season. The sun smiles weakly through the patchy cloud cover, and the wind is creating a bit of a chop which in turn puts some colour in the water – classic perch fishing conditions according to Nigel.

Haversham Lake is very uneven in depth and Nigel reckons a deep hole is where you find fish at this time of year. He plumbs up, looking for deeper water.

Eventually he finds an area of water over 3m (10ft) deep about 20m (65ft) out from the east bank. The bottom continues to slope away to even greater depths and Nigel is pinning his hopes on a leviathan lurking out in the deeps.

As it turns out, weed isn't the problem – it's the wind. The drag it creates pulls the line out of the clips, setting off the bite alarms. He changes to thinner line, but now the wind blows the bobbins, pulling the line out of the line clips – and guess what? It sets off the bite alarms.

Nigel replaces the bobbins with a line clip-cum-bite indicator of his own invention. This solves the problem and he's able to concentrate on perch once more.

1:10PM Carefully does it

Nothing's happened for over an hour, so he changes his single lobworm for two smaller ones. Injecting them with a little air makes them sit slightly off the bottom, so they are easier for hungry perch to spot.

This requires a great deal of care, as Nigel is at pains to point out. If you don't give the syringe your full attention, you may inject yourself with air – which can be fatal.

NOON Windy wind-up

It's mid-day before he makes his first cast, but Nigel knows that perch are much more likely to feed later on in the day. He's fishing lobworm on one of his two Avon rods, with a roach livebait on the other.

To keep resistance to bites to a minimum, Nigel leaves the bail arm open and clips up the line. Bite detection is from two bite alarms with bobbins for drop-back bites.

Big perch aren't as reckless as their smaller brothers – that's probably how they got to be so big – and they drop a bait if they feel any resistance. Nigel's livebait rig is a float leger, which he has to cast carefully to avoid tangles. If there's one thing guaranteed to create resistance to a bite, it's a knotted ball of tackle with a bait hanging meekly to one side of it.

Nigel starts with an ordinary running leger for the worms, though he'll change to a float leger if the bottom is weedy. There's little point having a bait in the water if it's hidden by a foot of foliage.

▲ The bite alarm sounds on the right hand rod and Nigel is ready to strike. This time it was just the wind blowing the line, but perch can be so cautious, you've got to strike, just in case.

Fishery facts

- You can buy day or season tickets for the whole complex at local tackle shops or by post from: Len Gurd, Linear House, 2 Northcroft, Shenley Lodge, Milton Keynes. Bucks.
- An Anglian Water Authority licence is also required to fish at Linear Fisheries.
- There are specimen carp, tench, pike, barbel, chub, dace and eels as well as big perch and roach in the various waters at Linear.

Haversham Lake at Linear Fisheries

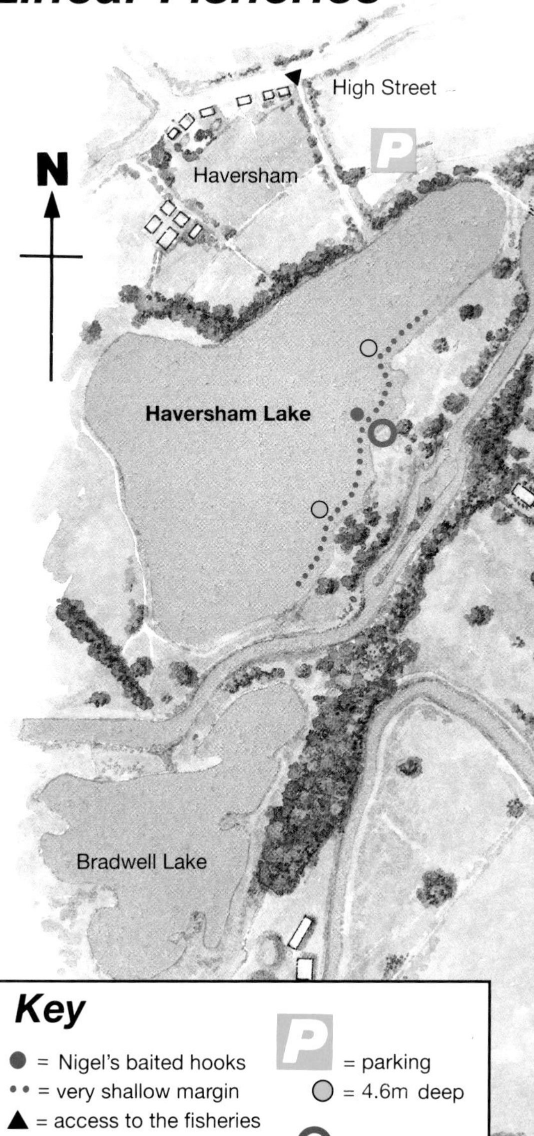

Key

- ● = Nigel's baited hooks
- •• = very shallow margin
- ▲ = access to the fisheries
- 1 = coarse syndicate waters
- 2 = trout syndicate waters
- P = parking
- ○ = 4.6m deep
- ◯ = Nigel's fishing spot

How to get there

- **By car** Take the A509 (Childs Way) off the M1 at junction 14. Go right along Marlborough Street then left along Portway, and right down Grafton Street to the end. Turn left and then right soon after along Haversham Road. Follow signs to Haversham, go left along the High Street then right to Haversham Lake parking.
- **By train** Wolverton is the nearest local station. Intercity services stop at Milton Keynes.

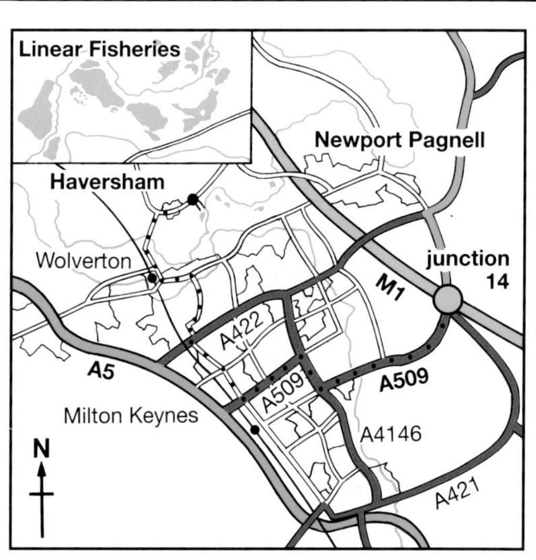

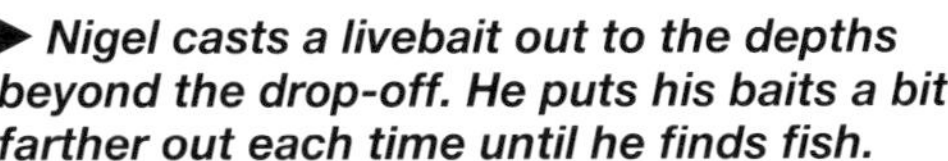

► *Nigel casts a livebait out to the depths beyond the drop-off. He puts his baits a bit farther out each time until he finds fish.*

▼ *The first fish of the day is a roach of around 1½lb (0.7kg). It proves there are fish in the shelter of the deeper water.*

"Perch won't be in front of you all the time. Pick a good spot and wait."

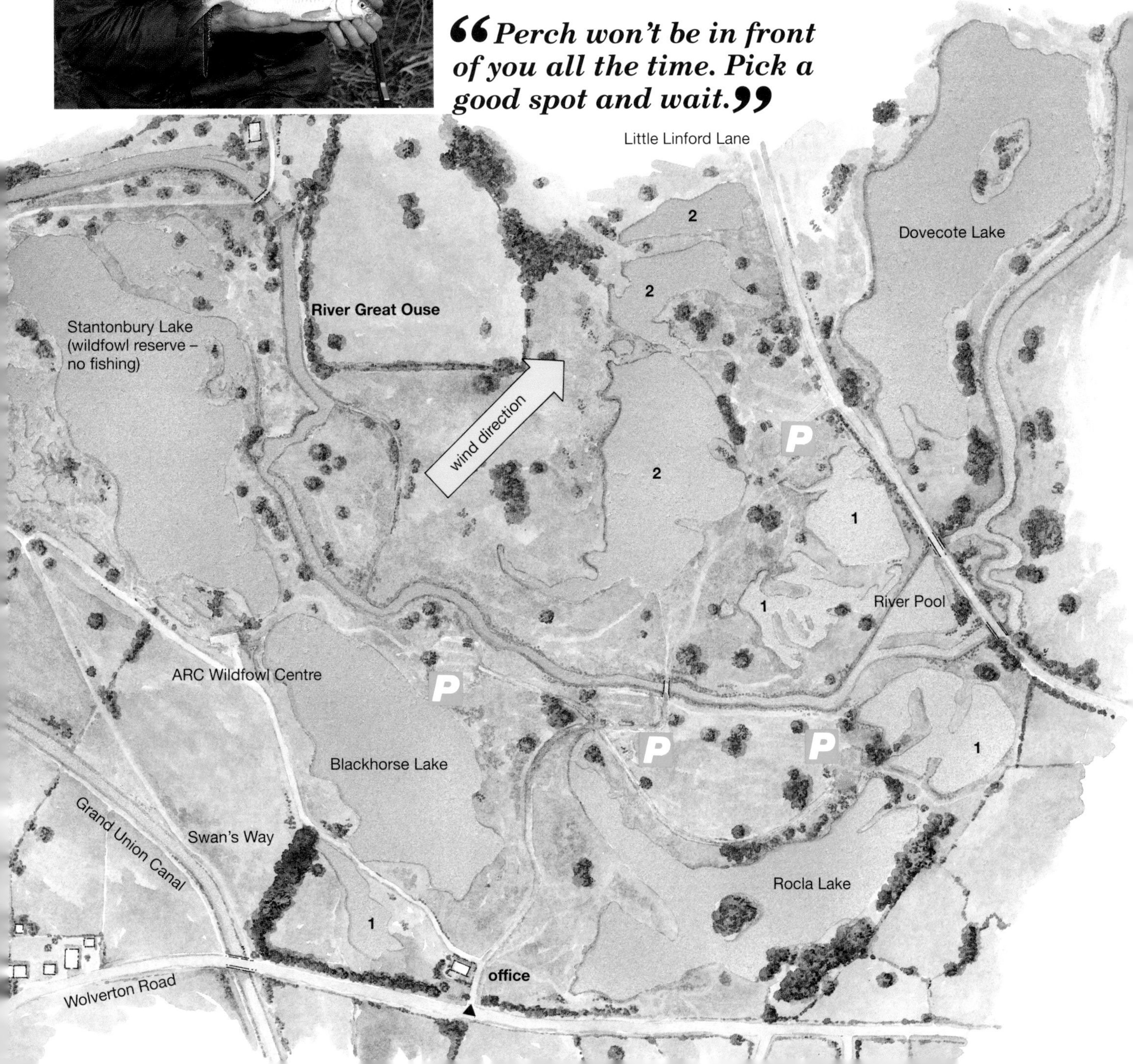

Little Linford Lane

Dovecote Lake

River Great Ouse

Stantonbury Lake (wildfowl reserve – no fishing)

wind direction

2

2

2

P

1

1

River Pool

ARC Wildfowl Centre

P

P

P

1

Blackhorse Lake

Grand Union Canal

Swan's Way

Rocla Lake

1

office

Wolverton Road

Specialist perch rigs

main line
swivel
size 4 or 6 hook
swivel
120cm mono trace
90cm leger link
Arlesey bomb

The running leger is a good rig for presenting the bait in a free-running way – which is essential for catching big perch.

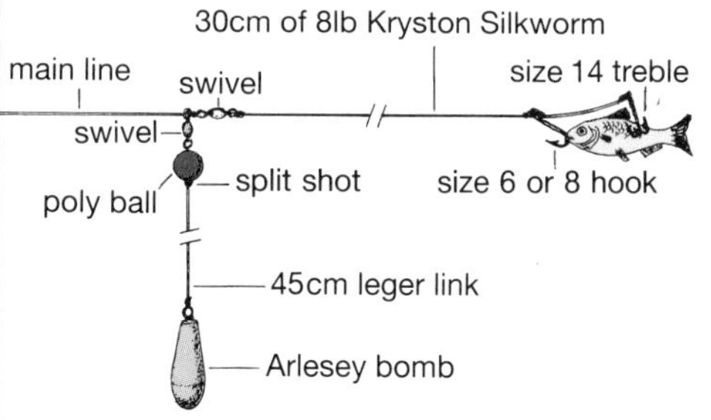

The float leger stops the livebait hiding on the bottom. It is quite prone to tangles however, so don't try casting a long way.

2:00PM Still nothing

Nigel changes his double lobworm bait to a single fat 'un. He casts a little farther too, so he's fishing a good 10m (33ft) beyond the drop-off.

The bite alarm sounds. It's the livebait that's gone and Nigel is quickly at the rod. He barely has time to find a bare hook when the buzzer goes on his worm set-up.

He winds down and tightens the line – he only strikes at extreme range. This time, the rod is not disappointingly straight – it describes a lovely thumping arc and Nigel begins to smile.

"I wasn't really expecting anything until sunset," he beams, "but I don't think it's a perch." Two minutes later he turns out to be right, as a plump 1½lb (0.7kg) roach comes out to have its photo taken. Not a perch by any stretch of the imagination but a worthwhile fish nonetheless.

3:00PM I'd rather jack

Not a lot's happening, but Nigel isn't worried – he's waiting for the sun to get low in the sky. In the meantime there's lots of time to talk about his fishing. He's not a great one for huge fish any more – odd for a specimen hunter.

Actually, he *is* interested in big fish. But nowadays he'd rather catch good fish from a small, tree-lined river than sweat it out at a concrete bowl for a monster. If he ends up with a 1lb (0.45kg) roach, then he's very happy with that.

Just as he's getting into his subject there's a run. A fit 6lb (2.7kg) pike goes tail-walking with the livebait. While he's landing it the other rod sounds. Which just goes to prove you can have too much of a good thing. Unfortunately, despite rushing the pike into the net somewhat (you don't hang about with a Kryston hooklength in any case), the second run doesn't develop.

▲ Waiting for the elusive big perch turned up a pretty big pike – all 29½lb (13.4kg) of her.

▼ Nigel casts out another livebait after unhooking a small jack. There were a lot of them about that day.

Tip You've got it taped

A roll of insulation tape comes in very handy for a number of jobs – from taping on a line clip to fixing on a rod ring in an emergency. Don't leave home without one.

▲ ***Strike! At long range you may have to strike to be sure you've overcome the stretch of the mono and have set the hook properly.***

4:00PM Farewell to jacks

Another pike – only this time it's caught by his companion Ben Eveling. It's the biggest to come out of Haversham Lake and weighs 29lb 8oz (13.4kg). Well, well, this is becoming a pretty interesting session.

Jacks have been at the livebaits all day, but as it creeps towards Nigel's favourite part of the day, they become noticeably less active. Nigel, on the other hand, is clearly more alert and a bit more tense than he has been up till now.

5:35PM Breathless

The sun is going down, the wind has dropped to a mere whisper of its former self and Nigel bubbles with anticipation. He catches himself at it and makes a feeble attempt to distract himself with conversation.

Bang goes the bite alarm and Nigel is there – strangely unhurried after the build-up. It's a better fish than the roach and a tenacious fighter. Could it be...? But you can catch anything on long range legered lobworm. No-one dares breathe.

It's too marvellous to be true, but there it is. A big hump-backed perch bristles into the landing net and everyone watching lets out their breath. "I knew it was a perch. I could feel it! But I didn't say anything just in case." Who says anglers aren't superstitious?

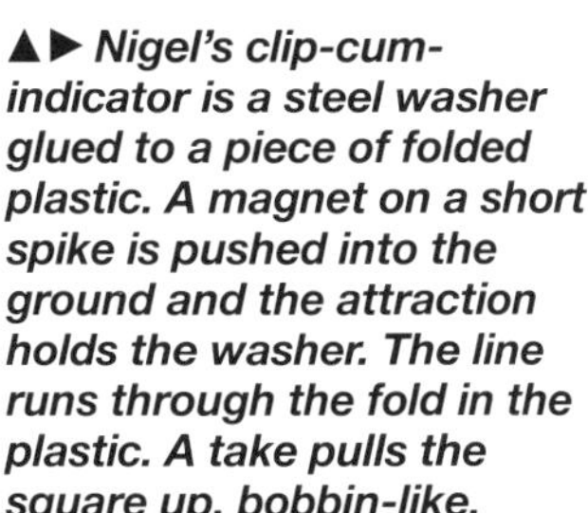

▲► ***Nigel's clip-cum-indicator is a steel washer glued to a piece of folded plastic. A magnet on a short spike is pushed into the ground and the attraction holds the washer. The line runs through the fold in the plastic. A take pulls the square up, bobbin-like.***

Tip Bait hints

- Big perch often gobble the bait down quickly, so strike fast and don't give them much time.
- Cut 5mm (¼in) off your lobworms before casting to create a scent trail.
- Livebait often does better for perch towards the end of the day. Pike also take livebaits, but with a wire trace you won't catch big perch. A Kryston hooklength won't deter perch and gives you a good chance with pike.

◄ ***As dusk approaches, Nigel begins to feel more confident. This is often the best time of day for big perch and after hooking up fresh baits, he settles back to wait for a run.***

Tip Confidence

Even if he's not catching, Nigel won't change rig. After years of perch fishing he's confident in his rigs. He just changes or adjusts the bait.

Changing location is no more likely to bring results than staying put if you're in a good spot. It's all about confidence.

There goes that livebait rod again. Maybe it's another one. But no, it's a pike this time. It has to be landed by hand since the perch is still nestling in the landing net – there's been no time to land it. Back goes the pike, and Nigel's dying to get another lobworm out 60m (66yd) to where the perch are feeding.

First he's got to unhook this one. Typically, it had gulped the bait down. Nigel pulls the hook through and cuts the line rather than force it back against the barb – easier for fish and fisherman. Next it's got to be weighed and returned. Wet the sling, steady the scales, 2lb (0.9kg) dead. Well, what a day.

But it's not over yet. On with another hook and out goes the lobworm again. Then it's time to change the livebait rig to another worm set-up – that's obviously what they want. Now he can relax. But of course he doesn't, not when perch are about.

▲ ***The bristling prize that Nigel came to Haversham Lake to find. Catching one first trip indicates a good head of big fish.***

▼ ***After a seven and a half hour wait and right on cue, here it is. Nigel holds the landing net ready as the perch does its best to avoid it. A big 90-105cm (36-42in) net is essential for any serious specimen hunter.***

▲ ***Nigel's best roach of the season at exactly 2lb (0.9kg) was a definite bonus and put the seal on a real red letter session.***

6:35PM *Specimen number three*

Nigel slowly begins to unwind, suggesting the end of the day is near, when the farther out of the two lobworms goes off for a spin in the mouth of a hungry fish. "This is a typical perch fight. It's really dogged." That's absolutely fine, until a fat *roach* slides over the net.

Well, nobody's perfect. And there are compensations. At 2lb (0.9kg) exactly it's his biggest of the season and the third specimen-weight fish of an amazing session.

7:10PM *A last fling*

Time to pack up, and continue the gloating over a drink. It's really dark now and it's quite difficult to see what's going on. It's not hard to hear a last blast of the bite alarm, though. A roach of 1¼lb (0.6kg) is almost a disappointment. It really is time to go, or we'll be here all night. Maybe next time.

Hooks and traces for pike

Choosing the right hooks and traces saves both you and the pike a lot of trouble. Experienced pike angler Barrie Rickards can't believe there are still some anglers who don't use a wire trace – condemning fish to a slow death.

The pike hasn't gained its reputation as the freshwater shark for nothing. To combat those sharp teeth you need proper equipment. Fortunately, pike anglers today are in the excellent position of having a good choice of hooks and trace wires from which to make up their various rigs.

Wire traces

Never – ever – fish without a wire trace for pike. Just don't do it. Incredibly, even some experienced anglers try without on occasion. It is grossly unfair to risk leaving hooks in pike.

The wire for traces comes in two basic forms, single strand and cabled.

Single strand wire is rather stiff and cannot be used for spinning – but it is fine for bait fishing. Alasticum is the brand usually recommended, but various piano wires can be used.

Cabled wire is the alternative, and this is the type of wire used by most pike anglers. There are two kinds: seven strand types, which are very fine; and thicker types such as PDQ and Alasticum. Barrie's preference is for PDQ – despite the fact it has a greater diameter than seven strand wire. He finds it rarely kinks, does not get 'the bends' when hooks are moved along it, and is very easy to work with the fingers.

Kevlar and steel is a new type of cabled 'wire' that has recently appeared. Barrie has started using it extensively and has found it superb for all forms of piking. One of its good features is that you can tie half blood knots in it! These should be fixed with instant glue – though unglued ones don't

▼ *A fair sized pike puts quite a strain on your rig. It should go without saying that you use a wire trace every time you go piking. Sadly there are still anglers prepared to risk fishing without wire. When a pike bites through the line it is left with trebles in its mouth, and could well die slowly.*

usually give trouble. Barrie is currently using both PDQ and Kevlar wires as a comparative exercise, though he believes it is rare to find that either kink without it being obvious at an early stage.

The traces

There are times during baitfishing when, during a cast, a deadbait may flick backwards so the hooks catch the reel line. In the event of a take, the pike mouths the reel line and – bite-off. This means you have a pike swimming around with hooks in its jaws.

For this reason many anglers now consider two traces are better than one. The lower trace, the one at the business end, carries the hook or hooks. The trace above merely has a link swivel on the bottom and an ordinary swivel on the top.

It might appear that one long wire trace would do the job just as well. But for some reason the wire still seems to flick back – a separate trace stops this.

The purpose of the upper trace is both simple and important – it prevents bite-offs. An upper trace prevents these completely and Barrie now always uses one in all forms of bait fishing for pike. Make the hook trace length around 30cm (12in) and the upper trace length from 30-45cm (12-18in).

Both traces need a swivel at the top end. If you are using PDQ you won't need to crimp the wire. Because of its relative flexibility an inch of PDQ can be threaded through the swivel and then twisted back a number of times around the trace. With Kevlar it's even easier. Simply tie a half blood knot. Attach a link swivel to the bottom of the upper trace.

Snappy tackle

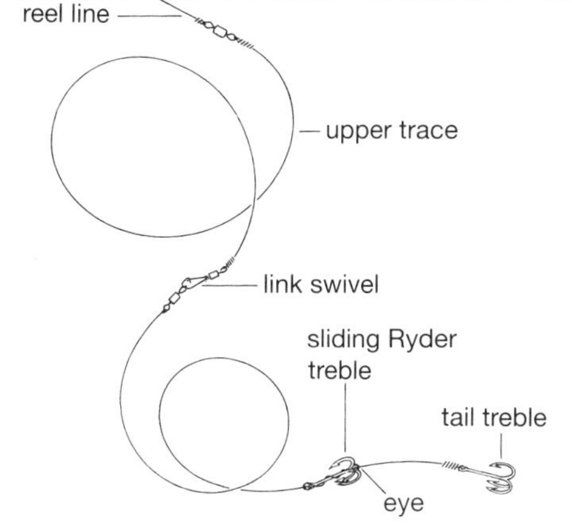

This is Barrie Rickard's recommended snap tackle rig – incorporating a sliding Ryder treble hook. It means that the size of the snap tackle rig can be altered to suit the deadbait you are using, and that one of the hooks can move even if the other hits bone.

Strong stuff

When fishing with a wire trace your reel line should be of around 10-12lb (4.5-5.4kg) b.s. Wire strength should be about 20lb (9kg) b.s.

Barrie Rickards strongly recommends a second wire trace 30-45cm (12-18in) long. He says that in theory the upper trace should be longer than the lower one – but in fact it doesn't seem to matter.

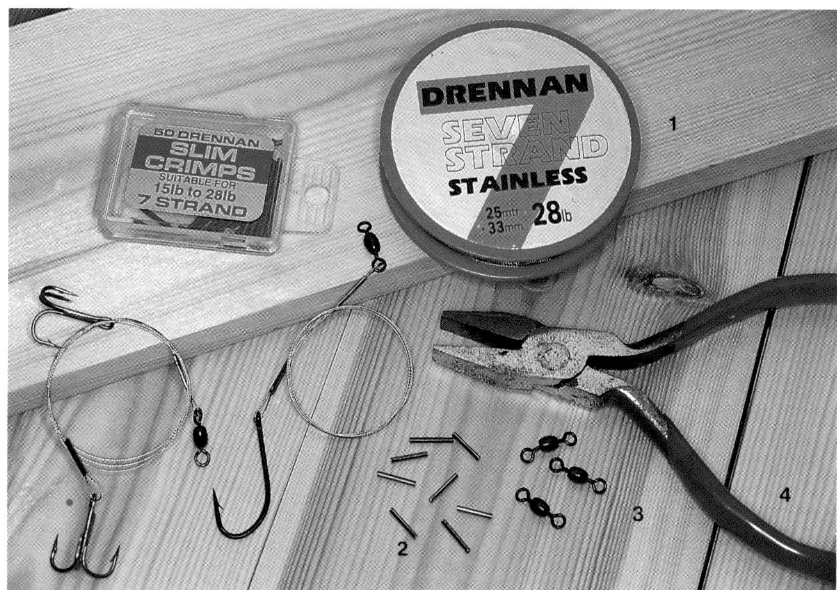

▲ A selection of equipment useful when making traces. Shown are seven-strand wire (1) – suitable for deadbaiting and spinning rigs, – crimps (2), swivels (3) and a pair of pliers without serrations (4) so they grip without cutting.

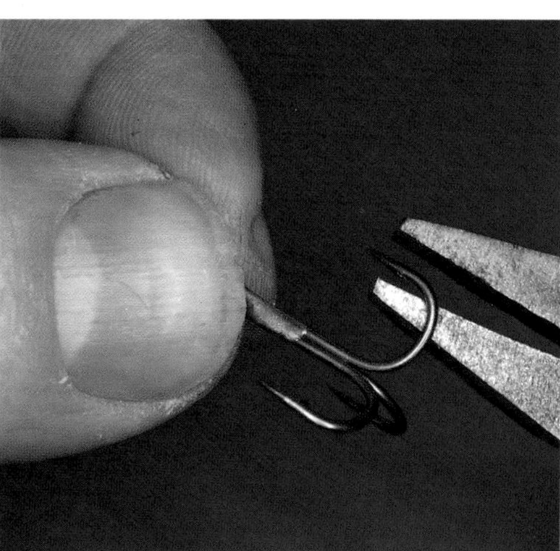

▲ Barbed hooks are difficult to free, particularly if the pike has swallowed the bait deeply. Most trebles come barbed, so flatten them with pliers.

Head first

Research shows pike usually swallow whole fish head first. Try keeping the hooks back, as near to the tail as possible. By mounting the fish this way, the pike won't swallow the hooks so deeply when it bites.

The hooks

Barrie's personal preferences are for small treble hooks, from size 10 to 6. Most of today's 'fish-friendly' anglers use barbless hooks because they are much easier to remove from a pike when it has been deep-hooked.

However Barrie, who has fished barbless hooks for many years, is not convinced. Very occasionally, he thinks, they harm fish by coming adrift during playing – tearing at the pike as they do so. But he shares the view of other anglers that barbed hooks are all too likely to damage fish.

As a solution Barrie would like to see micro-barbed hooks. These won't come loose during playing, yet are easier to unhook than barbed ones.

Currently there are no genuine micro-barbed hooks on the market, so Barrie fishes small treble hooks with the smallest barbs he can find, or presses part of the barbs down with pliers until they are little more than whisker barbs. These give a securer hold than barbless hooks but are easier to unhook than barbed ones.

◀ *This angler is set up ready to float fish a deadbait, in this case a complete small fish on a snap tackle rig. The snap tackle incorporates one treble hook and a single hook at the tail root of the bait – to hold the fish in position. This is because the pike is likely to swallow a bait whole – and the fewer trebles there are the fewer points there should be to unhook.*

▼ *Two ways of deadbaiting herring. Top is a rig for float fishing a suspended herring. The top size 8 treble is threaded through the back of the fish and the bottom treble mounted behind the gill.*

The bottom herring has been mounted through the tail and flank for legering.

Snap tackle

Usually snap tackle has two sets of treble hooks fixed in position. This is perfectly effective.

Anglers have also developed other rigs – often 'fish-friendly' ones. One such rig sets the snap tackle closer to the tail, so that a pike swallowing a bait head-first won't take the hooks so deeply.

Another rig uses just a single hook at the base to avoid more hooks snagging pike than are necessary to catch.

However, as an alternative, Barrie says that there's no reason for the upper treble in a snap tackle rig to be fixed in position. Using a snap tackle rig is much easier if the upper treble is easily moved. With PDQ wire or Kevlar this is possible without introducing bends into the wire.

To prepare such a rig, first fix your upper swivel. Next attach a Ryder treble to the rig (a Ryder treble is like a normal treble hook but with two eyes, one at the top and one at the bottom). Thread the wire through the top eye, giving just one turn or even half a

Tip Securafish

If you have attached your deadbait firmly to the treble hook there is no reason why it should come off. However, if you do feel the urge to break casting distance records, try tying the tail of the fish to the snap tackle rig to make doubly certain.

turn of the trace wire around the shank, and then thread the wire through the other eye.

Move the hook 15cm (6in) up the wire and finally tie in the tail treble with either a 2.5cm (1in) twist of wire or, when using Kevlar, a half blood knot. Now move the Ryder hook carefully along the trace to suit the size of the bait. A moveable snap tackle rig offers greater flexibility in bait size.

In addition, the moveable Ryder has a great advantage over a fixed hook. If both

▲ Storing rigs made from wire traces can be a nightmare. Well-known pike hunter Ken Whitehead has a corking answer to the problem with this cork trace holder.

◀ Get the hooks and traces right and there's no reason why you shouldn't land a good pike. But skimp on rig preparation and the fish could get away with a mouthful of trebles.

your hooks are fixed in position, and one of them fetches up against bone in the pike's mouth, the other hook is stuck in the same relative position – probably dangling uselessly. No matter how hard you pull, if the first hook is lodged the other won't move. As soon as the pike opens its mouth, out they both fall.

If the Ryder can slide on strike, then – even if the Ryder catches in the bone – the fixed hook is still free to move towards the Ryder. This is because the fixed hook is attached directly to the line – which slips straight through the eyes of the caught Ryder. It can be pulled through, until, the angler hopes, it finds a softer part of the pike's mouth to catch.

Experimenting with rigs

The above rig is recommended by Barrie as the best basic rig. But he is currently experimenting with an idea thought of by two friends, Archie Braddocks and Colin Dyson. It uses a large (size 4 or 2) VB (Vic Bellars) hook. A VB hook is basically two singles back-to-back – one being smaller than the other. This is attached by elasticated cotton so that the hooking hook stands proud of the bait.

The advantage of this is that the hook seems to lodge – almost invariably – in the scissors of the pike's jaws. This aids unhooking – freeing pike from single hooks in the jaw is easy if you use forceps. Barrie is now comparing VB hooks with kevlar traces. Traces are still evolving! Whichever he chooses, he knows both are good rigs.

▲◄ ***Barely 15 minutes after casting, Martin strikes into the first tench.***
Martin, from Corby, began tench fishing aged 16 and discovered Sywell three years later. He's had tench over 7lb (3.2kg), pike to 26lb (11.8kg) and double-figure zander but he also enjoys trout fishing.

Martin Blakeston and the early season tench

The pre-dawn mists roll gently over the tranquil waters of Sywell Reservoir as the sun begins to rise. It's June the 16th and you can practically smell the tench...

At three in the morning the car park by Sywell Reservoir in Northamptonshire is already half full. And Martin Blakeston, specimen tench hunter, thought he was going to have his pick of swim! Perhaps that was a trifle optimistic, given that Sywell is well-known for its massive tench.

In the dark, it's impossible to tell which parts of the bank are occupied until you've actually bumped into another angler or had his headlamp in your eyes. Because of this, Martin doesn't think it's worth walking all the way round to the other bank. All the decent areas may be occupied by the time he gets there.

3:00AM *Baiting up*

Instead, he opts for a fairly productive area about 50m (55yd) from the dam wall. It's close to the car park and it's empty, making it altogether too tempting. The first task is to mix up plenty of crumb groundbait, adding a fair few maggots to help it break up on the bottom.

Next Martin demonstrates long range baiting up by catapult. "There's no point fishing an area that's less than 30-40m (33-44yd) from the bank – where you've got about 3-4m (10-13ft) of water."

After a fairly intense barrage, Martin tackles up in the darkness. He doesn't seem to find threading 5lb (2.3kg) line through the rings of his two 1¼lb (0.6kg) TC carp rods at all difficult in the gloom. Martin can use such comparatively fine line because the bed of the reservoir has just a light covering of weed this early in the season.

Later on, in a hot summer, there can be so much weed that you need 12lb (5.4kg) line to have even an equal chance of landing a determined tench. Not that Martin does this. "I enjoy tench fishing, but dragging a fish through the weeds on heavy carp gear isn't my idea of fun," he says.

3:20AM *First light*

As the first hint of the pre-dawn light begins to show in the sky, wisps of mist drift over the water. There's a breeze in Martin's

▼ ***Baiting up at range in the dark can be difficult but Martin aims for a tree silhouetted against the skyline. He has to get the mix stiff enough so that it won't break up in mid-air.***

▲ ***Early in the season (and later on if he can get away with it), Martin likes to use traditional tench baits.***

▼▶ ***The open-end feeder filled with crumb or maggot. A feeder filled with maggots, with maggot on the hook, turned out to be the most successful combination.***

How to get there

● **By car** From London or Leicester, leave the M1 at junction 15, taking the A508 towards Northampton. Take the A43 towards Kettering and Corby, then the A45 to Wellingborough. Turn left on to Nene Way before Earls Barton. Cross the A4500 and take the first left along Washbrook Lane. The car park is the first right turn. If you come to the main gate, you've gone slightly too far.

● **By train** Northampton and Wellingborough are the nearest BR stations.

▲ ***Martin ready to cast. Most of the fish caught at Sywell are taken in deep water – more than 30m (33yd) out from the bank.***

face and the hazy cloud promises a fine day once the sun has burnt it away.

The first cast lands in the middle of the baited up area, followed shortly by the second. Martin places the rods on the bite alarms, sets up the monkey climbers and sits back to wait for a run. With dawn on the way, it shouldn't be too long.

4:15AM *Paydirt*

Martin retrieves his tackle and pulls off a few strands of Canadian pondweed. He rebaits with a bunch of maggots, and fills his open-end feeder with more of the same. As soon as he's cast, he brings in the other set and repeats the process.

After recasting the second rod, he catapults another few balls of groundbait out to his feed area. On top of regularly casting the feeders, he likes to keep balls of feed going in – tench can polish off a bed of

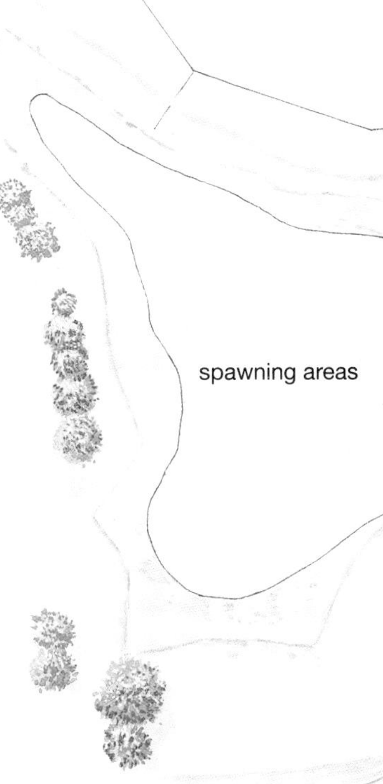

Tip A tench on!

As with many other reservoirs, the water at Sywell tends to be very clear. This means that the tench do not venture into the shallow margins unless it's dark and you are quiet. Fish for them in deeper water well away from the banks.

► ***The first female of the day – and despite her deep body, she's no monster. Fish of around 3lb (1.4kg) are usually a pretty rare catch in Sywell's 68 acres, so to catch any fish like this is a bit of a surprise. Still, within a couple of years she'll be a five-pounder (2.3kg) too.***

Sywell Country Park

“Tench fishing should be fun. I do prefer using 'old fashioned' baits and fairly light gear. That way I really enjoy every single fish I catch.”

Fishery facts

Sywell Reservoir has a big stock of huge tench and decent roach. On opening day five tench over 8lb (3.6kg) were reported with one over 9lb (4.1kg)!

Fishing is controlled by Wellingborough and Dist. Nene AC. You must have a ticket and a National rod licence before you fish – season tickets from local tackle shops, day tickets from the ranger's hut (Tel 0604 810970).

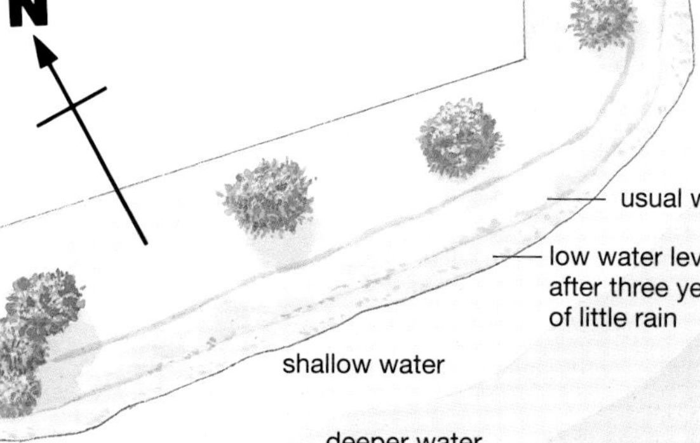

Martin's feeder rigs

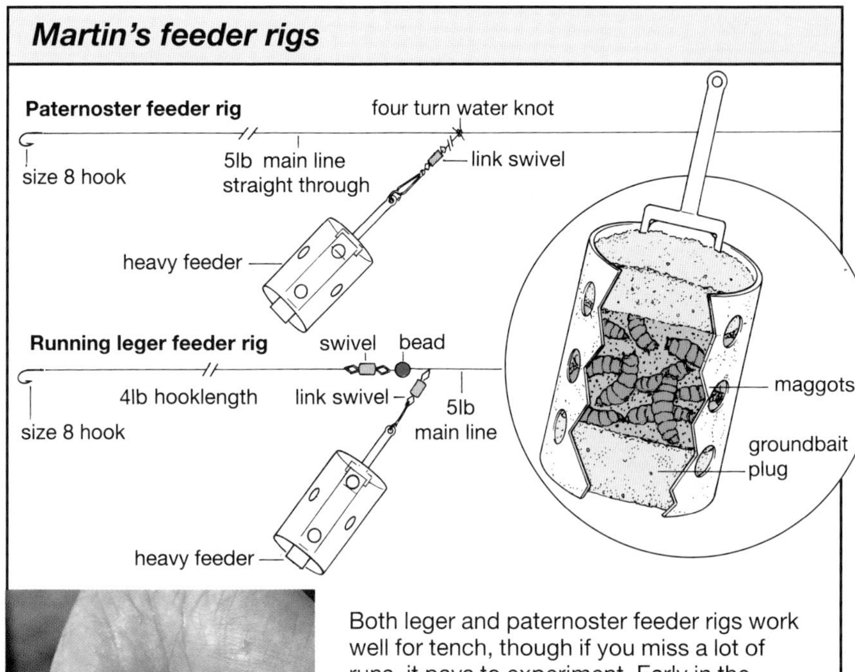

Both leger and paternoster feeder rigs work well for tench, though if you miss a lot of runs, it pays to experiment. Early in the season, team them with a bunch of maggots.

crumb in no time.

He lays down the catty and almost straight away there's a bleep from the bite alarm on the first rod. He ignores it – one bleep doesn't make a run. But more follow and his climber slowly starts climbing.

He ignores it no longer, and strikes. At long range this involves picking up the slack line first by winding down, but in Martin's hands it's one smooth movement.

Eureka! Martin's in and a swashbuckling tench goes off on a series of short, jagged runs. In typical tench fashion, it's dogged and hard to budge, but budge it he does, and soon its dorsal fin is waving in the shallows. But there's a bit of a surprise – it weighs only about 3½lb (1.6kg).

In many other waters, that's a nice fish, but in Sywell a fish this size is rare. The usual size is around 5lb (2.3kg), with quite a few much bigger. Ah well, a surprise is an interesting start.

5:00AM Oh yeah?

The bite alarms aren't giving Martin much time to relax – there's a bleep or two every few minutes. After a few of these bleeps, Martin retrieves one set of tackle. "I thought so," he says. "There are lots of roach in here and some small ones are at the bait." As proof he offers the maggots – they have been extensively chewed.

The bleeping continues, making it very difficult to spot a real run. It's also hard to know when to strike. After missing a couple of runs, Martin changes down from size 8 to size 12 hooks, to give the fish more confidence.

He also changes his strike pattern. "With finicky fish you've got to vary the strike until you start connecting." Having tried waiting for runs to develop, Martin decides to hit the bites on the second or third bleep – to see whether some of these twitches are caused by tench.

Minutes later the monkey climber jumps,

▼ Martin strikes as the climber rises. The exposed bed and rushes behind him provide evidence of the low water levels in many of Britain's reservoirs.

◀ ***Martin strikes quickly after a couple of bleeps on his bite alarm and is rewarded with a good fighting curve in his rod.***

Tench waters

There are many other good tench pits and reservoirs in Northamptonshire.

- **Ditchford Lakes** Another Wellingborough and Dist. Nene AC water.
- **Ecton Pits** Controlled by Northampton Nene AC.
- **Hollowell Res.** Day/season tickets in advance – Pitsford Fishing Lodge, Tel 0604 781350.
- **Thrapston Pits** Tickets from BP Tackle, Kettering.
- **Welford and Sulby Reservoirs** Season tickets in advance – John Ellis, Tel 0442 235400 or Bill Williams, Tel 0858 575394.

the alarm bleeps once, and Martin strikes. Almost to his own surprise, the rod assumes a fighting curve. This fish makes little effort to escape so Martin hurries it through the shallows. And guess what? It's smaller than the last one – about 2½lb (1.1kg). This is not what's supposed to happen at Sywell Reservoir.

Ten minutes later, there's another of those shy 'Is it, isn't it?' bites – Martin strikes and connects. Like the other two, it came on maggot – and like them it's a male. It's between the other two size-wise, weighing around 3lb (1.4kg).

6:15AM Turn of the worm

Martin's given sweetcorn, bread and lobworm a turn but all the bites so far have come on maggot. Obviously this has to change – and Martin has two runs in quick succession on lobworm. He's so surprised at this development, that he misses both.

The sun ought to be quite warm by now but that early morning haze has turned nasty, grey and thick. The wind which might have blown it away has dropped – making for a cold, dour opening morning.

Martin's getting plenty of exercise to warm his chilly muscles. A couple of slow taps turn into a full-blooded run, which he hits right away. Have you ever heard of tail-walking tench? Probably not, but this female is so overjoyed to be caught that she leaps from the water several times.

Once she's in the net it's obvious that she too is a three-pounder (1.4kg). Martin is puzzled. "I've never heard of anyone

▶ ***Unhooking a big male in the water. This can save the fish a lot of trauma and damage – if your net is big enough to allow you to get at the fish without it escaping.***

Tip Rods & sods

For long range tenching you need a rod that casts and picks up line on the strike well. A fast taper carp rod does this but more than 1¼lb (0.6kg) TC can kill the fight. Martin uses a pair of glass rods which are quite stiff but let him feel a good fish.

► A fine 6½lb (2.9kg) female which fought all the way to the bank. Fish of this size are quite common in Sywell Reservoir.

▼ Martin holds up the largest male in a bag of seven fish up to 6½lb (2.9kg). Not a bad start to the season.

catching four tench this small here. Still, it's good really – it means there's plenty of small fish to make the next generation."

9:10AM Big males

After a bleak and blank hour and a half, it suddenly starts to happen again. That's what tench fishing on a reservoir is often like. Long periods of nothing followed by a short burst of action as a group of tench moves on to your bed of feed.

In quick succession Martin makes the most of two runs, bringing in two larger males. At 4½lb (2kg) and 5½lb (2.5kg) they are, at last, 'average' Sywell tench!

By half past nine the sun at last makes an effort to shift the blanket of cloud, and smiles weakly down on the first day of the season. By eleven it's almost pleasant and it's easy to slip into that 'fishing since very early' stupor as the sun's warmth penetrates your third windcheater.

It's not so easy to stay stupefied when the tench are about, though. Suddenly, the monkey climber shoots off the top of the spike and the reel handle starts spinning.

The result is a really solid-looking curve in the 1¼lb (0.6kg) TC rod. Having had the whole of the close season to forget about being caught, the fish takes a while to wake up. But when it does, it takes off for London. Fortunately, this early on, there isn't too much weed, so Martin can afford to give line – letting the fish tire itself in the deep water.

After a series of kiting runs, the tench finds itself in the shallows and from there it is soon splashing its way over the rim of the net. Up on the scales, this is the one Martin's been waiting for – a 6lb 9oz (3kg) specimen. On top of six other tench to 5½lb (2.5kg), one of the more respectably-sized residents of Sywell makes a fine start to the season.

Catching big river roach

Roach wizard John Bailey has a very simple approach for big river redfins – he legers a nice fluffy piece of flake. The hard part is finding the fish...

By tradition, any roach of 2lb (0.9kg) or more is a specimen. This weight remains a kind of magical national target, reinforced by the angling press, but from many British rivers it isn't a realistic one.

At the top of the scale there are rivers like the Hampshire Avon, Wensum and Dorset Stour, where a 2lb (0.9kg) roach is a good one – but they have to be over 2½lb (1.1kg), at least, to be considered 'big'.

From most other rivers, however, a 2lb (0.9kg) roach really is the fish of a lifetime, so don't destroy yourself chasing 'super-roach' if they simply don't exist in the rivers you fish. Roach of 1¼-1¾lb (0.57-0.79kg) are very big ones anywhere and monsters from most rivers.

Big roach in residence

Choice of swim is vital. Look for one with slightly greater than usual depth. In water averaging 1.2m (4ft) deep, 1.5m (5ft) will do. If the river is generally 2.4m (8ft) deep, then look for a 3m (10ft) hole. Big roach just love such depressions, probably because they act as food traps.

Water speed is important too. Look for a

▲Roach don't have to weigh 2lb (0.9kg) or more to be classified 'big', says John Bailey. Any roach over 1lb (0.45kg) is a good specimen from most rivers in Britain.

◄John Bailey legers for roach on his beloved River Wensum in Norfolk. Big roach tend to like a still bait.

Titbits

"When looking for roach in a swim you have regularly prebaited with mashed bread, watch the water surface closely," advises John Bailey. "Sometimes foraging roach dislodge small bits of bread which float back up to the top."

slightly slower area, close to the main flow. It doesn't have to be still, but big roach definitely favour the slacks just off the current – provided the bed of the river is reasonably clean. They will not tolerate too much rubbish or mud, preferring harder sand, gravel or chalk.

Overhanging trees play their part as well. Many of the best river swims for big roach slide under alders and willows, possibly because their branches keep a little light out of the water and provide some shelter from cold winds.

Marginal reed beds are also important; big roach like to forage around the roots for beetles, snails and shrimps.

Not all these features guarantee the presence of big roach and you will have to show some 'fish awareness'. Try to get down to the river at dawn, the best time to see big roach rolling. Observe the swim very, very carefully, for big roach often send up tiny strings of bubbles as they forage.

Winter warmers

The prime months for big river roach are from about the beginning of October to the end of the season. The very best conditions at this time of the year are when air temperatures in the day are around 7-12°C (45-54°F), with a westerly wind bringing cloud and light rain. Conversely, the worst winter conditions are an easterly wind, clear skies, overnight frosts and daytime air temperatures below freezing.

But whatever the weather, don't despair – big roach always feed at some time. Generally, they feed best at dusk, or even in

John Bailey's simple leger rig

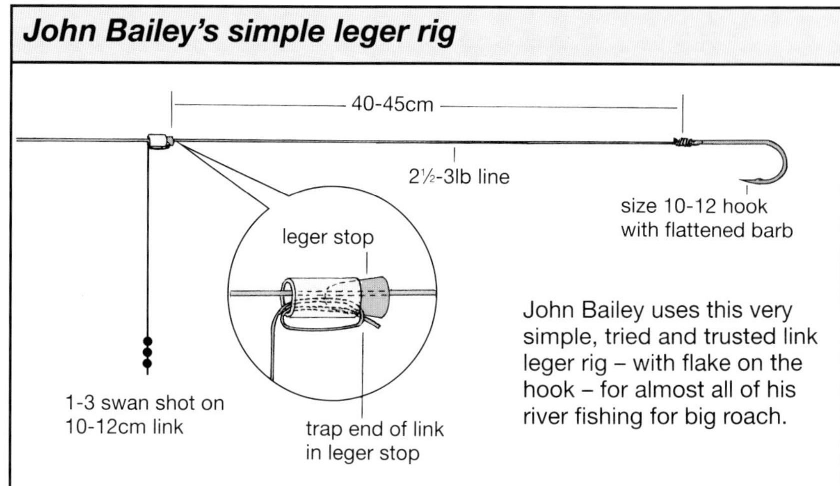

John Bailey uses this very simple, tried and trusted link leger rig – with flake on the hook – for almost all of his river fishing for big roach.

Flake faith

John Bailey's absolute belief in breadflake for big river roach is easy to understand when you consider that this bait has caught him more than 300 two-pounders (0.9kg)!

Caring for your catch

A big roach is a wonderful sight... at least it should be. The unfortunate fish shown above has no top lip – the result of careless unhooking by a thoughtless angler.

This is why John Bailey recommends flattening the barb on your hook with pliers – roach have such delicate mouths that it is all too easy to damage them when trying to remove a barbed hook.

A fat specimen winter roach in almost perfect condition (right). Such fish might be caught many times over the years. Only when they are handled with tender, loving care by their captors do they stay in good condition. Bad handling not only spoils the good looks of a fish; scale, fin or mouth damage can make it susceptible to disease and might even stunt its growth.

A classic encounter

John Bailey well remembers his first 'super-roach' and the feeling of absolute awe it inspired in him...

"I had reached the River Wensum in the late afternoon and by the time I had settled into my favourite swim, fed in some pieces of bread and set up the tackle, the January dusk was falling.

"I was on a slight bend where the flow steadied and eddied a little. In front of me was a thick bed of died-back sedge and above was an alder tree. The water was tinged with colour but not chocolate – I could see about 12-15 inches into it.

"A piece of legered breadflake followed the free offerings about three or four yards from the the rod tip. As the current was so slow I decided to use a bobbin indicator at the butt.

"My first two casts lasted 20-25 minutes each – longer, and the bread is probably off – and at last, after about 15 minutes of the third cast, the bobbin twitched. It hung still for ten seconds, then shot up!

"The battle that followed was dour and undramatic – the fish was anything but! It weighed a massive 2lb 13oz (1.27kg), and although it carried old scars of disease and heron attack, to me it was the most beautiful creature in the world."

the late afternoon if the weather is mild. Strangely, the worse the conditions, the later they tend to come on the feed. Often this is between 8:00pm and midnight – if you can stand the cold.

Dawn is another excellent time to catch big roach. This is especially true in summer, but first light can also be a good time to fish through the autumn and winter, particularly if the night hasn't been too cold and

▲ Prebait your chosen swim with mashed bread to wean big roach on to the bait, advises John Bailey. But mind not to overfeed them!

▼ Expert river angler Andy Orme with a magnificent winter river roach. Always take a camera with you to record your success.

True weight

"Many is the 1lb 15oz (0.88kg) roach that has been called 2lb (0.9kg), and many the 2lb 14oz (1.3kg) roach that has become a fabled 'three' (3lb/1.4kg)," says John Bailey. "This is a shame, and the anglers concerned are only really cheating themselves. For your own peace of mind, weigh roach accurately and know that your triumph is real."

the wind is slight.

Of course, big roach can sometimes be caught in full daylight, but generally they strongly favour the protection of the low light levels of dawn and dusk.

River in trim

For your best chance of a big roach, the river should be neither too clear nor too coloured – a slight tinge so you can see 30-60cm (1-2ft) into the water is perfect.

Think bread

Make no mistake, bread is THE bait for big roach. Other baits do work, of course, but nowhere near as well or as selectively.

Prebait your chosen swim or swims with mashed bread as often as you can – at least once a week and ideally every day. Once bread starts appearing in a swim, big roach begin expecting it and stop there in their wanderings to look for it.

How much bread you put in a swim – either when prebaiting or actually fishing – is crucial. You must put enough in to tempt them but not so much that it fills them up. Weather and river conditions dictate this decision. As a guide, in cold, clear water a big roach might eat half a slice of bread, while in mild weather when there's a touch of colour in the water it might eat a whole one. Given that most shoals of big roach number only three to six fish, the mathematics are easily worked out.

Big roach tactics

The best way to catch big roach is to leger a piece of breadflake firmly on the bottom. Float fishing does work occasionally, but most of the time big roach prefer to pick food up off the river bed at their leisure.

A simple 1-3 swan shot link – depending on the flow – with 2½-3lb (1.1-1.4kg) line straight through to a size 8-12 hook is all you need. A white quivertip in a torch beam is easily seen, though a butt bobbin is excellent in slow water. Bites are generally confident and hard to miss.

▼ John Wilson gently returns a specimen roach to the water, fit to live on and fight another day – and provide other anglers with the chance to catch what many regard as the most special of all coarse fish.

Gord Burton on Loch Lomond

The cold bleak expanses of Loch Lomond are forbidding at any time, so you'd have to be a madman to fish it in winter. Enter Gord Burton, the man whose heart and soul lie somewhere in the Crom Mhin bay.

Hoist the Jolly Roger! Fire up the Seagull! Don your sou' wester... Ace pike buccaneer and Lomond predator addict Gord Burton has come for another fix of those tailwalking, deep-running Loch Lomond pike. "Don't think you've caught pike until you've 'ad a Lomond monster. They're not the same species. These fish really *fight*."

The evening before the expedition Gord is down on the jetty catching bait. The sunset is calm and rosy, so it's hardly fair when the dawn brings a gusty force 4 westerly and February drizzle arrived, making it easier to surf than catch fish. By ten o'clock the wind had eased a bit, and we set off.

So, armed with a boat that seems pitifully small to deal with the tooth-filled terrors that Gord describes, off we chug from Balmaha for the first of two days in the Crom Mhin bay. The very name of it sends shivers down the spine... The Crom Mhin bay... the hottest hotspot of them all.

10:45PM The bay

The bay is surrounded by reed beds. So while the wind whistles about the ears, the boat lies steady. Gord puts out two baits – a live float-paternostered dancer (dancing dace) and a float-legered sardine. He also throws out a plug – a 20cm (8in) trout patterned Whopper Stopper Hellcat Magnum.

Most people don't bother with plugs even in summer, when tradition says they work best, and in the winter... Well, it's just sheer folly. Which is why it's no real surprise when it's taken in a flurry of spray. Despite the head shaking antics and a quick angry leap, it isn't long before Gord is unhooking a fish of about 4lb (1.8kg) in the water.

"You see 'ow that fish went. You can imagine what a big one is going to do. That's why you 'ave to use 'eavy lines 'ere. Nothing under 15-18lb (6.8-8.1kg) 'as the stopping power to 'andle a big old girl 'eading off towards the snags by the bank."

He stops plugging to check the livebait. It doesn't look very happy. The wind creates turbulence in the 1.5m (5ft) deep water, making it difficult for the dancer to swim. Gord puts it back in his bucket to recover and replaces it with a dead smelt.

He recasts the plug. "There's a channel which runs along the bank from the mouth of the bay. It swings out when it reaches the burn there. It's not deep but the pike cruise along it into the bay. That's what I'm casting the plugs over."

▲ Gord Burton, the flying Lancastrian, at the helm of the 'Creek Chub' in search of Esox magnus – the mammoth pike.

One of Britain's best-known pike anglers, Gord has fished obsessively for his favourite species for over 20 years. In that time he has had many amazing catches. One day in June 1986 he had 25 fish from the Crom Mhin bay to 17lb (7.7kg) by 11am!

Time-saver

One cheap way to simulate the effect of fishing Loch Lomond is simply to take a powerful fan on a long power lead into a walk-in freezer. At regular intervals a friend should throw a bucket of icy water over you, allowing the fan to blow it into your face, while you say, "There's nothing like fishing on the vast bleakness of Lomond." It's a (mad) man's life.

◄▲ Around midday Gord strikes into a fish on sardine (left). Despite putting up an amazing struggle, after unhooking (above) it weighed in at a mere four pounds (1.8kg).

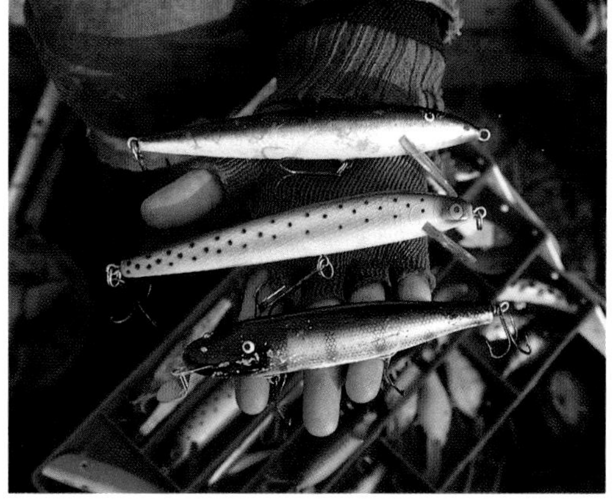

◄ *Gord prefers big lures in winter – a sluggish pike might not be prepared to move to take a small bait. The water was also a little coloured, so a bigger lure gives the pike more to see.*

Three of his favourites are (from the top) a Rapala, a Hellcat and a Creek Chub Pikie. He is so fond of the last-named, he named his boat after it.

How to get there

Balmaha
B837
LOCH LOMOND
Drymen
River Endrick
Gartocharn
A809
A811
Balloch
A82
N
Alexandria
to Glasgow
A813

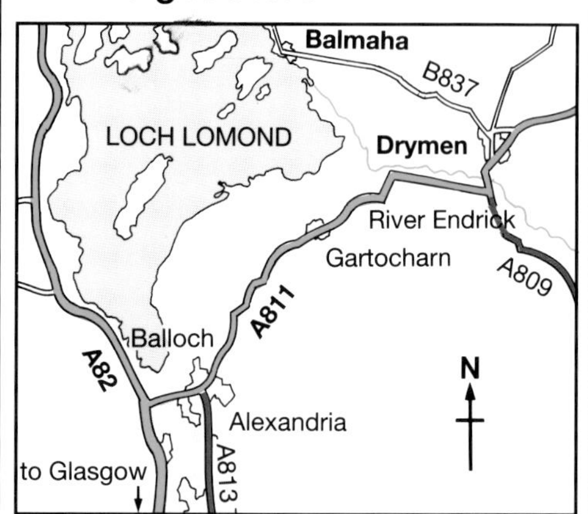

● **By car** Take the A82 from Glasgow through Alexandria, then turn on to the A811 towards Stirling. Shortly after the road crosses the Endrick, turn left on to the B837 at Drymen which takes you to Balmaha.

● **By train** The nearest station is Balloch. From there buses run to Drymen (and direct from Glasgow too) where you can take the local taxi to Balmaha.

Which action?

In summer, work your plugs hard and fast to give them plenty of action. In winter, however, the fish are more sluggish so aim just to amble the plug along about 30cm (1ft) under the surface. Pike have their eyes on top of their heads, and a plug mooching along above them often tempts a take.

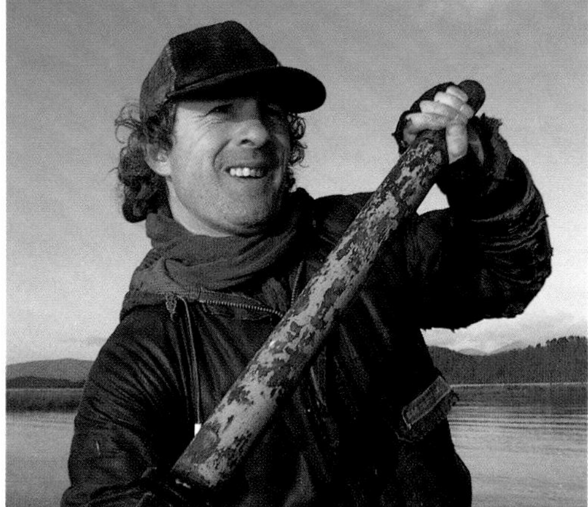

◄ *Day two of the expedition dawns bright and clear, and before long Gord is quietly positioning the boat in Crom Mhin bay.*

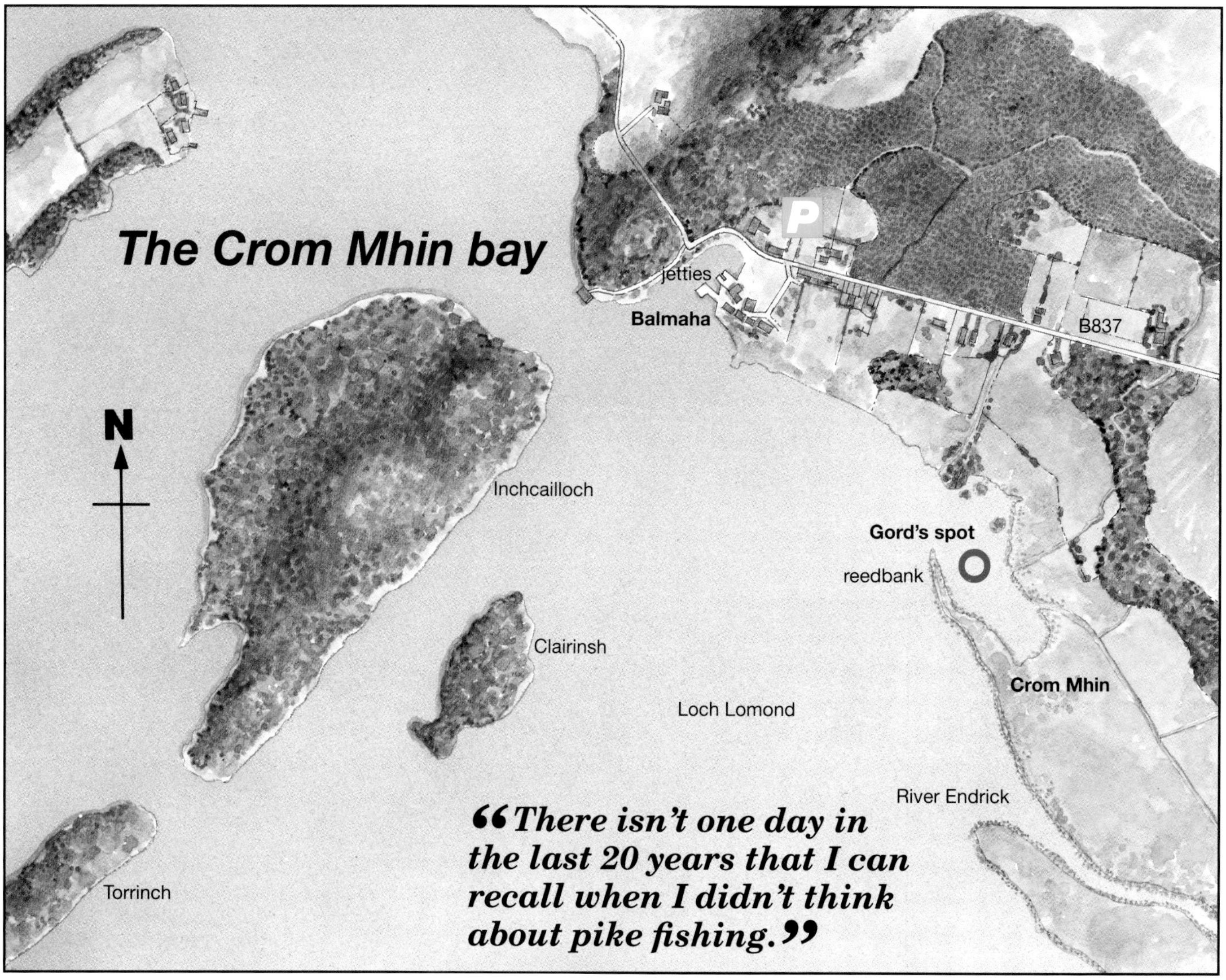

The Crom Mhin bay
P
jetties
Balmaha
B837
N
Inchcailloch
Gord's spot
reedbank
Clairinsh
Crom Mhin
Loch Lomond
River Endrick
Torrinch
"There isn't one day in the last 20 years that I can recall when I didn't think about pike fishing."

▲ *No matter how cold it is, Gord is always ready to have a chuck with a plug. Fished slowly they can be very effective in winter.*

Fishery facts

The Crom Mhin bay is half an hour by dinghy from Balmaha. Bring your own boat and pay a small launching fee, or rent a boat there.

Mrs Lucy Fraser runs *Moniack*, the nearest B & B, though you will have to take your muddy boots off. If you can't handle the thought of behaving properly, there is also a caravan available for hire by fishermen. Lucy will be pleased to give you details (tel. 0360 87357).

The Crom Mhin bay is superb in February because the big females come in to feed up before spawning. In summer it can host a pack of decent pike, especially when the water level is high, but is often home only to jacks.

Tip Fishmongers

Buy deadbaits fresh from a fishmonger, rather than blast frozen from the tackle shop. You don't know how long the bait has languished in the shop's freezer. You can't check the eyes of frozen fish for freshness and clarity, as you can with fish on a fishmonger's slab.

11:30AM Sardine jack

The drizzle which has been around all morning solidifies into a steady downpour. The texture of the rain is very much improved by the wind which drives it straight under the hat and into the eyes.

However, Gord is undeterred. "I love this place. You know all about it when you're out on the vast bleakness of Lomond in February. There's nowhere to touch it." His eyes mist over as he imagines the take of a Loch Lomond monster.

For a while nothing happens, except that the rain actually eases. Then the float on the sardine bait starts edging towards the submerged trees along the bank. Gord picks up the rod, calmly winds down to the fish and hits it. A pike erupts from the water and tailwalks away from the boat.

"Look at that! It's only a four-pounder, but it thinks it's a twenty." Even in the coldest weather, the fish fight like fury. These are no ordinary pike.

Sadly though, that's it for the day. After seven hours in the rain, it's good to get back to the warmth of *Moniack* – our B & B. But there's no supper for Gord until he's checked all of his lines. He doesn't want one breaking on the first good pike.

Day Two: early start

Our second dawn couldn't be more different from the first – blue skies, hardly a breath of wind and glassy calm. Gord stops the Seagull engine and rows into position. He's going to try farther inside the bay this time, near the mouth of a burn which runs into it. We're not alone; another boat has moved in to sample the pike fishing.

Gord moves silently and efficiently around the boat as he casts out a smelt and a herring. "When it's this calm, you don't want any noise or unnecessary movements, or you'll put the pike down," he whispers.

Once the baits are out and in position, he repeats yesterday's drill, going through his armoury of big plugs. But when, by half

Gord's rigs for Lomond monsters

A dancing dace deadbait is suspended on a paternoster link. The long 60cm (2ft) wire trace helps prevent bite-offs if a pike misses the bait.

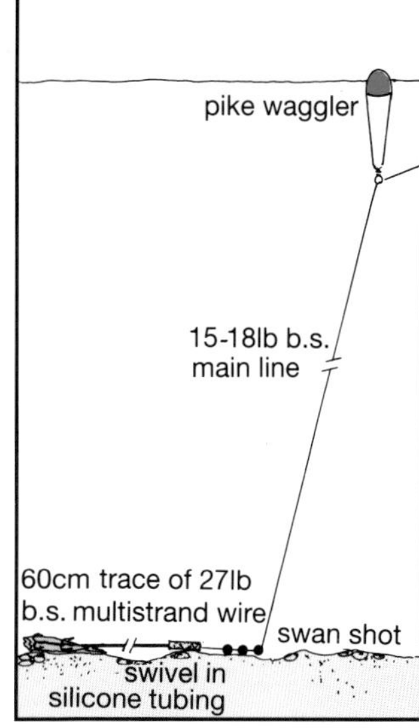

A float leger is ideal for deadbaits, especially well scented sea deadbaits. The waggler holds the line above any weed and indicates runs.

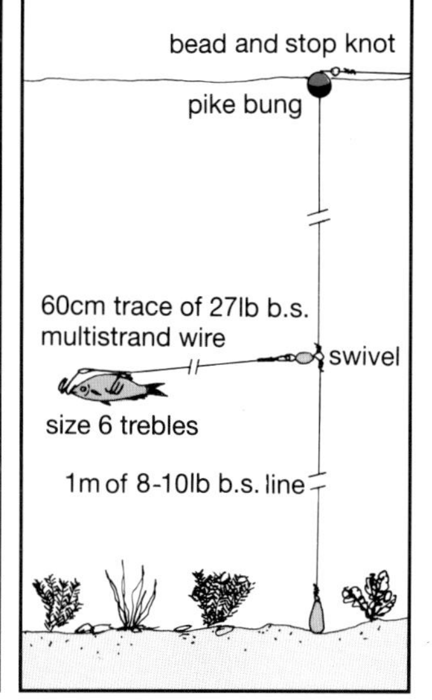

A float paternoster is best for livebaits and suspended deadbaits, particularly freshwater deadbaits such as the dace on the left.

Tip I'm a frayed knot

One of the plug-caught pike swam through another line and pulled it in. Gord made a point of checking the line and knots, to make sure there was no damage from the pike's gill rakers or the wire trace.

past ten, there still hasn't been a run, he retrieves the smelt to put on a live dancer.

The wind gets up slightly, making a bit of a ripple and bringing home the February cold. Despite this, Gord keeps up a quiet banter, recounting courageous piking exploits of the past. Every so often Lomond inspires him and he breaks into verse. "But no matter 'ow brave or bold, you put your gloves on when your hands are cold." And he does.

He looks about, drinking in the atmosphere. "This is what piking's all about for me. The bleakness, the emptiness. It's so vast, there's always the chance of a 'uge

▲ Gord is a great fan of multipliers for piking, as they yield line smoothly to a big fish, and don't cause line twist. Note also the rod rests that he has made for his boat fishing. They hold one or two rods out of his way.

▼ Clamping down hard on the spool as a decent Lomond pike makes a break for the snags. This is the place for pike that really put a bend in your rod.

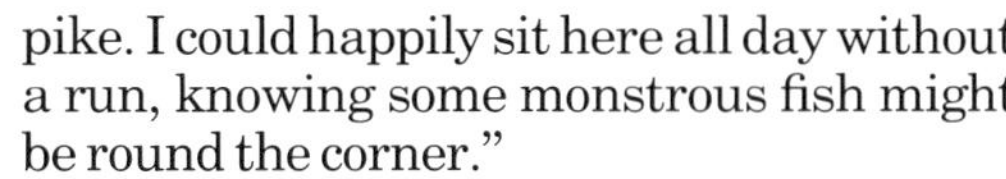

pike. I could happily sit here all day without a run, knowing some monstrous fish might be round the corner."

11:40AM Root problem

Gord tries to retrieve the dace livebait, but finds it stuck. "Ah. My little dancer has found sanctuary in some far distant weed bed. And it is my sad duty to pull it out." All around the inner part of the bay there are extensive potamogeton weed beds in summer, and the roots provide a ready-made system of snags during the winter.

Almost as soon as the dancer is repositioned out of reach of the roots, the float marking the legered herring vanishes, to reappear much closer to the boat. Gord winds down but feels no resistance. When the bait comes in it's been savaged. "That was probably only a jack. They tend to do the most damage to a bait."

Gord quickly recasts with half a mackerel and then clips a home-painted golden Rapala to his spinning trace. "Let's see if there are a few pike over there then." So saying, he casts the plug over to where the run had come from. There isn't long to wait.

Third cast produces a take. This fish doesn't leap but runs parallel to the boat. Gord draws it in and every run brings it closer to the net. Eventually he has it and shortly after slips the lean 8lb (3.6kg) fish back into the frigid Lomond waters. That's two fish on plugs and just one on baits. So much for conventional thinking.

12:45PM Hardly a mark

Having only had one fish, our fellow pikers in the bay head off to another spot. Hardly have they left when the livebait float stops

▲ A Loch Lomond demon tamed by a golden Rapala – at 8lb (3.6kg) it's no specimen, but it certainly knows how to scrap.

► *In just 1.5m (5ft) of water it's hard to avoid the potamogeton roots which cover the bottom of the far end of the bay.*

bobbling around and shoots off left. Since the last bait was dropped, Gord hits this one quickly. For a second the rod testifies that this is a good fish, then the line falls slack. Gord retrieves to find the bait almost intact.

"That's the sure sign of a big bold Lomond pike. They can 'old a bait right inside their mouths, without putting a tooth into it."

About a minute later, the other bait – a half mackerel – goes off for a slow wander towards the reed bed. "That's a good fish. See 'ow slow it's swimming – it isn't worried about anything, it's just looking for a good place to eat.

Gord waits. "With a big bait like 'alf a mackerel you can afford to let the fish 'ave a bit of time." Eventually he's happy and he tightens up to the float and bends into the fish. "This is a better one all right," he grins, as the fish takes off.

A very determined pike is attached to Gord's line and it swims powerfully and unhurriedly off towards the reeds. "I've got to stop 'er in open water," he manages between grunts as he strains to turn the fish. "This is why you need strong line."

The fish stops and shakes its head, trying to dislodge the annoying thing in its jaw. Gord draws it close, and once it sees the boat, it stands on its tail and crashes back, trying to frighten this impudent and irritating intruder. At no time does it think it might be beaten.

"She's a really good fish," says Gord. "Just look at the way she's pulling." Finally he manages to trick his adversary into

Greased lines

Grease the line above the float for paternostered baits, particularly livebaits. If you don't, it can sink to the bottom and a pike may pick it up along with the bait. The fish can then bite through the line above the float, so you lose everything.

▲ *We have lift off! A Lomond pike attempts to become the first Scottish fish in space, as Gord tries to keep it under control. Even the smaller pike from this forbidding water don't know when they're beaten.*

Bait saver

Baits, especially deadbaits, tend to go in cycles on Lomond. Herring is currently good, but a few years back, you couldn't get a bite on a sea bait. However, smelts have proved an enduring choice since they were first tried.

Don't throw your deadbaits away at the end of a session, particularly if you are going to fish that mark the following day. Giving pike a free meal just fills them up and makes them less inclined to feed and take a bait.

◄ *The hunchback of Crom Mhin bay – not every pike is a sleek, lean specimen. Some, like this one, may look a little strange, lumpy back and all, but with that huge dorsal, tail and anal fins, you can certainly see where its power comes from.*

▶ ***Gord contemplates the rugged emptiness of the surroundings, which speaks to him of the elusive possibility of a truly enormous, almost terrifyingly huge fish.***

swimming too close to the net and she's trapped. "She's not as big as I thought. I must 'ave forgotten 'ow 'ard these pike fight. Still, she's a double."

She's neatly hooked in the scissors, so Gord clearly didn't wait too long. On weighing she turns out to be 11lb 15oz (5.4kg) – a fine, boldly marked pike.

1:15PM Go crazy

No sooner is the fish weighed, returned and a bait recast, than the livebait begins to move. Gord gives it plenty of time – the fish seem reluctant to take a bait properly today. The float slows down and then slides off in a new direction, and Gord strikes.

It's not the size of the last, but for a six-pounder (2.7kg) it puts up an amazing tussle. Once in the boat, Gord admires the build of a typical Lomond fish. "Look at the size of that tail... built for speed. A lean, mean fighting machine."

For the next two and a half hours, it's all action, as Gord winds into a succession of fish from close to the mouth of the burn. In most cases the float dithers then shoots off, but with one, it cocks irregularly for a couple of minutes, moves a couple of feet nearer the boat, stops and moves back again.

When do you hit a 'run' like that? The answer is, when you think the fish has taken the bait well. But don't wait too long – far better to miss a few fish than to gut-hook one. Striking as the float moved away again produced a muscular eight-pounder (3.6kg) hooked in the scissors.

At about half past four Gord decides it's time to head back, before darkness maroons us in the bay. He smiles as he steers back to Balmaha. "Seven pike in February. Who'd 'ave believed it?" He stares wistfully at the engraving rivetted to the side of his boat, *Esox magnus* – the mythical monster pike. "Next time. Maybe next time... "

▼ ***The biggest fish of the day is this near twelve-pounder (5.4kg). February is usually the time to catch few, but big fish. This particular February trip it was different, with plenty of smaller pike.***

Man with a mission

In the 1970s, when Gord fished Lomond whenever he could, he would collect baits most evenings to make his regular weekend trip up to Lomond. "It wasn't a question of enjoyment, it was an obsession. I just 'ad to be 'ere." A weekend without a big Lomond fish was a disaster, but now he's more relaxed about it and actually enjoys his piking.

Chris Yates on the Hampshire Avon

Many anglers consider Chris Yates eccentric because he uses vintage fishing tackle. Join him for a day on the Royalty Fishery, read what he has to say about his methods and decide for yourself...

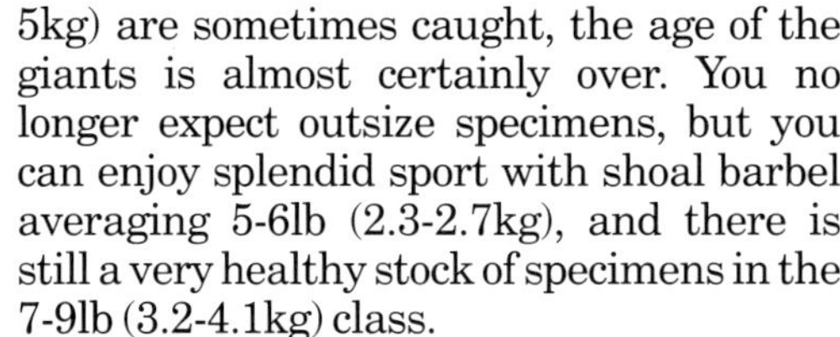

► *Man in harmony with the water. Chris Yates, complete with felt hat – the perfect specimen hunter – waits for the bite of a monster.*

▼ *In high summer the water is at its lowest. The best places for barbel are where the river is weedy and the current fastest – as it is here at Watersmeet.*

The Royalty Fishery on the lower Hampshire Avon is the most famous stretch of barbel river in Britain. For over sixty years it has produced not only great numbers of barbel, but many outstanding specimens. The current record of 14lb 6oz (6.52kg) was taken there in 1934 and, ten years before, in the close season, a monster of 16lb 4oz (7.37kg) was landed by a salmon angler after it grabbed his spinner.

Nowadays, though barbel of 10-11lb (4.5-5kg) are sometimes caught, the age of the giants is almost certainly over. You no longer expect outsize specimens, but you can enjoy splendid sport with shoal barbel averaging 5-6lb (2.3-2.7kg), and there is still a very healthy stock of specimens in the 7-9lb (3.2-4.1kg) class.

Nor do you fish the Royalty if you are looking for peace and quiet. There are many stretches of the middle Avon where you may also find excellent barbel fishing and have perhaps half a mile between you and the next angler. On the Royalty you are lucky to have ten yards, especially at weekends.

But nowhere on the Avon will you find such a concentration of barbel in such a short length of river. This is why, when the fishing has been a bit slow on my favourite, more pastoral stretches of the river, I occasionally fish the Royalty. It can restore a barbel angler's faith in himself. Such was the case one sunny day in late September.

More like a canal

The summer drought had caused the level of the Avon to drop alarmingly. I have never seen the Royalty so low and I guessed the barbel might be unusually difficult to tempt. Not only had there been no rain for months, much of the river was being stolen by the water authorities' pumping stations. For the first quarter of a mile downstream of the Great Weir, which marks the upper limit of the fishery, there was hardly any flow at all; the mighty Hampshire Avon was more like a canal.

Only after the confluence with the Parlour stretch, at Watersmeet, was there any appreciable current. It was here, then, that I chose to begin fishing.

◀ ***Chris, who fishes light for maximum mobility, searches the weedbeds and gravel runs of the Royalty Fishery for any signs that indicate barbel as he makes his way upstream towards Watersmeet.***

The weedbeds looked lush and thick and, using polarizing glasses, I could see a clean bed of gravel shelving down between and beneath them. With the extra push of water from the Parlour Pool, it made a textbook barbel swim.

Simply the best

In all my fishing, I like to keep things simple. The art of angling is not about encumbering yourself with a mountain of flashy, unnecessary gear; it is about harmony between the angler, the fish and the fish's habitat.

Once the angler – through knowledge and appreciation – has become closer to his quarry, then the actual catching of the fish is a relatively simple matter. If you can present a feeding fish with an acceptable bait and not arouse its suspicions you will, within reason, hook it, no matter what

Watersmeet on the Royalty Fishery

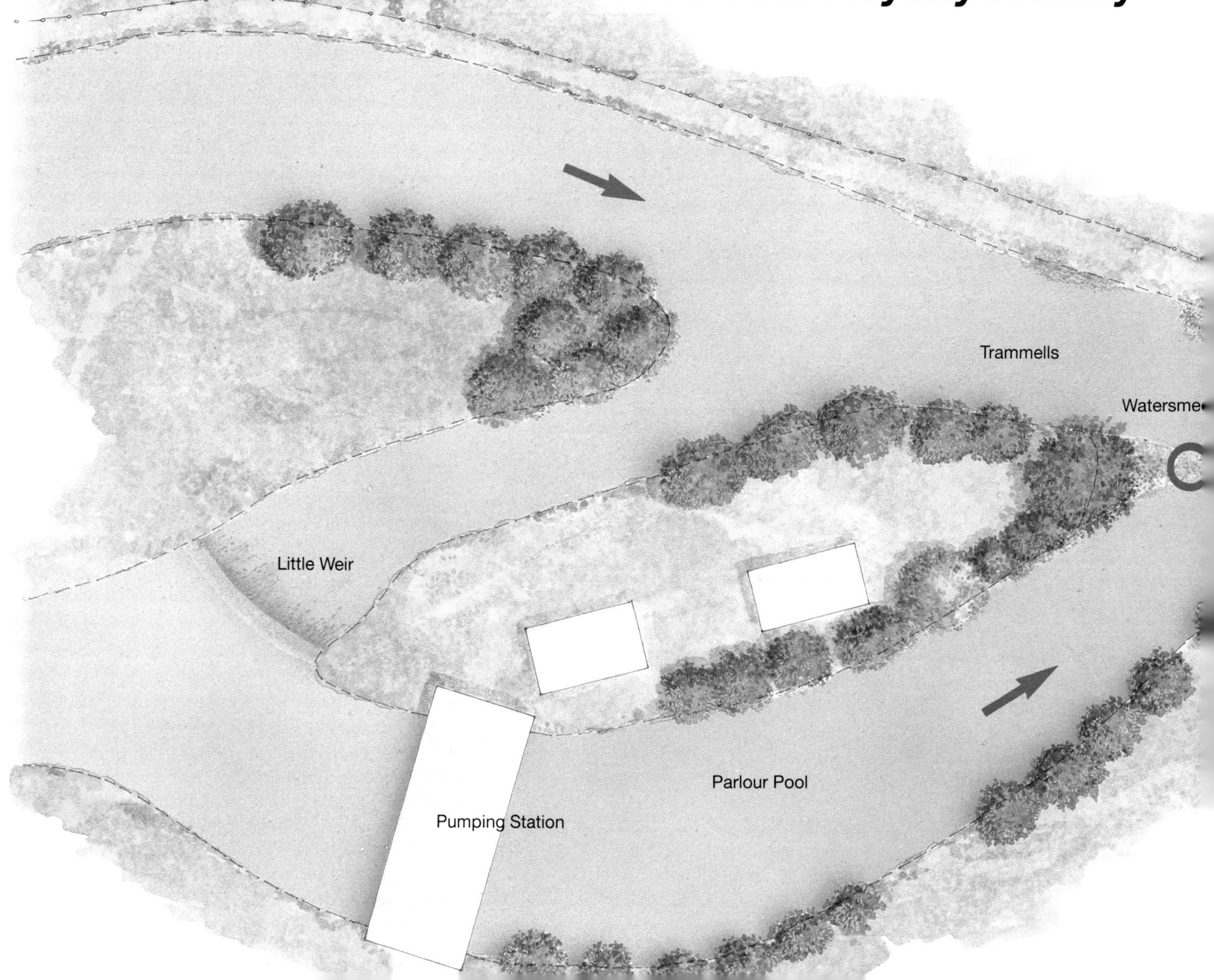

Trammells
Watersme
Little Weir
Parlour Pool
Pumping Station

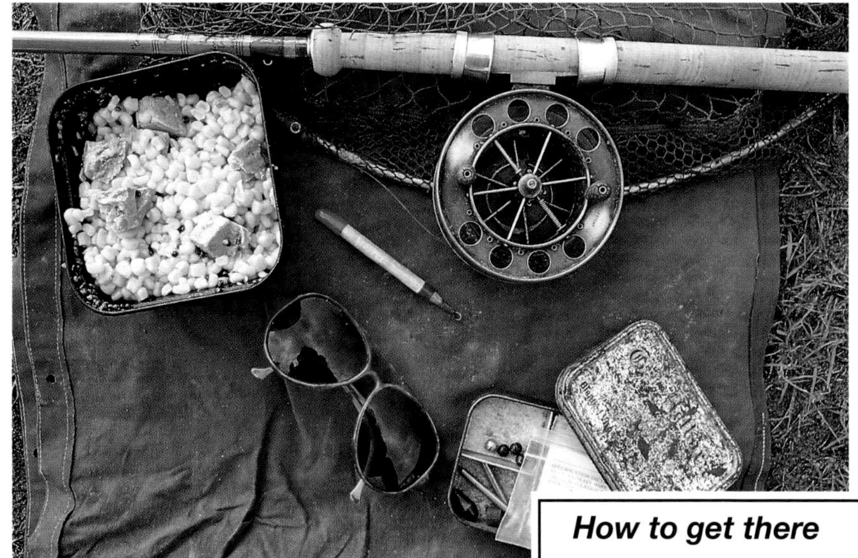

▲ *All the essential equipment a barbel angler should need – a rod, reel, float, baitbox with bait, polarizing sunglasses and tackle tin with hooks, swan-shot, weights and leger stops. Chris finds that this is all he needs to tackle even the largest and shyest barbel.*

> ***" In all my fishing I like to keep things simple. The art of angling is not about encumbering yourself with a mountain of unnecessary gear. "***

method you adopt or whether you're using a high-tech graphite rod or a beanpole from the garden.

My rod was specially designed for me by Edward Barder. It is 11ft 9in (3.58m) long and crafted in split cane, which I regard as superior to any of the synthetic materials now available. It is called the *Barbus Maximus* and is quite simply the best split cane rod I have ever used.

My reel is a beautifully sweet Allcock's Aerial centrepin; 4in (10cm) in diameter, with a wide drum, it runs as smoothly today as it did when it was made, seventy years ago. Because of the dense weed I had loaded it with 8lb (3.6kg) line.

How to get there

- **By car** Take the A35 from Southampton – Christchurch and after the road crosses the Avon turn right up Bargate. Just after Davis Tackle turn right into the Royalty car park. From Salisbury, take the A338 until the road passes under the A31 then take the B3347. Go west on the A35 at the roundabout.
- **By train** Take the Waterloo-Bournemouth line to Christchurch.
- **Day tickets** from Royalty hut in the car park until November, then from Davis Tackle.

N
Royalty Fishery
A338
A3060
A35
Christchurch
Bournemouth
Christchurch Station
Hengistbury Head

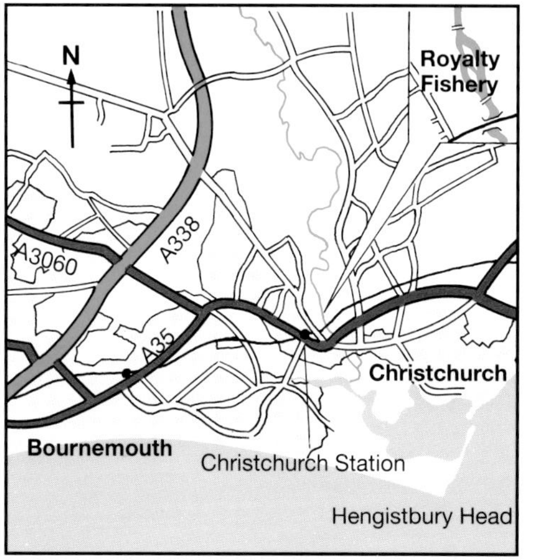

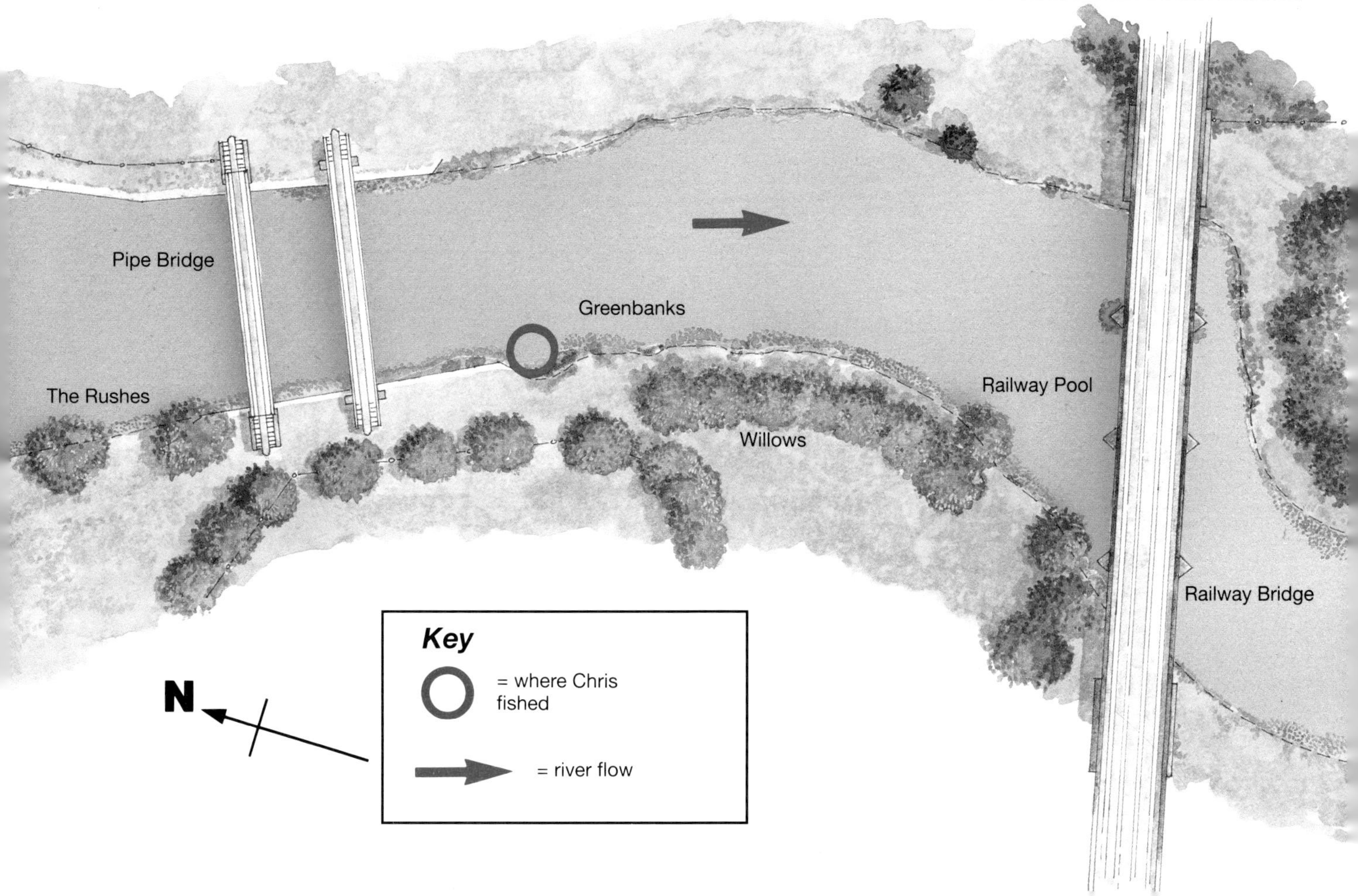

Pipe Bridge
Greenbanks
The Rushes
Willows
Railway Pool
Railway Bridge
Key
= where Chris fished
= river flow
N

▲ ***During that biteless hour, when the sun is too bright and the fish are skulking in the weedbeds, there is only one sensible option for the barbel angler.***

▼ ***Using the Wallis cast, Chris casts directly from the drum of his centrepin. This presents the bait accurately and delicately at up to 30m (33yd) range.***

I like to travel light, so that I can move quickly from one swim to another as my mood or the mood of the fish dictates. All my bits and pieces are contained in an old tobacco tin: a dozen swan shot, a stubby quill float, a few legers and leger stops, and half a dozen packets of forged, eyed hooks in sizes from 6 to 12.

My bait for the day was a can of sweetcorn and a can of luncheon meat, the latter cut into irregular shapes and sizes and mixed with the corn in a bait box. This flavours the meat with the corn and the corn with the meat.

Casting at shadows

I began fishing at about noon – not the best time for barbel on such a sunny day. They prefer cloudy days or times of low light at dawn or evening. But I saw a familiar dark shape shadowing across the gravel – a barbel of about 7-8lb (3.2-3.6kg) – and I felt hopeful as I scattered some corn and meat into the swim.

I had waded out into mid-river and it was a simple matter to cast a two-swan leger almost to the far bank then let the current bring the bait – four grains of corn on a size 6 hook to a 1m (3ft), 6lb (2.7kg) trace – round and down.

Once I felt the two swan-shot bumping across the gravel I gently let the reel unwind so that the bait travelled naturally down the middle of the swim. Occasionally I held it stationary for a few moments and then, after a pause, twitched the rod tip, nudging the bait on downstream. I find this the most effective method of searching every inch of the river bed in clear water and between dense weedbeds.

Bites are detected by touch: the line runs across the fingers of the left hand and you are immediately aware of the slightest change in pressure. Sometimes there is the merest vibration as a fish picks up the bait and hangs steady in the current. Sometimes a fish grabs the bait and turns downstream with it, abruptly tightening the line and banging the rod tip over: impossible to miss.

Chris's leger rig

Chris's rig is simplicity itself. In a slowish river like the Avon in drought, he uses just two touching swan-shot as the weight. The 6lb (2.7kg) hooklength ends in a size 6 hook at one end and a loop at the other. The 8lb (3.6kg) reel line is attached to the loop by a 10-turn half-blood knot. With this rig Chris can search out all the fish-holding areas of the pool he is fishing while staying in contact with the hook. In this way he can feel the very shyest of bites.

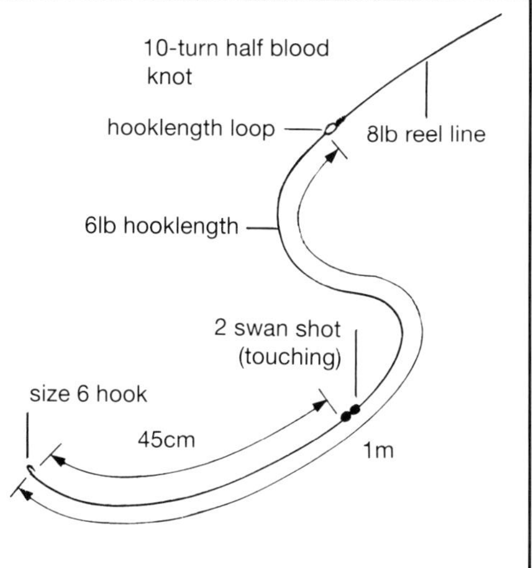

For the first hour I had only one feeble bite which I didn't even attempt to strike. Then I changed the hookbait from corn to a small chunk of luncheon meat and had a good thump of a bite almost instantly. The strike connected me to a fish that did not bore and haul in the manner of a barbel, but jagged violently like a chub.

Indeed it was a chub, quite a good one by the look of it. But as I began to ease it towards the net, it threw the hook. Of course this was a perfectly acceptable loss. I was, after all, using a *barbel* rod.

Time for a nap

Being a weekday, the Royalty was not as crowded as it often is at weekends, yet there were still half a dozen other anglers within fifty yards of me. By mid-afternoon only one of them had caught a barbel. "It's going to be hard going," said the bailiff Alan as he walked up the bank opposite. "The sun's too bright and the fish haven't got enough water over their heads."

In such difficult circumstances there is really only one sensible option for the barbel angler. So I wound in, waded ashore, found a shady spot and took a short siesta.

I awoke refreshed at about five o'clock and walked down the bank to see how the other anglers were faring. They had nothing to report, but as I peered into the water below the Pipe Bridge I saw the tell-tale flash of a barbel. You can see this quite wonderful phenomenon in even fairly deep water and it means that a barbel is scouring its flank on the gravel. I always associate it with feeding fish and am therefore always optimistic if barbel are flashing in my swim.

The sun was curving towards the Christchurch rooftops and we were rapidly approaching that optimum fishing time, the witching hour, the last hour of daylight.

▼ The sun is curving down towards the Christchurch rooftops and Chris knows he is in with a chance. The best fishing time is the last hour before dusk. Even if the barbel have failed to feed all day, there is still every chance they will do so towards sunset.

▼ After hours of searching, casting and hoping, the first barbel is reward indeed. All Chris has to do now is land it – with the persuasive pressure of his split cane rod.

I hurriedly fetched my tackle and began casting well out into midstream, dropping the meat bait above the fish and letting it bump down towards them.

Rocketing beauty

After about a dozen casts the bait was decisively taken even before it sank to the river bed. The sensitive tip of the rod quivered then hooped over and I struck into a powerful barbel.

The fish ploughed straight upstream into the weeds so I quickly marched down the bank and applied pressure from below, persuading it out of the clutching fronds and into the clear pool in front of me. It surfaced and lashed the water with its tail. It looked a good one and argued convincingly against coming to the net.

But eventually, after a last rocketing surge towards the far bank, I eased it over the rim, into the mesh; a beautiful specimen of 7lb 14oz (3.57kg) and well worth the rather long wait.

A few minutes later, casting into the same narrow run between the weedbeds, I hooked another, smaller fish which turned out to be a lovely, bright golden barbel of just over 5lb (2.3kg).

On my last cast, not long before sunset, I had a vague, trembling bite and hooked a huge-feeling fish that just began pushing slowly and determinedly upstream under the Pipe Bridge. Pressure from below or from the side had no effect and the barbel – I don't believe it could have been anything else – simply continued on its way. Then, sickeningly, the carefully sharpened hook sprang free. Perhaps there are still monsters in the Royalty after all...

Tip Sensitivity

Chris rarely uses a rod rest, prefering to feel for bites. Sometimes, when the barbel are feeding shyly, there is only the vaguest trembling of the rod tip to indicate a bite.

Using a rest, most of these bites are easily missed but by holding the rod you can respond instantly, sometimes converting even the tiniest tweak into a surging barbel. If they're being really finicky, don't wait for a firm pull – strike at the first indication you get of a possible bite.

▲ In the end, after a last magnificent surge towards the far bank, the fish is on its way into the net. When landing a big barbel, always try to manoeuvre it upstream before leading it towards your net.

Tip Upstream

In especially difficult conditions, fish a stationary bait upstream and strike when the line flutters, jerks or falls slack. This is the most sensitive legering method.

▲ After a hard fight, Chris holds up a beautifully coloured, perfectly proportioned Royalty barbel of 7lb 14oz (3.6kg). It took luncheon meat legered with very little weight due to the low levels, on a size 6 hook down a narrow run between dense weed beds.

► Barbel always fight till exhausted and should be held in the water, nose upstream, while they recover their strength. Without this nursing, a fish could roll over on the surface and be swept to its death.

Catching the mighty red-eye

Jim Gibbinson has been fishing for specimen tench for over 15 years with a variety of tackle and tactics. Here he passes on some of what he's discovered.

Tip Hot tenching

A heatwave can all but kill most sport but is often ideal for tench. Some really top catches come on days when you need high protection sun cream to fish in the sun.

In the last 20 years or so there has been something of a revolution in tench fishing – the average and maximum size of tench has shot up. Until quite recently, a 5lb (2.3kg) tench would have been considered a specimen. Nowadays, in the 1990s, even a seven-pounder (3.2kg) is not that unusual.

No-one can be absolutely sure why this has happened, but it may be partly due to increasing water weed in British waters. Rivers, lakes, ponds, pits and reservoirs certainly have become much weedier, possibly because farmers have been using more artificial fertilizers to bump up the yield of their land.

Much of this fertilizer is washed into rivers and still waters where it encourages strong water plant growth. More plants mean more insects and a richer supply of the tench's natural food.

With more big tench around there has never been a better time to get to grips with a specimen. Unfortunately, the increase in weed means that these big fish are harder to get out of the water. There are few places left where it is possible to fish light lines and expect to land that huge tench.

All this means you need to take some fairly hefty tackle to many big tench waters. However, try to remain flexible in your approach so you can take advantage of any less weedy waters by fishing with lighter tackle. That way you'll enjoy your tenching more and get better results.

◄As waters have got weedier, so tackle has had to get heavier to cope with pulling big tench out of the weeds. Here the author poses with the end result.

Big tench waters

- **Johnson's Lakes,** near Maidstone, Kent. Day/season tickets on bank.
- **Leisure Sport Pits,** Thames, Lea, Kennet and Darenth valleys. Permits from Leisure Sport, Thorpe Park, Staines Rd, Chertsey KT16 8PN.
- **Savay Lake,** near Denham, Bucks. Day tickets from some local newsagents, season tickets from the fishery manager, 309 Shirland Road, London W9.
- **Various other gravel pits** around Britain where big tench have grown unmolested and unsuspected. Check them out just before dawn in a spell of settled weather near the end of the close season. If tench are there in numbers you'll see them rolling. Don't fish a virgin water on spec.

Tip Roll up

Tench are quite territorial and remain in an area for several weeks before moving, often for no apparent reason. Don't flog away at a once-productive swim in the hope that it'll come good again. Look instead to see where the tench are rolling and fish there.

▲▼ ***You need heavy tackle (like that above), fixed-lead rigs and particles or 16mm (⅝ in) boilies to have a realistic chance of landing a specimen tench from most waters.***

Fixed-lead rig

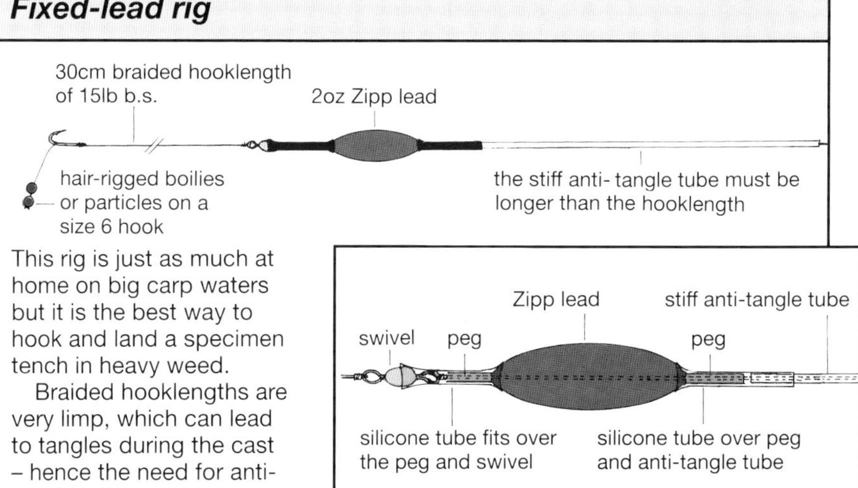

This rig is just as much at home on big carp waters but it is the best way to hook and land a specimen tench in heavy weed.

Braided hooklengths are very limp, which can lead to tangles during the cast – hence the need for anti-tangle tubing.

Tackling the weed

Many tench waters become heavily weeded, aquatic jungles in the summer and you must use appropriate gear. You need a 2¼lb (1kg) TC carp rod, coupled with about 200m (220yd) of 12lb (5.4kg) line on a sturdy fixed-spool reel.

Terminal tackle is a size 6 forged hook on a 15lb (6.8kg) braided hooklength. Fixed-lead, anti-tangle rigs are most effective in heavy weed. There's no getting away from it – you need carp tackle to get a big tench out of a weedy water.

Standard carp baits – boilies and particles – work best with carp gear. Tench seem particularly fond of fruity, creamy flavours such as Maple Creme and Strawberry Jam. If you make your own baits, use a milk protein or bird seed base with these flavours. Tench also readily take fish flavoured boilies based on a fish meal mix.

The best of the particles are sweetcorn, black-eye beans, chick peas and maple peas. Fish both particles and boilies on a 2.5cm (1in) hair. Fish 16mm (⅝ in) boilies singly, but use particles and small boilies in tandem or as a trio on the hair.

An electronic bite indicator with monkey climber or swinging drop-off arm gives an accurate audible and visual signal of runs and drop-back bites. While not the most sensitive form of bite detection, if your rig and bait presentation are right you will only get sailaway bites.

Tip Times and places

The shallows are a good bet early in the season with lots of fish on the spawning grounds. Later many move into water up to 6m (20ft) deep.

Don't ignore the margins – you are just as likely to catch close in as at long range.

Don't fish the night and pack up at breakfast time. In pits the best time is often between 7am and noon with night time the worst.

A bit of subtlety

Where weed hasn't quite reached the horrendous proportions of the watery jungle, it's possible to be a little less brutish in approach.

Tackle can be lighter with 1¾lb (0.8kg) TC rods, 8lb (3.6kg) main line and a forged size 8 or 10 hook. A simple running leger with a ½-¾oz (14-21g) bomb works well with this particular set-up.

With an extending hooklength the leger becomes a fairly sophisticated rig. Devised by Ken Townley for carp fishing, it works equally well for tench in allowing the fish to take line without feeling resistance. This produces very confident takes.

Use the rig with a slack, drooping line. This gives a taking fish some low-resistance line and makes sure that the last few feet of line lie flat on the bottom – reducing line bites. Where drag caused by the wind or floating debris makes this impossible, use a small back-lead to avoid those liners.

Particle baits work well with this rig, as do mini-boilies. The best size for these is about 10mm (⅖in) across. Use them singly or, more commonly, in twos or threes.

▲ Feed 2-3 pouches of hookbait samples. At short range loosefeed with hemp and casters but farther out use groundbait as a carrier.

Crumbs before tench

Jim Gibbinson makes his own groundbait:
6 measures (by volume) of fresh white crumb
2 measures of layer's mash hen food
1 measure of roughly ground roast barley
1 measure of fish meal or finely ground trout pellets

Concertina rig

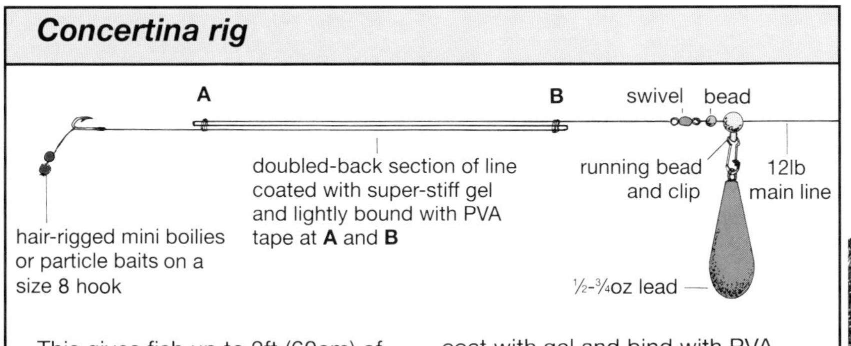

This gives fish up to 2ft (60cm) of line without resistance. Fold 2-3ft (60-90cm) of Dacron into a Z-bend, coat with gel and bind with PVA tape. The gel and tape dissolve in water, leaving a folded hooklength.

▼ Where weed allows, use 1¾lb (0.8kg) TC rods and a running leger. It's an enjoyable and effective way to take big tench.

Ultra-light

On a very few lightly weeded venues you can still fish very light – 1¼lb (0.6kg) TC rods, 4lb (1.8kg) line, fine-wire size 12 hooks and a feeder. Where this is possible, it is without doubt the most effective way to catch numbers of big fish.

A hooklength of at least 3ft (90cm) on a helicopter (rotary) rig works best. However, tench sometimes take delicately presented baits with such confidence that they become deep-hooked unless you use a shorter hooklength. With anti-tangle tubing above the feeder, this rig is as near tangle-free as a paternoster can be.

Feeding is easy – catapult two or three tangerine-sized balls of groundbait into the swim and cast your ready-loaded feeder rig into the centre of the spreading rings. Don't feed again until you've had a couple of runs or you'll put the big tench off.

The best bait for this type of tenching is a gilt-tail worm which looks like a redworm with a bright yellow tail. Look for them in the muck heap on a pig farm. You won't find many, but you will find lots of redworms which are a close second best.

Concentrate your efforts on the edges of the heap, where it's fairly cool. Near the middle of a muck heap it's too hot for redworms and gilt-tails – all you find are brandlings and these are greatly inferior as a tench bait.

If you do know of a virtually weed-free water that holds big tench – give light feeder tactics a try. The fishing is an absolute joy and well worth all that grovelling in pig heaps.

Rotary feeder rig

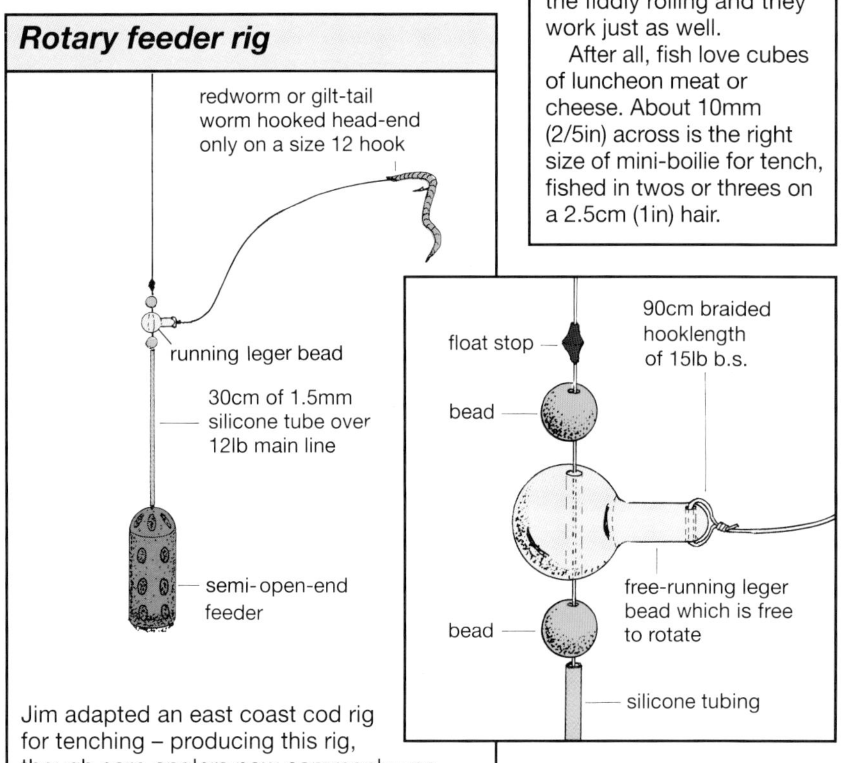

Jim adapted an east coast cod rig for tenching – producing this rig, though carp anglers now commonly use variations on it. The feeder is filled with maggots and plugged with groundbait.

Tip: A cubist approach

If you want to make your own mini-boilies, you'll find it easier to make cubes instead of the usual round shape. It avoids all the fiddly rolling and they work just as well.

After all, fish love cubes of luncheon meat or cheese. About 10mm (2/5in) across is the right size of mini-boilie for tench, fished in twos or threes on a 2.5cm (1in) hair.

▼ At waters without much weed you can land tench like this on light feeder gear. Give it a go and don't fish heavier than you need.

Bryan and Jon Culley at Hollowell Reservoir

Hollowell Reservoir holds some monster roach/rudd hybrids and tench. Join Bryan and Jon Culley who aim to tempt a specimen during a night session in early autumn.

It's six o'clock on a fine evening in mid September, and it looks as though there's going to be a beautiful sunset. Bryan and Jon Culley (father and son) are all set for a night session on Hollowell Reservoir.

The main target is Hollowell's head of big roach/rudd hybrids – and they are big, growing to at least 4¼lb (1.9kg) – but they're also going to have a go for some of the decent pike the water holds.

The water's very low, revealing thick muddy margins. The wind doesn't make it easy for Bryan and Jon to put up brollies, but it takes more than that to put them off.

7:30AM Rigs and things

They are quite confident of success. After three weeks of dry weather it rained in the morning, freshening the water. With any luck the fish'll be in the mood for food.

They tackle up, starting with their pike rods. The idea is to have at least one pike rod out at dawn and dusk, and fish a couple of leger rods for hybrids, up to the maximum of two rods each.

Jon casts a freelined sardine, closely followed by a freelined half mackerel. Bryan uses two half mackerel. The gear is standard – 2¾lb (1.2kg) TC fast taper pike rods, 12lb (5.4kg) line on Baitrunner-type reels. With 20lb (9.1kg) multistrand wire ending in two size 6 semi-barbless trebles, the set-up is complete.

Bite detection is a little less orthodox. They use Optonics on the front rod rest with plain drop-off indicators on the line, instead of electronic drop-offs, which buzz as soon as the line is pulled from the drop-off clip. Their set-up gives better indication of a run.

With the pike rods set up, Bryan and Jon

► *Bryan (right) and Jon (left) Culley, part of the well-known angling family that has had specimens of almost every type of fish that swims in British waters.*

Tip Timed strike

Timing the strike for big pike means making sure you hit them before they're deep-hooked.

You must have the proper unhooking kit including gloves and long forceps – but never use a gag.

▼ *Jon hurls out his freelined sardine before setting up his feeder gear for the big hybrids. It looks as though it's going to be a clear, crisp night.*

Tip Feeding time

Bryan and Jon aim to cover about five square yards with feed per rod. "Fish stay around longer if the bait is spread thinly but widely. They have to root around for it." They don't usually replenish the feed except with feeders unless they catch a lot of fish, though they may put more in before dawn for tench.

► ***The sun has set by the time Jon and Bryan fire in the groundbait. They believe that constant feeding spooks the fish.***

turn their attention to the groundbait. It's made up of half a gallon of water with enough brown crumb to absorb it, three tins of sweetcorn and two pints of maggots. It has got to be stiff enough to hold together to the bottom of the lake where the wriggling of the maggots breaks it up.

The feed goes in 40m (44yd) out where there's 1.8-2.4m (6-8ft) of water and Bryan and Jon tackle up for hybrids. The gear is 1¼lb (0.6kg) TC fast taper leger rods, 5lb (2.3kg) line to 4lb (1.8kg) hooklength, open-end medium-sized feeders with size 8 hooks for a breadflake/maggot combination and size 12s for multiple maggot and maggot/corn cocktails.

◄▲ ***Jon displays the 20½ pound (9.3kg) pike which was the first fish of the day (left), while Bryan holds up the second (above) – a near thirteen-pounder (5.8kg).***

7:40AM Mackerel mate

As Jon threads the line through the rings of a leger rod, he hears a ringing of a different sort. Well, more of a bleeping really. A pike has grabbed the half mackerel. Jon winds down and gives it what for.

Not to be outdone, the pike retaliates and from the healthy bend it's putting in the rod, it's a decent fish. After three powerful runs parallel to the shore, it has had enough

◄ ***Some anglers prefer to use electronic drop-off bite indicators for pike, but the Culleys use an Optonic at the front as this gives better indication of a run.***

► ***This type of bobbin works well with an Optonic. The Dacron tethers it to the front rod rest and you can pinch on swan shot to stop it swinging in the wind.***

Hollowell Reservoir

“ Wherever you fish, whether you catch or not, the main thing is to enjoy yourself – fish are the icing. ”

and Jon can guide it into the waiting net. “Not a bad start,” says Bryan, by way of congratulation.

A bad start it certainly isn’t. Once in the sling, it pulls the scales round to 20lb 8oz (9.3kg). Long, slim and handsome, it’s better looking than Paul Newman.

9:00PM Darkness falls

These hybrids like to go a roamin’ in the gloamin’, so now’s the time. The wind has got up slightly, making it very chilly out of the shelter of a brolly. A half moon gives enough light to see by.

Bite detection on the leger rods is also by Optonic – pretty much essential for night fishing. Bryan and Jon use bobbins with Betalights inside for visual indication. With the wind, it takes two swan shot to steady the bobbins.

The evening quiet is shattered by a screaming Optonic – a second pike falls for mackerel. Bryan grins and hits the run. “This is another good fish.” True to his word, a few minutes later a $12\frac{3}{4}$lb (5.8kg) fish lies sullenly in the net.

Bryan recasts and straight away gets another run. But after a minute or so, it comes off. “Ah well, it felt like a small fish,”

How to get there

● **By car** From Northampton take the A50 towards Leicester. Some way after Spratton turn left to the village of Hollowell. Take the first turning on the right through the village down to the sailing club. Park outside the gate.

● **By train** The nearest main line station is Northampton on the Euston-Birmingham line. It’s a long taxi or bus ride to Hollowell.

Fishery facts

You must get your day or season permit to fish Hollowell Reservoir in advance. You can buy them from Ravensthorpe or Pitsford Reservoir Fishing Lodge, Tel 0604 781350.

The reservoir is infrequently fished and holds many big tench up to double figures, as well as the hybrids and a good head of pike up to mid-twenties.

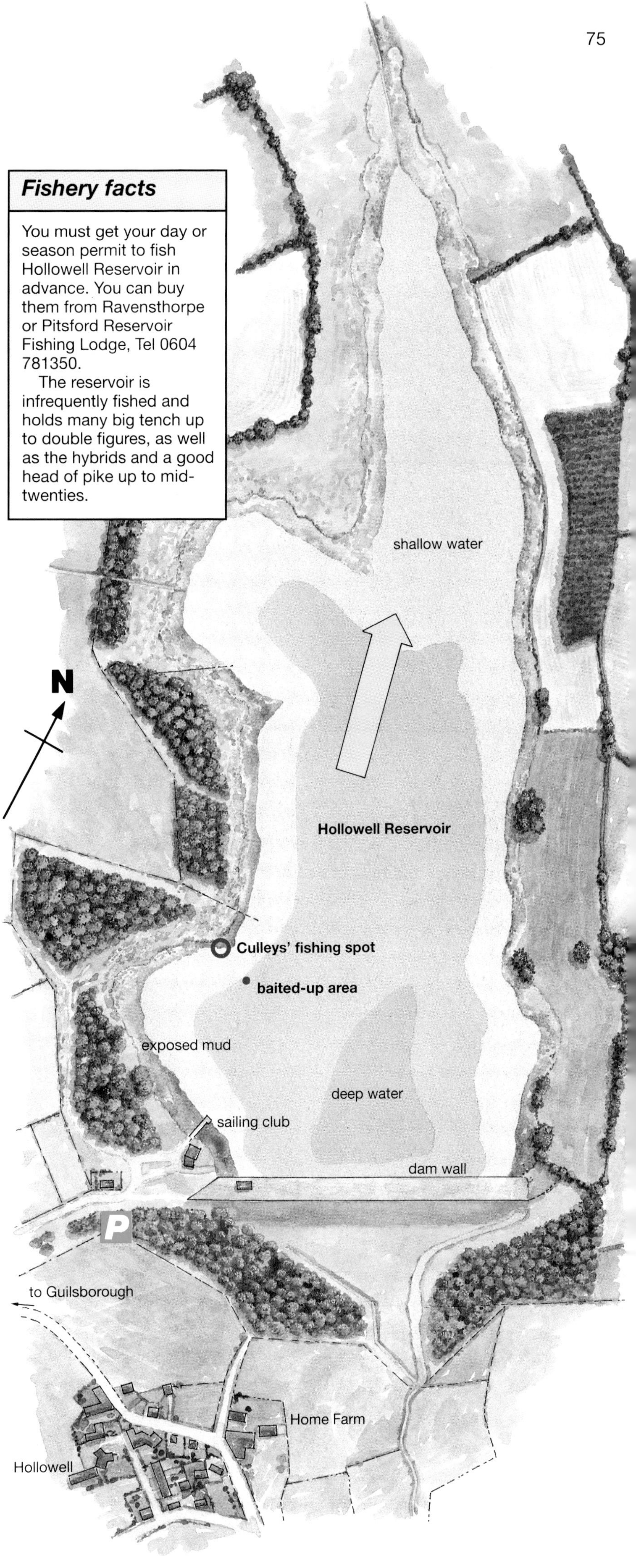

N
shallow water
Hollowell Reservoir
Culleys’ fishing spot
baited-up area
exposed mud
deep water
sailing club
dam wall
P
to Guilsborough
Home Farm
Hollowell

▲ Sunrise proves to be as lovely as sunset, and the fish are almost as obliging. Jon brings in a five pound (2.3kg) pike which snaffled his half mackerel. Dawn is often the best time for pike at this time of year.

▼ This near four pound tench (1.8kg) fell for a flake/maggot combo which proved deadly on the day. Both tench and hybrids found it irresistible, though sweetcorn cocktails can also be killers.

says Bryan, consoling himself.

Once the excitement's over, they check the hybrid set-ups. Inspection reveals the first signs of hope. A couple of maggots are flattened at one end – something must be interested. After that hopes are high.

They bring in the mackerel to concentrate on the leger rods. But a few more chewed maggots, without so much as a bleep from the indicators, quells the rising tide of optimism.

10:40PM *Bleep and Booster*

It's time for bedchairs and sleeping bags to make their appearance – there's a definite chill in the air. But what do you expect in mid September? In this muddy mire, trying to keep it all clean will be fun.

As these preparations get underway, Bryan is interrupted by the occasional bleep from the Optonic guarding a hybrid set-up. The bobbin rises and falls irregularly. Five minutes pass and there's still no sign of a run, so he decides to strike next time there are three bleeps in succession.

Three quick bleeps later there's a good bend in the rod. "Well, it feels like a hybrid," grunts Bryan as the rod tip thumps satisfyingly. The fish moves off left and before he can stop it, it has taken Bryan into the weed (figuratively of course – it's actually taken itself into the weed).

Now it's just a question of whether the snag or the line is the stronger. The line wins and a weedy hybrid comes kicking into the net. After removing the salad, it weighs 3lb 2oz (1.4kg) – a real morale booster.

That's all that happens for about an hour until Jon gets a single bleep. He waits but after five minutes of occasional bleeping, frustration strikes – and so does he. Much to his surprise, it produces a fish, though it's less than hand-size.

MIDNIGHT *Moonset*

With no-one else on the water, it's so peaceful it's almost a crime to speak. The moon is going to set within an hour and brief clouds across its face hint at the real darkness to come. If you haven't night fished like this before, you don't know what you're missing.

Despite the cold, you gently doze as you

▲ ***Roach, rudd or hybrid? This is one of the many small fish which attacked the baits from sunrise till Jon and Bryan left.***

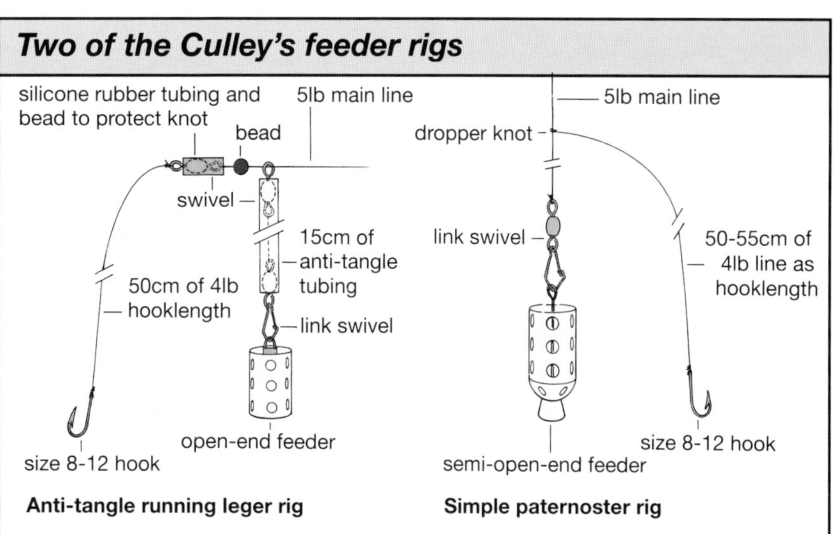

▲ ***The flake/maggot cocktail which outfished all other baits on the day (and the night). Sweetcorn and maggot also works well here.***

▼ ***Jon replaces his feeder with a bomb in an attempt to get the baits out to where the big fish are rolling and avoid the hordes of small hybrids closer in.***

wait for the Optonic to wake you to a run. Hope springs eternal as you slip into a light sleep. Whoops. What's that bleeping? I wasn't asleep was I? Surely not.

Where Jon's fishing there isn't too much mud, so he's able to set up his bedchair right by his rod. Bryan, on the other hand, is fishing knee-deep in muddy quicksand and he can't actually get his bedchair down there without it sinking. He has to set up his gear and his umbrella about ten paces away.

So when his Optonic goes he stumbles in the complete dark down through the thick mud to where he thinks the bleeping is coming from. Then he's got to hit the run.

2:10AM Dropping-off

Just as sleep begins to overtake the body, (making you forget about the blocks of ice at the end of your legs masquerading as feet), Bryan stumbles down to his rods. In the dark it's hard to see whether he is actually up to his knees in the mud or not, but a few minutes later, a night-snacking tench comes struggling and splashing into the shallows.

Fifteen minutes later Jon is awakened in the same way but as he strikes he feels only the resistance of the feeder. The maggots are crushed when he retrieves. Fish are on the prowl, so Bryan decides to spend half an hour by the rods instead of on his bedchair, just in case.

3:55AM Twitchy hybrid

Nothing has happened for over an hour, Bryan has returned to his bedchair and peace has returned to the reservoir. Not a bleep disturbs the silence.

Jon is asleep when a short sharp sound has him rubbing his eyes. The bobbin rises, then falls. Once more it jumps and still Jon waits (though that might just be because he hasn't woken up properly). Finally the bobbin rises to the rod and the Optonic goes crazy. Jon winds down and strikes into a decent fish.

The fish splashes noisily in the shallows, but it's hard to make it out in the dark. Bryan (roused from his slumber) navigates by sound to slip the landing net under another plump hybrid. At 2lb 11oz (1.2kg), it's a personal best for Jon.

5:45AM Predator sunrise

Nothing much has happened for hours and there's been plenty of time for anticipation-filled dozing. Then, as if someone had turned on a tap, twitches start coming on the hybrid set-ups. Fast and very hard to hit, they produce fish of no more than 12oz (340g) and averaging half that.

At six o'clock the half mackerel are recast, and half an hour later the expected morning pike run produces a five-pounder (2.3kg) on mackerel head. Twenty minutes later Bryan strikes into a another run. It's obviously a better fish. When Jon finally nets it, it's a low double of 11lb 12oz (5.3kg).

Just after that run, our intrepid duo fire in another barrage of groundbait, to entice any passing tench and to replace the feed scoffed by the shoal of small hybrids. These

▲▶ *Bryan (right) retrieves to rebait after an abortive run, completely ignoring the fact that his feet are completely stuck in thick mud. It can make moving at night quite tricky, though apparently hippos like it.*

herring-sized fish are beginning to make a real nuisance of themselves.

About 60-70m (66-77yd) out there are bigger fish rolling on the surface, so Jon and Bryan exchange feeder for bomb to boost casting range. For the moment though, there's nothing doing.

As the sun comes up, the feeling returns to parts of the body you'd forgotten existed. Eventually, it might even be warm.

8:30AM Shallow swirls

It's all happening on the fish activity front now. There are fish, big and small, rolling on the surface, and pike are swirling in the shallows. After he has a small hybrid mauled by a pike on its way in, Jon tries a chub deadbait in the margins – but to no avail.

It's turning into a bright, warm day and the fish obviously appreciate it. Just to prove it, Bryan connects with another run on flake and maggot, and brings in a four pound tench (1.8kg), but it's hybrids he wants.

Just as they decide to pack up, Jon hits a run on a mackerel tail. The fish is so small he almost lands it on the strike. It only weighs about a pound (0.45kg). Still it would take a hard man to grumble about the sport. Three pike in double figures including a twenty, two fat hybrids and a couple of tench. Who could ask for more?

There's just time to photograph the hybrids in the clear sunlight before going off for some real (and well-deserved) kip. The silvery-golden scales flash in the morning air. It's the perfect end to a great introduction to night fishing.

Tip Range finder

When fishing over a bed of feed at night, sort out your casting distance in daylight. Get used to the 'feel' of the distance. Don't rely on an elastic band on the spool which may cause problems with a big fish on in the dark.

◀ *Bryan and Jon pose and the hybrids gleam in the morning sunlight. Bryan's weighs 3lb 2oz (1.4kg) and Jon's 2lb 11oz (1.2kg).*

▲ *"You'd swear it was a rudd if you didn't know better," says Bryan of Jon's fish. It's hard to be sure when there are hybrids about.*

Big perch from small rivers

Small rivers and streams don't always look like the sorts of places to catch specimen perch. But follow Nigel Witham and you might find bigger, more pristine fish than you'd believe.

One thing you soon learn about perch is that they are not fussy about the size of water in which they grow big. All they seem to need is an abundance of fodder fish, and little competition for it. This happy situation has resulted in lots of small rivers and streams throughout Britain holding big perch which have never seen a net.

Forget complications

When you're after a single species of fish on a small river, it's usually better to carry a minimum of tackle and to fish as many good looking spots as you can. Remember you're fishing for perch which have rarely been hooked, so sophisticated bait presentation is rarely necessary – a simple set-up is fine.

Whatever you do, don't lumber yourself with too much gear. Take just one rod and one reel and a small selection of tackle.

Rod choice is important. Some anglers prefer a short rod for roving and fishing inaccessible swims, but for this type of fishing a long rod is much more useful. It allows you to fish well back from the bank, out of sight of the fish.

A 13ft (3.9m) hollow tip float rod with a bit of backbone is ideal. An Avon may be a little heavy, while a spliced-tip match rod is too light. The rod should have a soft, flexible tip for casting light baits and to help in detecting bites when freelining or legering.

You need a small or medium fixed-spool reel which balances your rod, though a centrepin is also good, and much more fun. Fill your reel with 4lb (1.8kg) line.

Take a small bag filled with the rest of

Comeback care

Perch are beginning to recolonize British waters in decent numbers after the worst ravages of the perch disease that all but wiped them out in the 1970s. However, they are still not as common as they were, so good care of your catch is important. Don't keep perch in a keepnet – their spines always get caught and they suffer badly.

If you must keep them, use a well-submerged carp sack, and release them each time you move swim. Try to weigh and photograph them and return them well away from the main shoal as quickly as you can.

Small river set-up

Everything you'll ever need for small stream perching: a bankstick **(1),** landing net **(2),** forceps **(3),** catapult **(4),** 13ft (3.9m) hollow tip float rod **(5),** a tub of mixed split shot **(6),** and boxes of nos. 8 and 10 shot (in tackle box), a selection of plastic Avon floats **(7),** a centrepin **(8)** or fixed-spool **(9),** nail clippers and snatchback **(10),** leger bobbin **(11),** a container with float rubbers, leger stops and leger beads **(12),** packets of hooks – sizes 6-10 **(13)** and a box to hold it all **(14).** You also need a bag to carry this gear, and some polarized glasses are very useful in summer.

Nice 'n' easy for small river perch

Keep it simple when fishing small rivers for perch. If you wish to change from freelining to a float rig, slide some float rubbers over the hook, attach your Avon, add the required shot and you're away. If a freelined bait won't reach the bottom, and you need a couple of shot to get it down, put the float rubbers on before you add the shot (below). That way you can quickly slip on your float whenever you want to float fish (right).

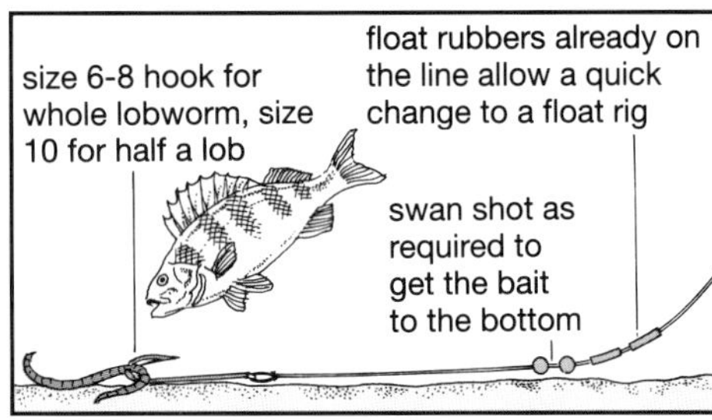

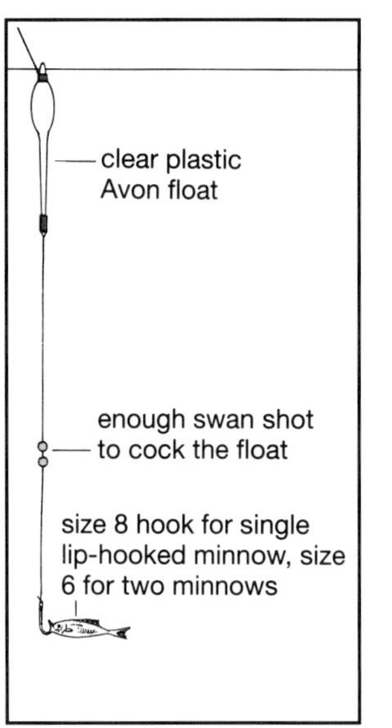

▼ ***This fine perch of about 12oz (0.34kg) fell for a live minnow freelined into a deeper, slower section of river close to a fallen tree. Note that the perch tried to spit the minnow out, pushing it up the line, but too late – it was already hooked.***

your tackle. A variety of Avon floats (the clear plastic ones are hard to break, so a float tube isn't necessary), a tub of mixed split shot, some float rubbers, leger stops, leger beads (for making a link leger with swan shot) and some hooks (sizes 6-10) are all you need. You might also want to take a bobbin for bite detection when watching the line or rod top is difficult.

Trap-ease artists

Worms and minnows are by far the most consistent baits for small stream perch.

With worms, the bigger the better – lobworms are the absolute first choice. Fish a whole lob on a size 6-8 hook, or half a worm on a size 10.

Minnows are easy to catch with maggot or pinkie on a size 22 hook, or with a bread-baited minnow trap. You can make one of these with a couple of plastic drinks bottles. Cut the bottom off one and staple the top from the other in its place, forming a funnel.

Keep minnows in a small bucket with an air pump to aerate the water. Fish them singly on a size 8 hook, or in pairs on a size 6, hooked once through the upper lip only.

Rigs are simplicity itself – big perch are sensitive to resistance from the rig, so the less complicated the better.

Freelining works well, though you must watch the line all the time. With a big worm, let a fish have up to 1m (39in) of line before striking to allow it to take the bait properly. With minnows, don't tighten right up to the hook – leave some slack line and strike when the fish has taken up this line.

If you need weight to get the bait down through the current, add a swan shot. If you need more than one swan, a link leger may be better. To change to float fishing, slide a couple of float rubbers over the hook and turn your rig into a float set-up.

A wanderin' perch fisher, I

Location is the key to good catches, so keep moving until you find the fish – that's why you should travel light. Perch generally live in mixed shoals, in fairly localized areas, so once you've found a few fish, expect more of varying size. They prefer a moderate current, siding with roach on the question of flow, rather than the faster-water chub.

Cover is important too – perch need somewhere from which to ambush prey. It can take many forms: overhanging or submerged plants, especially reed and lily beds, and the old favourites – tree roots and fallen branches. Consider also the river bed – perch are generally much more common over a gravel bottom than over mud or silt. Lastly, depth is important – a slow deep hole with cover close at hand is ideal.

Weir pools are often a particularly good place to try. They, along with deep pools and holes, are the only places where you are likely to find perch in mid-stream. After the first heavy rains of late summer or autumn, a weir pool is hard to beat.

Under the sill of the weir the current forms a vertical eddy. Near the river bed, there is often almost no flow. Freeline a big lobworm or minnow into the white water. It is often swept up under the sill to stay there until you move it. If the current on top is too strong for this, add the smallest amount of shot it takes to get the bait down quickly enough, about 50cm (20in) from the hook.

You can spot bites either by touch or by watching the rod top, but make sure you leave some slack so the fish have time to take the bait properly before they feel any drag on the line. If you don't get any bites, search the rest of the pool thoroughly, letting the bait work back towards you and roll down in the current.

▲ Swims such as this are good places to find perch all year round, especially in autumn and winter. The water is deeper and slower than the surrounding areas and there is plenty of cover where the fish can lie in wait for their prey.

Tip: Good times, bad times

Hot summer days when the sun is bright on the water are rarely good for perch, and bites are also few and far between after dark. But in most other conditions perch usually oblige – time of day is not that vital. Bigger fish come most often at dawn in summer and dusk in winter, but shoals are generally of mixed size fish, so there's always a chance of good sport.

◄ You must keep a low profile when fishing a small stream for perch since they spook easily and you are never far from the fish you are trying to catch. A long rod of about 13ft (3.9m) allows you to freeline or float fish while sitting well back from the river, out of sight of your target – the big, wary perch.

The outside of a bend, particularly where there is cover from an overhanging tree, can be another good place. The current runs close to the bank, and this often scours out a deeper area, slowing the current down. For winter perch, the deeper the water the better these swims are.

Try freelining a lob or minnow under the bank, or cast a float upstream under the tree. Set the float well overdepth, with the bulk of the shot about 30cm (12in) above the hook. That way the bait lies on the bottom, and you can easily hold the float back hard. Feed around your bait with chopped lobs while you wait for a bite.

Reed beds are another classic place to look for perch, especially after a summer flood. Perhaps the best way to fish them is to trot a float along the side of the reeds, with the bait set well off the bottom. The closer you can get the bait to the reeds, the more likely you are to tempt a bite from a fat, river perch. The same is true of any snag when it comes to fishing for perch.

These are just three types of swim that are fairly common on small rivers – each one requiring a different approach. But remember, though the swims you come to fish may share many features with these three, every swim is different, and they all call for changes in tactics to suit the particular problems they pose.

However, it's not all hard work. As you get to know a river, you find that the perch tend to stick to certain spots. Once you've caught them in a swim or length of river, you tend to come across them in the same places time and again.

On most rivers, perch feed in just a few areas, so it's a question of finding the right one on the day. Because of this, you mustn't fish one area for too long without a bite. If the perch are around and you haven't scared them, you soon know about it.

Perch fishing on small rivers is a mobile game, so it doesn't appeal to every angler. But if you fancy some challenging and potentially highly rewarding fishing, load up a small back pack and get down there!

▲ An angler trots a lob beside a reed bed, hoping for a good perch. The urban setting doesn't affect the fishing if the water's clean and the food plentiful.

▼ Any river containing perch like this bristling beauty of around the ¾lb (0.34kg) mark, has a rich enough food supply to produce bigger fish too, so keep at it!

Down the drain with John Watson

You're always taking a risk when you set out to catch zander from a Norfolk drain. They can be here today and 10 miles off tomorrow. Predator expert John Watson chances his arm for us.

► *John Watson is one of Britain's leading pike anglers. Having come down with a bad case of zander bug, he now hunts them every hour he can get off work.*

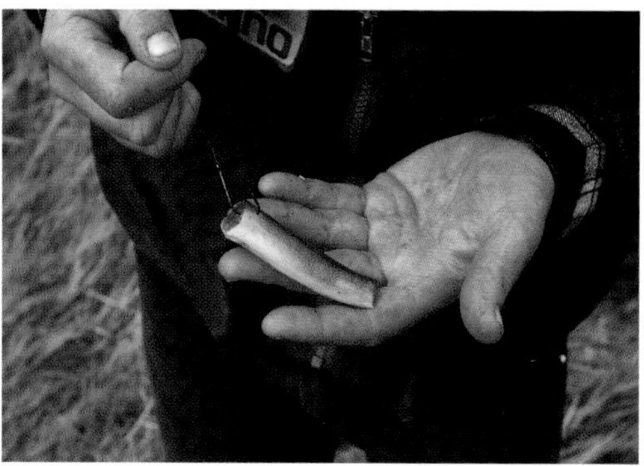

► *Eel section is perhaps the best bait for zander. John uses a 1/0 single hook which improves his hook-up rate.*

▼ *Fish on! John recommends that you have a spare rod set up so that you can keep two baits in the water even while you're rebaiting or tying on a new rig.*

Since the mid-seventies, when the British population of zander really took off, many have fished for this elusive, good-looking predator. For some anglers, the fear that this invader from the Continent would strip our waters of fish drove them to hunt and kill. For others, such as John Watson, the hunting is enough, with a big zander worth many days (and nights) fishing.

The Fens in Norfolk around the Great Ouse are a prime spot for big zander but you can never guarantee a brush with the toothiest grin in British waters. You just have to pick your spot and hope.

Day One – The Delph

The Delph is 16 dead straight miles cut

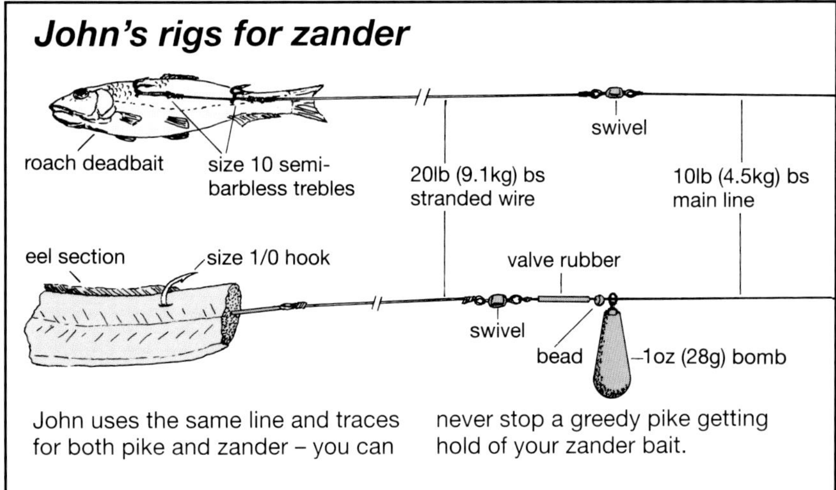

John uses the same line and traces for both pike and zander – you can never stop a greedy pike getting hold of your zander bait.

◀ The bite indicator arms are clipped to the line. The buzzer goes when the line is pulled which drops the arm – showing the bait taken.

through the flat Norfolk landscape, and only a cast away from a similar water – the Old Bedford river. They both start and end in the Great Ouse and are superb fisheries, but the Delph has the edge for zander.

7:00AM Perfect conditions

With a good colour in the water, conditions are ideal – a reason John chose this venue. Zander seem to like murky water – perhaps preferring to hunt by smell and vibration.

He sets up two through-action pike rods with a test curve of 2¾lb (1.2kg) to fish the drop-off on each side of the drain. The soft-ish action means that even a small fish can produce a decent bend, while the rod retains the power to deal with a monster.

John casts a 15cm (6in) freelined bream deadbait to the far side and on the near side he legers an eel section. The eels come from the Delph itself and John has found that on waters with a big eel population, three inch (8cm) lengths are a zander bait *extraordinaire*. The bream is rigged up to two size 10 semi-barbless trebles which are easier on the fish than fully barbed hooks, especially for unhooking. They also make it quicker and easier to remove the hooks. The eel section is hooked on a 1/0 single hook. This allows the point to rest well clear of the tough eel body, giving excellent hooking where a treble's points might be masked.

Once you've set up, there are two approaches to fishing a drain. If you know that fish are in the area you can stay in your chosen swim. Or you can move down the bank, one rod at a time, until you get a

The Delph below Welney

hawthorn

undergrowth

reeds

shelf (60cm deep)

main channel (2.4-3.1m deep)

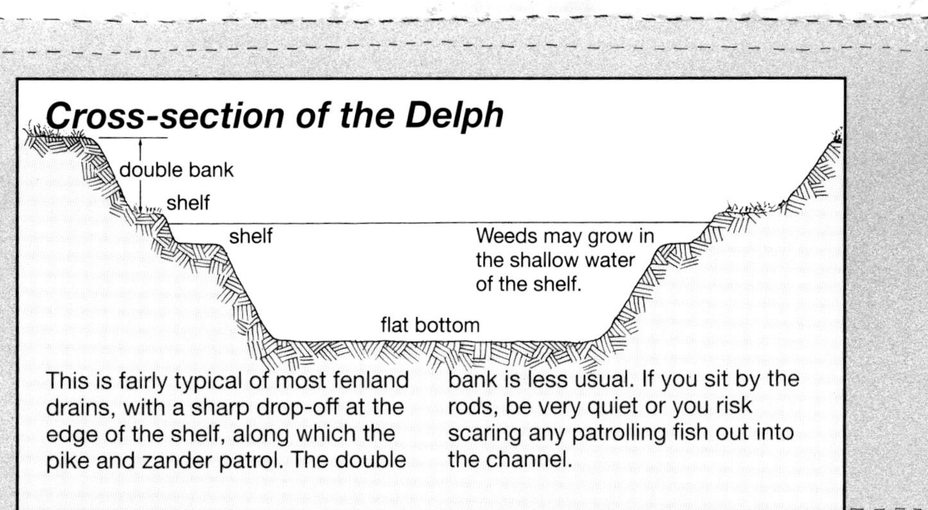

This is fairly typical of most fenland drains, with a sharp drop-off at the edge of the shelf, along which the pike and zander patrol. The double bank is less usual. If you sit by the rods, be very quiet or you risk scaring any patrolling fish out into the channel.

shelf (60cm deep)

alder

lower bank

N

“The fish could be anywhere along the river, so keep moving or you may never come across them.”

run. John's had a double-figure zander and several smaller fish from this swim in the last week, so he's going to stay put.

7:30AM False alarm

The buzzer goes but it's a false alarm. John has electronic bite indicators clipped to the line by his reel which react if the line is pulled from the clip. He waits for further signs of interest in his bait before striking.

9:10AM The bream deadbait

This time it's a run on the bream deadbait, but it's dropped. When John reels it in there are tooth marks everywhere. A smallish zander probably picked up the bait and then realized that this mouthful wasn't going to fit. John changes to a smaller deadbait, a 6cm (2½in) perch, in case it is still keen, but it has decided to hunt elsewhere.

There's a discouraging pause for a couple of hours. Not because you don't expect long blank periods when specimen hunting, but because if the zander were still in the area, John would have expected a fish by now. About mid-day he decides to move farther down the drain to another favourite spot. It really is time the fish showed up – even the usually plentiful baitfish are reluctant to show themselves by topping and bubbling.

▲ Something's playing with my bait... John waits for a tentative pluck at the line to turn into a full-blooded run. Don't strike if you aren't sure whether the fish has the bait fully in it's mouth. Remember that pike and zander mouth the bait before swallowing it whole.

How to get there

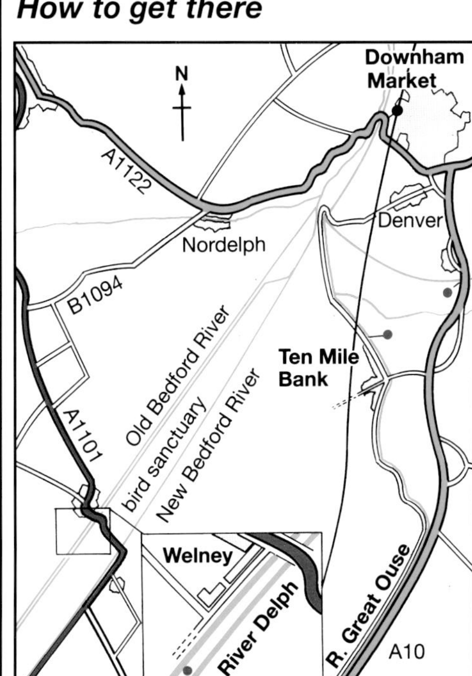

● **By car** Turn off the A10 to Ten Mile Bank for the Great Ouse. Most of this stretch is controlled by Kings Lynn AA (permits on the bank). For the Delph at Welney take the A1101 off the A10 at Littleport. The north west bank is controlled by Welney AC (permits from the post office). The other bank is a bird sanctuary with no access.
● **By train** The nearest station is Downham Market on the Cambridge-Kings Lynn line.

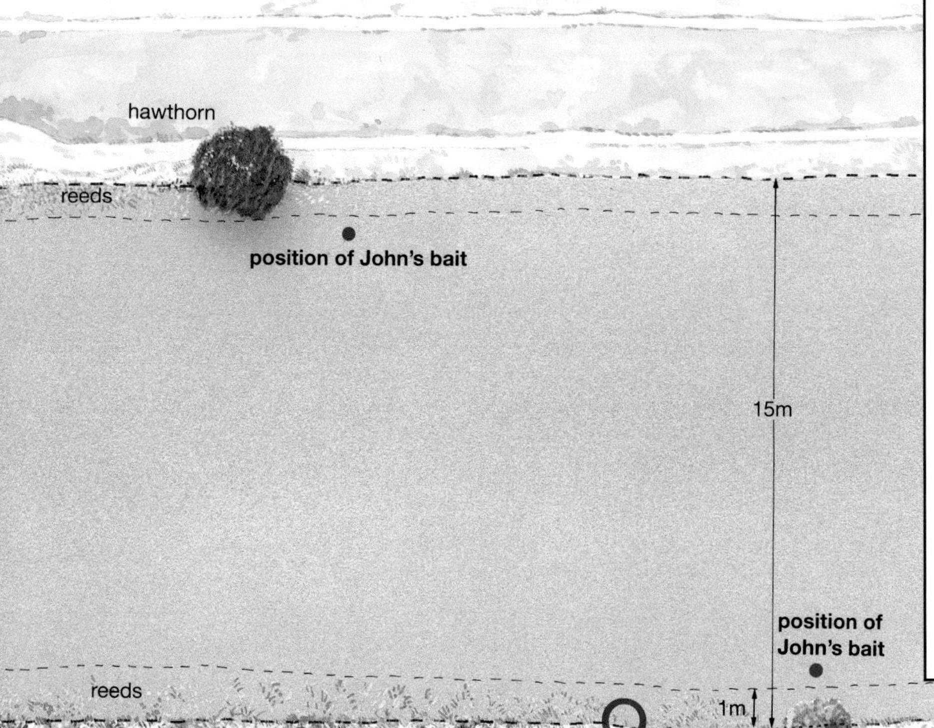

► *We are not amused. A distinctly unhappy looking pike surrenders to the 2¾lb (1.2kg) test curve of John's rod. It's just a shame it wasn't a zander.*

▼ *Unhooking a pike needn't be a traumatic experience for either party if you keep a cool head. Lay the fish down, and if you can't reach the hooks through the mouth, try the gills – carefully.*

▲ *And here it is – a nice (but small) pike which John puts at around 4lb (1.8kg). It snaffled the deadbait meant for a zander.*

12:25PM The perch deadbait

John strikes into a run on the perch deadbait and after a nervous second's pause, connects with a real scrapper. Dogged to the last, the fish tries to stay deep, suggesting a zander, but as John works it to the surface it's a pike's snout which appears.

Once it's safely landed, he unhooks it through a gill cover, scratching his knuckle on the gill rakers in the process. He explains as he returns the fish, "It's better to damage yourself rather than the fish, and I don't use a gag or gloves because this way's quicker." Fair enough, and the scratch is minor.

He settles down to wait for more – after all, one fish of round about 4lb (1.8kg) is hardly enough – and begins to explain his tackle. "On most waters..." and there goes the buzzer again.

12:40PM A creeping take

Sadly, the take doesn't develop. Inspecting the roach deadbait shows it has been savaged. John reckons it's mostly zander which drop baits. Pike usually finish what

they start – unless it's twice their size!

Back to the tackle then. Even though zander are the quarry, John doesn't go as light as the fish deserve. It's no use being sporting when you might hook a 20lb (9.1kg) pike. You can't risk leaving two trebles and a wire trace in its mouth.

Although John does get one more run on the eel section, it is dropped. It can't be his day – that's the first run on eel section he hasn't connected with since he changed to the single hook set-up. We're going to need another go at the zander.

Day Two – The Great Ouse

After the zanderless day on the Delph, John had a phone call from a friend who had been fishing the Cut-off Channel where the A10 crosses it and had caught a sackful of zander. For the next couple of days there was a bit of a zander spree, so this was clearly the place to try.

▲ John demonstrates the best way to slip a pike back into the water. Even the wrong fish deserves careful handling; otherwise you shouldn't be fishing at all.

► Onward and upward in search of zander. John and his inseparable companion Sally move further up the Ouse to try to find a pack of marauding fish.

▼ Is it or isn't it? John tries to work out whether the movement of the line is something playing with the bait, or just frustrated imagination.

7:00AM Fishing frenzy

Despite the attentions of some 20 anglers (or perhaps because of them) the zander won't oblige. John uses a heavy swimfeeder filled with fish scraps to attract any passing fish to his hook – rather than the one next to it. Unfortunately, there are no passing fish.

10:00AM Moving on

There's not a sniff of zander, so John decides to move on to the Ouse. There aren't as many of these sleek predators there, but at least if he doesn't catch one there's a good chance of pike. It's only 20 minutes by car, so John has his rods in the water by 10.30am.

While he waits, John explains that pike and zander usually patrol up and down the edges of the shelf along miles of these drains. Last week's hotspot can be this week's blank swim. However, even if you're not catching, there's always a chance that in half an hour they'll be crawling up the bank.

11:20AM Along the bank

There's some movement, though not by the fish. John retrieves one set of tackle and moves it past the other along the bank. That way he explores a larger area of water without ever taking both baits out of the water. This method is especially effective if you fish with a partner as you can always cover the shelves on both sides of the river between your four rods.

11:55AM Coffee break

John pours some coffee; of course the buzzer goes just as its cool enough to drink, but no run develops. The bait shows no sign of having been attacked so it's coffee time again.

At least today there are plenty of baitfish topping and bubbling merrily. Unfortunately, that's all that seems to be going on. The only thing to do is to keep moving and keep trying.

3:30PM Time to go

John's covered about a mile of the Ouse without even a run – it's not warm and the coffee's running low. He begins to reel in the first rod but stops. "There's something playing around with this." He pauses. "No, it's just wishful thinking." He starts to retrieve again, but suspiciously this time. The rod tip dips. It can't be... can it? "There's definitely something down there." Yes it is, at last. At the end of the second day, there on the surface is what we've been looking for – only smaller. A perfect, petite zander of about 1lb (0.45kg). The deadbait barely fits in its mouth. This fish is the future of these waterways, and John treats it carefully. "I love zander. They always look like they've just been minted."

So the search hasn't been in vain, and though no more are forthcoming, it's enough. Getting to grips with these fish takes patience as well as skill, but once you've got the zander bug, you'll never want to give up – just ask John Watson.

▲ Last gasp fish! John connects as he reels in. It's not very big, which explains the amount of time it took to get the bait in its mouth. At first sight it looks like a small jack...

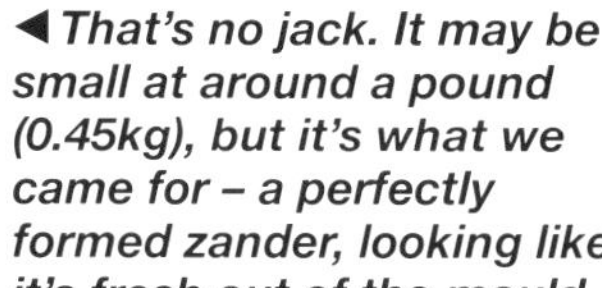

◄ That's no jack. It may be small at around a pound (0.45kg), but it's what we came for – a perfectly formed zander, looking like it's fresh out of the mould.

▼John puts it back to recover and grow. Now many anglers no longer fear the spread of these fish, one day they may not be quite so rare a catch.

Wobbling for pike

Top predator expert John Watson can't understand why more people don't wobble deadbaits. It's a hugely successful roving technique for pike, so stop just waiting for your buzzer and start wobbling!

Tip ***Scruffs work!***

Deadbaits suffer from repeated casting, and can end up looking very sorry for themselves. If you have lots of replacements, it's best to change the bait once it starts to look a bit tatty. You can catch on the scruffiest remains of a bait, however, so don't panic if you're running out.

Deadbait wobbling, also known as fishing sink-and-draw, is one of the most effective – yet unpopular – ways to catch pike. This simple method involves casting and retrieving a deadbait through areas which you suspect might hold pike. It is called wobbling because the way you mount the deadbait on the trace makes it wobble on the retrieve like a sick prey fish.

It's effective because it allows you optimum opportunity to present a bait to numbers of pike. As to why it is unpopular, it seems that most of today's pike anglers prefer to fish static, waiting for buzzer to sound or float to slide under. This has less to do with results than with laziness.

Deadbait wobbling is about keeping on the move, continually casting and recasting. You cover as much water, and therefore pike, as possible. That, in a nutshell, is the secret of its success. If one pike doesn't want a bait, you don't waste time fishing fruitlessly in front of it. After a short while you're off to find a pike that *is* interested.

When to wobble

There is no specific time or place to wobble – the method works at any time and in any kind of swim. However, there are a few situations where it can be especially effective.

From a boat you can cast 360° around you, exploring a section of water completely before moving on.

In an awkward swim wobbling allows you to get a bait near fish that are otherwise inaccessible. If, for example, on a river, the productive area is upstream of a snag, the current might push a static bait into the snag. That's when a wobbled bait can score.

Cast the bait set-up for wobbling downstream of the snag and work it upstream, over and through it. With any luck a pike lurking in its snaggy lair won't be able to resist the sight of an apparently injured fish limping past its nose.

On new waters wobbling keeps you on the move, allowing you to fish more swims and so learn more about the venue and the habits of the pike that live there.

Fishing a new swim where you aren't sure of the behaviour of the resident pike provides one of the best opportunities to wobble a deadbait. Put out a floatfished bait, or two if the local regulations permit,

▲ A beautiful pike, which fell for a wobbled deadbait, waits to be netted. Theswan shot on the line helps with casting and sinking the bait to the required depth.

◀ This angler wanders the bank, giving as many pike as possible a look at his bait – a great way to find feeding fish. Wobbling can bring results on all sorts of waters and on all sorts of days – from the depth of winter to the heat of midsummer. It's perfect for exploring a new venue and for keeping warm in winter.

Tip Wobbler's choice

You can use almost any small dead fish as bait for wobbling, from roach and dace to sprats, sandeels and pouting. Avoid sardines, however – they are so fragile they crumble after one cast.

Don't just throw discarded baits away while you're fishing – this just gives free food to the pike you're trying to catch.

and cast a bait set up for wobbling around and between the static ones.

Pike are attracted by the smell of the floatfished deadbaits and may take the wobbler as it whizzes past. This is particularly true in shallow water. Fishing like this is one of the most exciting methods at your disposal. A take from just below the surface in shallow water is enough to get even the most jaundiced angler's nerves jangling.

Baits to wobble with

Any fish about 10-20cm (4-8in) long is fine for wobbling. Both freshwater and sea fish can have their day. The simplest way of setting up the bait is the best. Use two semi-barbless trebles on a wire trace. The end treble is hooked about half way along the fish's flank, while the other one goes through the lips.

Give the fish some life by putting a slight bend in it as you hook it up. This produces the wobble on the retrieve which gives this technique its name. The bigger the bend the more pronounced the wobble. Experiment with the amount of bend to see which produces the most takes.

It's usually a good idea to add some weight by putting a few swan shot on the line above the wire trace. The number of shot depends on the size of the bait, the depth at which you want to fish, and how far you're casting.

A buoyant bait is best for this type of fishing. This has two advantages. If you're fishing a water with weeds, snags or litter on the bottom, make sure the distance between the swan shot and the bait is greater than the depth of the snags. That way you can let the whole set-up sink to the bottom, secure in the knowledge that the bait is floating above the snags.

A wobbling set-up

There are many ways of hooking up baits for wobbling – the right one really depends on the size and kind of fish you intend to use.

For most fish, the top hook in the flank and the other through the lips works best. But some large coarse deadbaits (above) take three hooks to hold them secure. It also helps them to stay in one piece for longer in the face of repeated casting and retrieving.

It's better to hook herring (below) and sprats in the eye socket instead of through their rather fragile lips.

Sink-and-draw – the art of wobbling

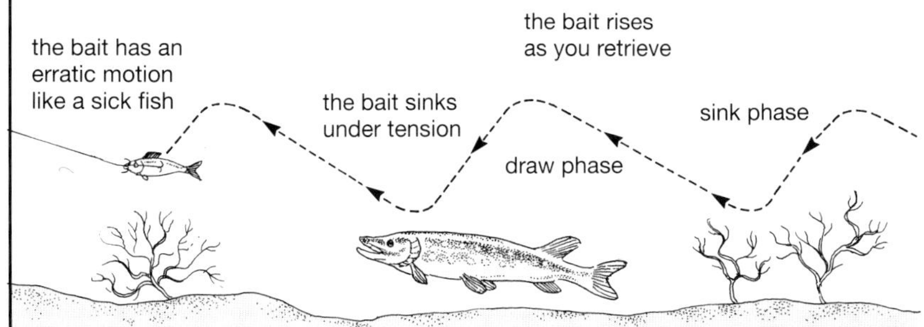

Fishing sink-and-draw literally means letting the bait sink before drawing it towards you. Repeat this process until the bait is at your feet. The zig-zag motion this produces mimics the behaviour of a wounded bait fish as it struggles to swim. Your bait fishes a range of depths like this – it doesn't just rise to the top and skim along the surface. It's one variety of retrieve that really is well worth trying.

The second advantage is that if you lose a bait, either on a fish, or by casting it off, it usually floats to the surface. A bait on the surface is less likely to be taken by the pike you're trying to catch. If you're in a boat you can recover it for re-use. Either way it usually prevents a pike from getting a free meal – and a hungry pike is a catchable pike.

Some freshwater baits have the advantage of being naturally buoyant, but it's easy enough to insert polystyrene rods down the fish's throat with a pair of forceps to give a sinking bait a little help in floating. Put in a little at a time and test it after each addition. It's set correctly when it just begins to float upwards if you push it under.

Wilder wobbles

The more bend you put in your bait, the greater the wobble and the more vibration it produces. Pike detect the vibration and home in on what they take to be a wounded fish.

But too great a bend can make the bait behave quite grotesquely in the water, putting off a cautious pike. Vary the degree of bend in your baits until you find the one the pike really want.

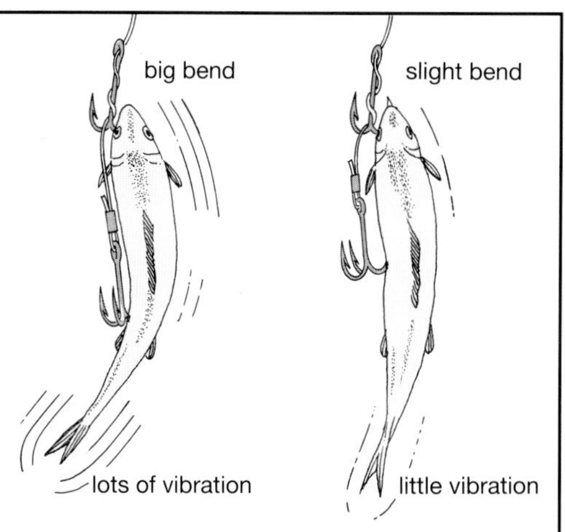

Wobble-ability

Wobbling has two chief virtues apart from its ability to take plenty of fish – it is simple and it adapts well to all types of water and conditions. At its most basic it consists of casting and retrieving the bait, but with a little more thought and effort, you can improve its effectiveness dramatically.

Try to imagine how the bait is behaving in the water, and aim to make it as appealing and as helpless-seeming (to pike) as possible. Its effectiveness depends on how enticing you can make it.

Vary the speed and the depth of retrieve for best results. You should also try an erratic retrieve – remember that you are trying to simulate the behaviour of a sick or wounded bait fish.

Generally baits tend to rise to the surface as you retrieve them because you are above the water. If you pause in your retrieve, the bait sinks again, giving an erratic motion to the bait. And if you vary the length of time you pause, you can get your bait to search through the depths for the fish. This is known as a sink-and-draw retrieve.

Tip *Wobbling the layers*

Cast out and count the bait down as it sinks through the water before you start retrieving. By starting to retrieve at a different stage each time, you can search through the water for pike to discover at what depth they are feeding.

A well-trained netsman waits for a pike which took a wobbled sprat to come over the rim of the net before making his move.

Tip Quick on the sink-and-draw

You can save a lot of fishing time by setting up your baits at home.

Hook up some baits on traces ready for wobbling. Freeze them individually as they are and take them to the water in a coolbox next time you go fishing.

Every time you need to change bait, it's a simple matter of taking one from the coolbox and clipping it on to your main line.

▶ ***John Watson likes to wobble deadbaits from his boat. It allows him to fish all round, thoroughly exploring a swim. But wobbling from the bank can be just as effective.***

Hitting the takes

Takes vary when wobbling, but they are generally fairly gentle. Often the line simply goes solid.

It can sometimes feel as though you've run into some weed, but don't just heave to get free. Always assume it's a fish. Pull off some line and wait about five seconds. If it *is* a pike, the line tightens as the fish moves off. That's when you wind into it.

If it is weed, you haven't lost anything through making sure. There's nothing quite as frustrating as getting a bait back all chewed up, knowing that if only you'd been a bit more careful, it could have been a fish on the bank.

All in all, wobbling a deadbait is a very easy method, requiring no special tackle over and above your usual pike gear. It gives you the opportunity to out-think your quarry, puts fish on the bank when static fishing is ineffective and keeps you warm on those cold winter days on the bankside. Give it a go – you won't be disappointed!

▼ ***Tricia King displays a mighty predator. On days when the fish won't come to your static baits, you have to look for them. A wobbled bait is often the best way to do this. It gives you the freedom to fish lots of spots for as long as you want – and it has accounted for many specimens as big as this one in its time.***

John Bailey on the Wensum

Norfolk anglers are battling to restore the River Wensum to its former glory. John Bailey, who knew Wensum roaching in its heyday, finds grounds for hope in the shape of three-pounders in miniature.

It's mid-autumn. After weeks of drought the Wensum at Lyng is low and clear and desperately in need of rain. With every gust of wind, leaves fall from the bankside trees into the river. Some carpet the surface, others drift in mid-water; yet more smother the bottom. Ironically, the rain has chosen this very morning to make its return. Prospects for fishing of any kind, let alone roaching, don't look good.

The downpour doesn't appear to be dampening John Bailey's enthusiasm, though, and he hardly seems to notice the water running down his neck as he leads the way through the trees to the river.

This stretch of the Wensum is one of two leased by the Norfolk Anglers' Conservation Association (NACA), a group dedicated to restoring the river and its roach fishing to its prime. John can remember the days when two-pounders were two-a-penny and the shoals so vast that Ivan Marks – a regular visitor – reckoned he could have caught them on pieces of his hat!

► ***With numerous articles, books and big fish to his credit, John Bailey stands alongside Chris Yates as one of the great contemporary writing anglers – someone who not only writes well, but catches big fish.***

▼ ***John fishing the millpool at Lyng. He would usually expect to find roach in the slow water on the near side of the main flow, but it was chock-a-block with leaves. With the river low and clear as well, the fish shied away to the tail of the pool.***

Fishery facts

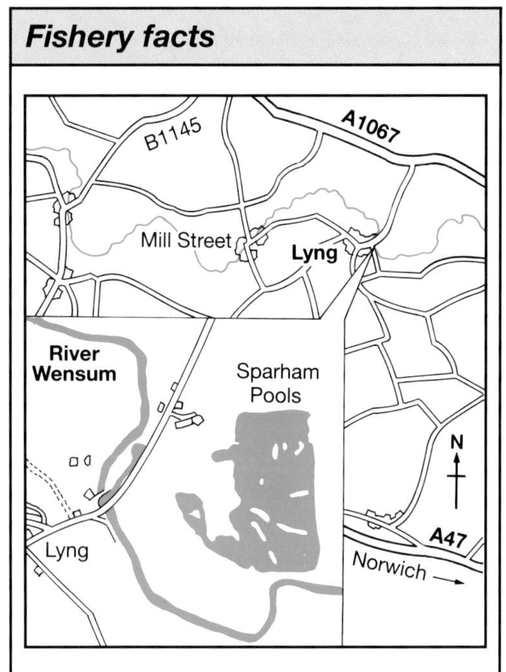

John fished the Wensum at Lyng, a village off the A1067 north-west of Norwich. The stretch is one of two leased by the Norfolk Anglers' Conservation Association (NACA).

▲ *With all his odds and ends on his back in a rucksack-cum-folding stool, John is able to move quickly and easily from swim to swim in his search for Wensum roach.*

"Two-pounders were two-a-penny and the roach shoals so vast that Ivan Marks reckoned he could have caught them on bits of his hat!"

The Wensum at Lyng

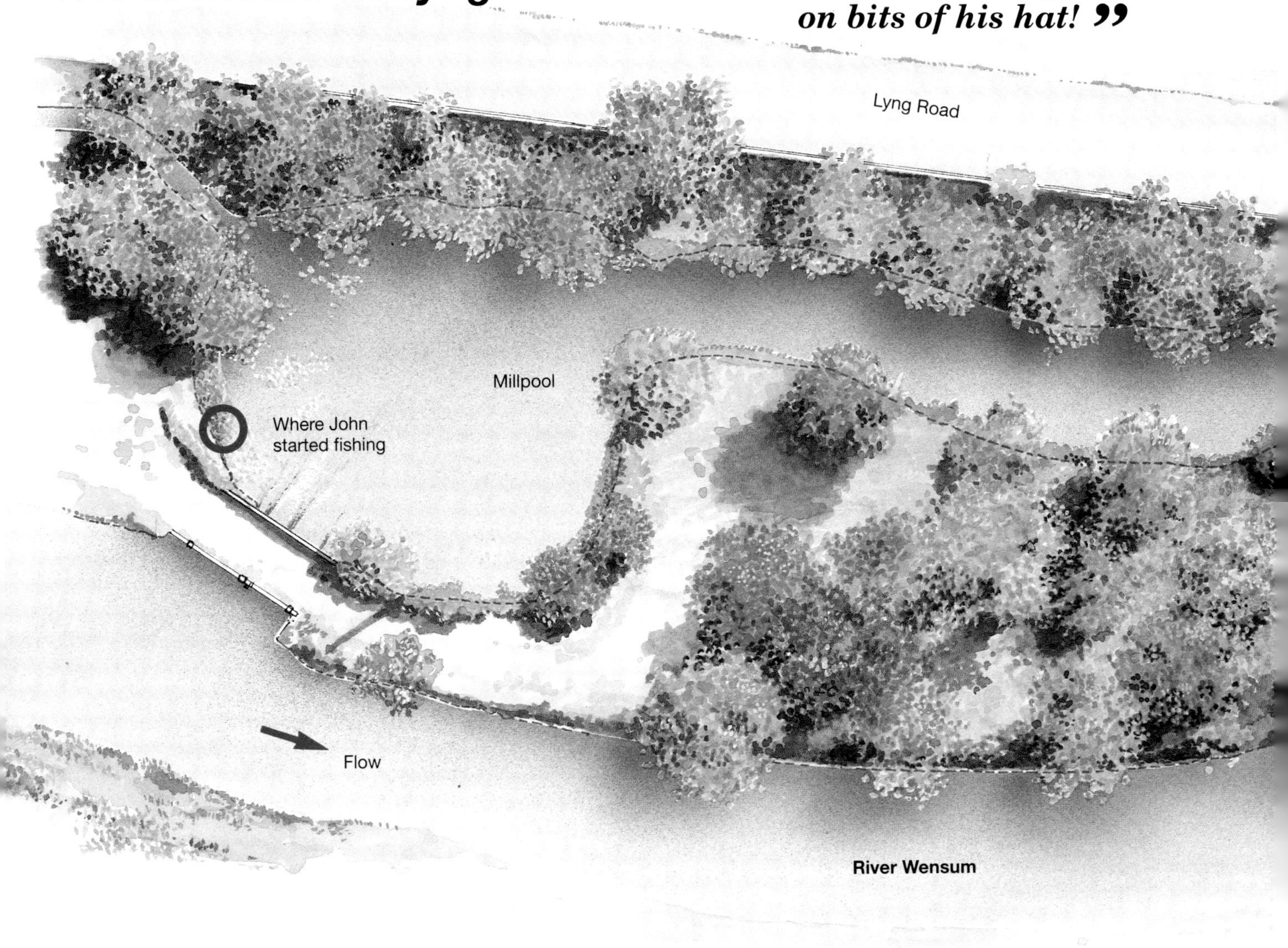

Then came the dredgers and the abstractors, and the Wensum went the way of so many other lowland English rivers. Its roach were unable to breed successfully and within only a few years they died off, leaving just the odd old, outsized fish.

For once, however, local anglers cared enough to act. No wonder John is so keen to start fishing, despite the adverse weather and water conditions: he's determined to catch some young roach, to prove that NACA is succeeding in helping the species to breed successfully again, and so show anglers in other parts of the country just what can be done.

9:30AM The old millpool

John starts in the old millpool above the weir. He chooses a pitch in the reeds at the head of the pool, a swim from which he can explore both the main flow and the slower water at the sides and tail. Even in the gloom and rain, it's an idyllic spot. Enclosed by trees, with the dominant sound the tumble of water through the sluice, you couldn't be farther away from it all.

▲ ***Right at the end of a long trot down a far-bank glide, John's float shoots under as a chub grabs the bait and the battle is on.***

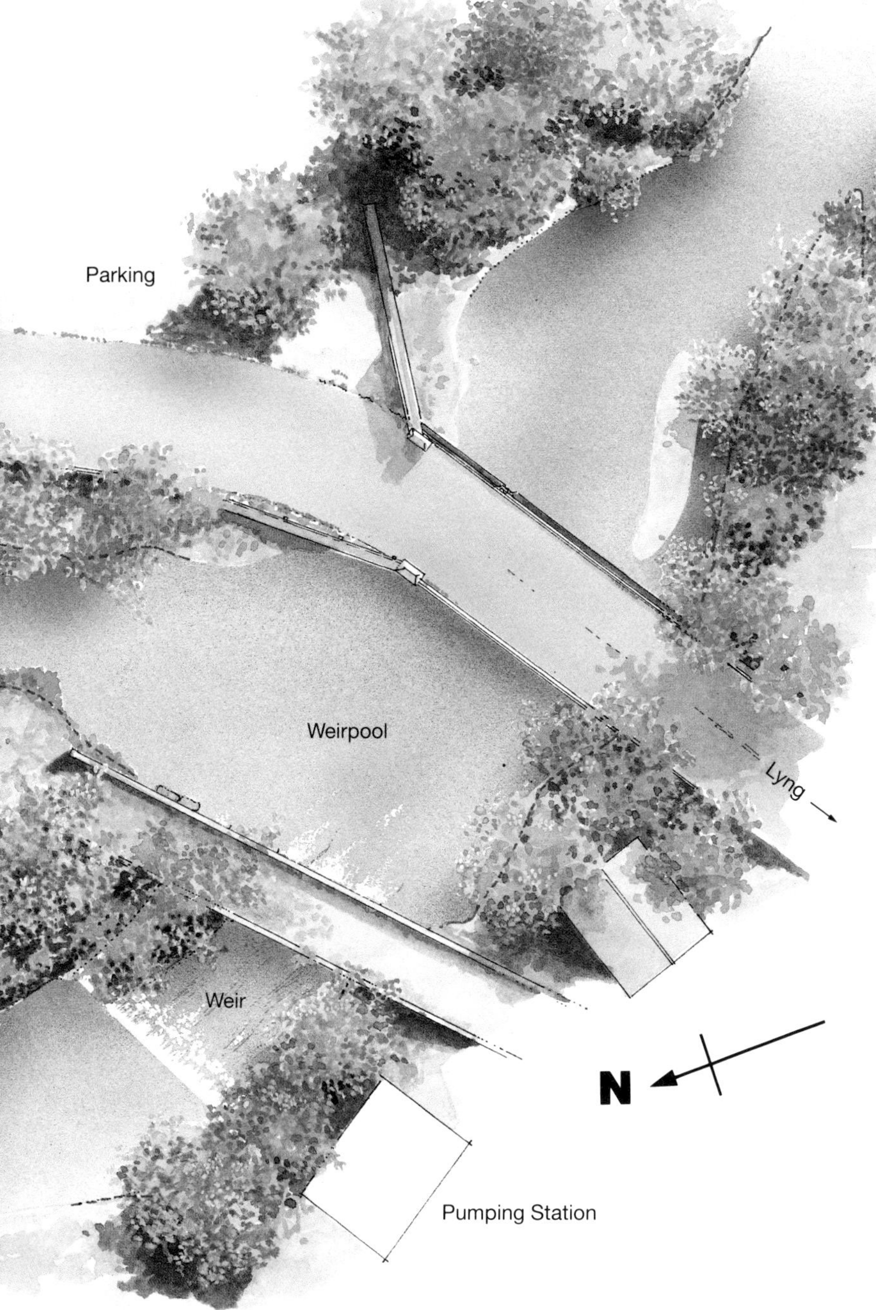

▲ ***John would rather this 2½lb (1.1kg) chub had been a 2½lb roach, but he was happy enough to catch it despite the driving rain.***

John mashes up some bread, squeezes out a few small balls and lobs them gently into the main flow. They break up as they sink, dispersing an enticing trail. By the time he has tackled up they should have whetted the appetites of any resident roach.

Float John sets up an 11½ft (3.46m) Avon rod and a fixed-spool reel loaded with 2½lb (1.1kg) line.

His float is a bulbous, buoyant, clear hollow-plastic 2SSG 'loafer'. He attaches it bottom-end only and shots it with a single SSG 30cm (12in) from the hook – this keeps the breadflake hookbait down in the flow. Undershotting the float allows John to long-trot it and still see it clearly. It also means he can trundle the hookbait along the bottom, or check the float's passage to make the hookbait rise, without the float dragging under.

John's hook is a forged size 12 tied direct to the main line. He flattens the barb so that it does less damage to the fish while retaining a secure hook-hold.

Leger John sets up an 11ft (3.3m) quivertip rod and a fixed-spool reel loaded with 3lb (1.4kg) line. He ties a forged size 10 hook, again with a flattened barb, direct to the main line. A swan-shot link slides above a leger stop, which he positions 30-45cm (12-18in) from the hook according to how the fish are biting.

10:00AM Fishing in the rain

John introduces some more mash, picks up his float rod and baits the hook with a pinch of flake. He flicks the float out into the main flow and lets it run down until it reaches the tail of the pool, where the bottom shallows up to form a natural food trap. He checks

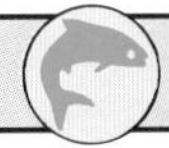

No to nets

John Bailey advises against the habitual use of keepnets for roach – indeed, for any fish. Apart from marring a fish's beauty, the loss of scales and splitting of fins that can occur in a net may stunt its growth. Far better to put the fish back immediately, after the minimum of handling.

JOHN BAILEY ON THE FIGHT TO SAVE THE WENSUM

▲ The way things were. A younger looking John Bailey with a 3lb 2oz (1.4kg) Wensum roach.

In the 1960s and early 1970s the Wensum offered possibly the best roach fishing in history. Incredibly, Wensum roach then were only really classed as big when they weighed over 2½lb (1.1kg). They were also numerous and huge bags were recorded: in one fantastic morning, two of us landed 400 roach the total catch weighing 250lb (113kg).

Then, in the space of only a couple of years in the late 1970s, the roach all but vanished from the Wensum. A few specimens remained but they were lone survivors in miles of water. By the mid-1980s a Wensum roach was an event and almost certain to be a very big, very old fish: in scores of sessions in the 1985-6 season I caught only three, weighing 2lb 10oz (1.2kg), 3lb 5oz (1.5kg) and 3lb 10oz (1.6kg). Clearly something was very wrong.

At first we suspected disease but, as usual, man was to blame. Abstraction had reduced flow, causing spawning sites to silt up, while flood prevention measures such as dredging had destroyed spawning sites and deprived fry and yearlings of slack-water shelter in winter.

Norfolk anglers got together and in 1986 the Save the Wensum campaign was launched to fight for the river and its roach. Shortly after, the Norfolk Anglers' Conservation Association (NACA) was formed. NACA plunged straight into the fray and ever since has fought for all of Norfolk's waters. It has acquired leases on two stretches of the Wensum where, among other improvements, it has put in riffles, which speed the flow to scour suitable spawning sites, and dug cattle drinks, to shelter fry and yearlings in winter. Already these improvements are paying dividends – in places the river now teems with young roach up to 1lb (0.45kg) or so. Thanks to NACA, the future of Wensum roaching looks much brighter.

NACA membership

For details of how to join NACA, write to: John Nunn, Heronsfield, West Somerton, Great Yarmouth. General enquiries should be addressed to: Chris Turnbull, 35 Rose Valley, Norwich. More than just fishing, NACA membership offers anglers the chance to put something back into the waters that give them so much enjoyment. Everyone who joins is encouraged to play a part – whether in waterside working parties or in campaigning for better waters. If every region had an Anglers' Conservation Association I know we would all enjoy much better fishing.

John Bailey

On a dredged stretch of the Wensum at Lyng, a cattle drink dug by NACA offers roach fry shelter in winter.

Also at Lyng, NACA has put a gravel riffle across the river to create a successful spawning site for roach.

On the same reach a NACA pipe helps oxygenate and speed the flow with water from nearby Sparham Pools.

the float's progress slightly, so that the flake flutters enticingly into the trap. The float reaches the end of the pool. Nothing. John strikes the flake off the hook and winds in, sets the float to fish a little bit deeper, rebaits and recasts.

Again, John checks the float at the tail of the pool, inching it down, almost willing the bait into a fish's mouth. This time, just before reaching the end of the pool, the float bobs once, then twice, then slowly but surely sinks out of sight. A smart, sweeping strike sets the hook and the as yet unseen fish heads determinedly up the pool towards the sluice.

► John's quivertip rod takes the strain as a small but fighting-fit chub makes a last-minute dash towards the head of the millpool.

▼John gently slips the chub back into the slow water to the side of the main flow, to allow it to recover from the tiring fight.

John soon gets it under control, however, and steers it into the side. It's a small chub, not one of the hoped-for roach, but a good fish all the same. He quickly but carefully unhooks it and slips it back.

11:00AM Wensum jewels

The rain is unrelenting, but John's concentration never wavers. He lets his float explore the slower water on the far side of the pool, and varies the depth setting in an effort to draw a response. Every now and then he throws in a little ball of mash. Despite the troublesome leaves constantly fouling the line and catching on the hook, several more small chub are fooled, plus a dace of almost ½lb (0.23kg). But no roach as yet.

John tries the leger, wondering if that will do the trick. Straight away the tip starts twitching and trembling as a fish

John Bailey's float and leger rigs

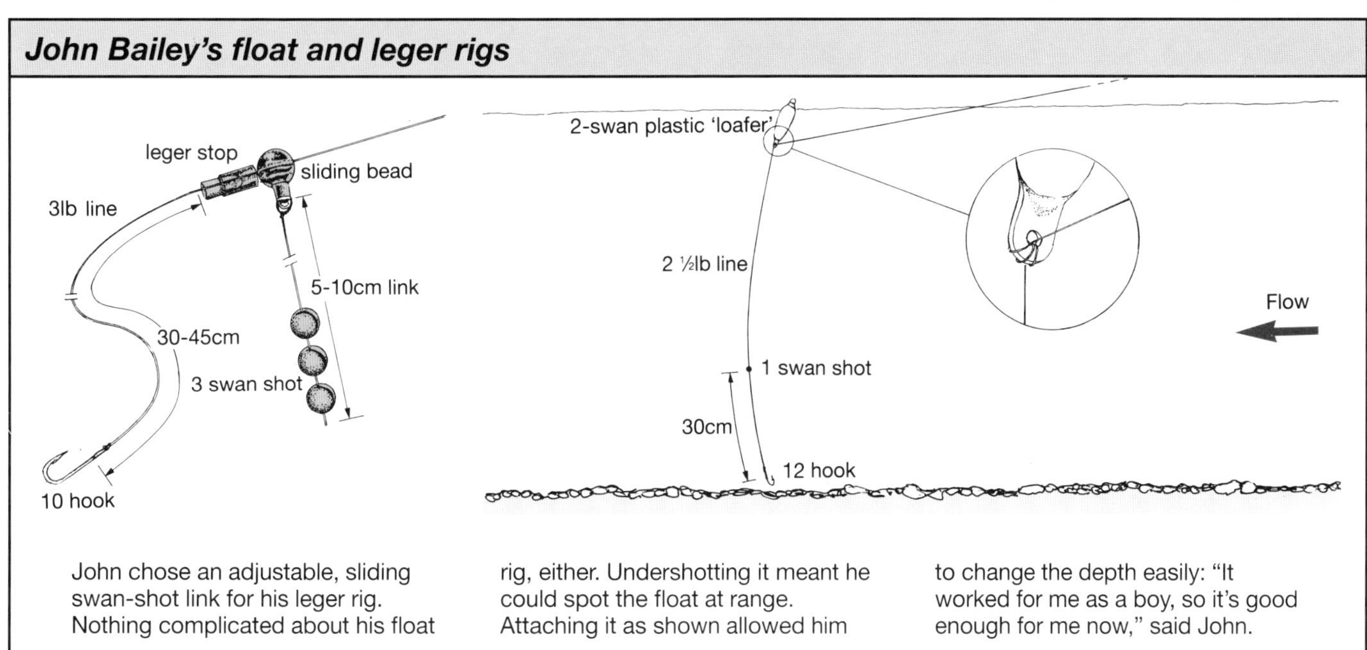

John chose an adjustable, sliding swan-shot link for his leger rig. Nothing complicated about his float rig, either. Undershotting it meant he could spot the float at range. Attaching it as shown allowed him to change the depth easily: "It worked for me as a boy, so it's good enough for me now," said John.

noses the bait. Two sharp pulls follow and he strikes into a fish – another chub.

Back to the float, and a roach is on! It only weighs a few ounces, but it's a young, perfectly formed fish and nothing could have pleased John more. Grinning broadly, he unhooks and returns it with loving care.

John tries the leger once more. After a long wait he strikes the wariest of bites and feels the characteristic thump, thump, glide of a good roach. A flash of silver shows in the clear water and a brilliant red dorsal fin breaks surface – a jewel in the Wensum. At around 1lb (0.45kg) it's a splendid specimen and, most encouraging of all, a young fish in mint condition.

Bites become cagey in the millpool and John thinks it's time for a move downstream. He stops here and there, trying different lies, and picks up a 2½lb (1.1kg) chub from a far bank glide, but the main river is really too low and clear for roach. With the rain still falling, the lure of the pub is too strong to resist.

2:00PM Fingers crossed

It did in fact stop raining in the afternoon, and John gave it another go in the millpool and on the main river. No more roach were forthcoming, but the morning's success was enough to show that, touch wood, Wensum roach are on their way back.

►▼ John lands a 1lb (0.45kg) roach (right). A young, unmarked fish (below), it has the distinctive bull-shoulders of Wensum roach – "like a three-pounder in miniature."

Spinning for stillwater perch

Stewart Allum of the *Perchfishers* takes a look at spinning – a neglected but deadly method of taking good numbers of big perch from lakes, reservoirs and gravel pits.

Anyone who spins for pike on a regular basis has probably caught the odd big perch. But all too often these catches are dismissed as freak captures, and spinning for perch is still largely ignored as a viable technique by most anglers.

This is unfortunate, since by making a few simple adjustments to your normal pike spinning procedures and observing a few basic ground rules, you can make some tremendous catches of big perch from all sorts of still waters.

▲ Early in the season spinning takes lots of perch from the shallows as they feast on the hordes of fry sheltering there.

◄ The author, Stewart Allum, with a fine late season 3lb 2oz (1.4kg) perch. Spring and autumn offer you the best chance to contact shoals of big fish.

Where and when

Perch hunt mainly by sight, so water clarity is obviously very important. If your lake is very clear then there's no reason why spinning shouldn't succeed. But if the water is cloudy, then static baits such as legered worm or deadbait – that perch can find by scent, are generally far more effective.

The early part of the season finds perch well spread along the margins of a typical still water. During the summer months, the margins are home to millions of fry (generally juvenile roach and perch), which form

Fish it deep!

In the colder months, too many anglers start the retrieve almost as soon as the spinner hits the surface. It's not much use fishing at 1m (3ft), when the fish are 6m (20ft) down. Perch move only slowly into the deep water, carefully adjusting their swimbladders as they go, so they aren't likely to rush up through the water to intercept a lure.

the staple diet of large adult perch.

Big perch, along with many other species, are at their most active during dawn and dusk in the summer. There is still enough light to hunt by, but the main force of the sun isn't beating down on the water.

You can often see perch chasing fry right up to the shore, and small fish leaping repeatedly across the surface in an attempt to escape a hungry perch. Armed with a light spinning rod, you can enjoy some tremendous sport by working a small spinner through these areas.

However, the best chance of taking a specimen comes in autumn. As temperatures fall, the large adults shoal and gradually head for deeper water. During this period they are hungry, active and extremely aggressive, with many large fish often packed into surprisingly small areas.

With the onset of winter, they become less active and move slowly into the deepest water they can find for the coldest months. At this time, they aren't often prepared to chase a spinner.

In early October they may, for example, be happily feeding at depths of around 4-6m (13-20ft), whereas by late November they may well be down as deep as 10m (33ft) or more, depending on the severity of the weather and the depth of the water.

▼ *A jack pike that has taken a red-bodied, silver-bladed spinner demonstrates the need for a wire trace.*

Spinning gear

Spinning for perch calls for a fairly light and sensitive rod, so that the tip actually bends slightly as you retrieve. Too stiff a rod gives you completely the wrong action, preventing the spinner from working properly.

Remember, you are trying to imitate a small crippled fish with your spinner, not merely dragging a chunk of metal through the water. A through-actioned Avon-type rod, 10-11ft (3-3.4m) long, with a test curve of around 1¼lb (0.6kg) is ideal.

Almost any fixed-spool reel which balances the rod will do. Load it with line tough enough to withstand the rigours of repeated casting and the odd underwater obstacle. It must, however, remain fine and supple enough to cut cleanly through the water without creating too much drag – 5-7lb (2.3-3.2kg) b.s. line fits the bill nicely.

Avoid pre-stretched lines as these aren't generally tough enough. A tough, abrasion-resistant, but moderately supple line, such as Maxima or Sylcast is fine.

Spinner selection

Don't blindly follow conventional thinking when picking spinners – small ones don't work any better than bigger ones. A 3lb (1.4kg) perch is perfectly capable of swallowing prey fish of all sizes up to 6oz (170g), so large spinners and spoons are quite attractive to them.

Also, a ¾oz (18g) spinner casts farther and bites the water better than a smaller one, sending out a stronger vibration and showing up more clearly to the perch. There are many thousands of patterns, but a few basic designs account for large numbers of quality perch year in, year out.

Barspoons are the ideal choice for bank fishing. The best patterns have a red body and a silver or gold blade. The blade is highly visible and red is noted for being a colour which seems to attract perch. The ABU Reflex is perhaps the most successful barspoon, with its well weighted body and feathered treble hook.

If you choose another make (Mepps are also excellent), put some feathers or red wool on the treble. It encourages a chasing perch to snap at it, much as it would the tail of a small fish in order to cripple it. The ¾oz (18g) size is ideal: it casts a long way, sinks quickly and the 4cm (1½in) blade bites the water well on the retrieve.

Spoons are generally heavier than barspoons and because of that they come into

Flutter-by fishing

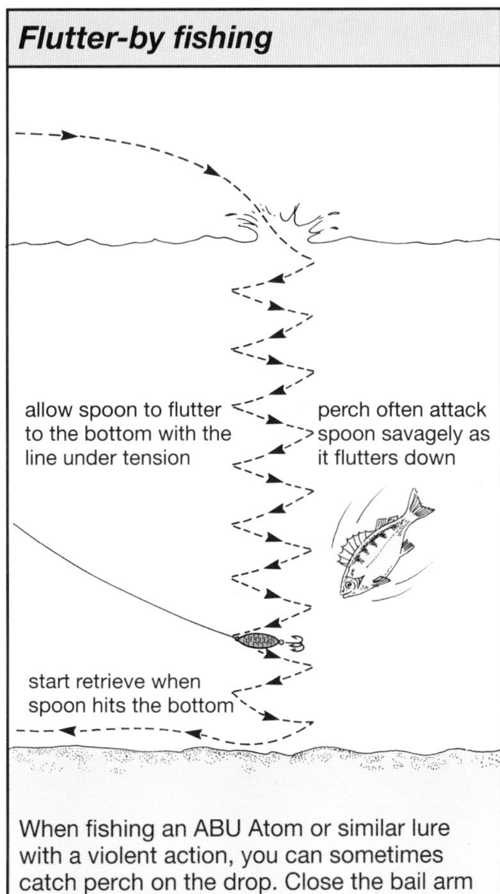

When fishing an ABU Atom or similar lure with a violent action, you can sometimes catch perch on the drop. Close the bail arm when the lure hits the surface, and allow it to flutter to the bottom under tension.

their own for boat fishing over very deep water. A dead slow retrieve keeps them working just clear of the bottom and they have an undulating action which is highly attractive to both perch and pike.

Two proven fish-killers are Toby-type lures and the ABU Atom in gold, silver, copper and perch-painted patterns of ¾oz (18g) and above. The Atom, in particular, has a very violent action, even at slow speed. It has the added advantage that it can sometimes account for fish on the drop since its body form allows it to flutter down attractively through the water. Big perch often strike at the lure as it sinks, and the takes can be quite savage.

Wire traces are strongly advisable to prevent bite-offs from the inevitable pike takes. Perch aren't deterred by the wire, especially since they usually attack a spinner from behind.

Boat fishing

A boat isn't essential for perch fishing, but if one is available, use it. It's much easier to cover a lot of deep water in a boat, including much that is inaccessible to the bank angler, with a wide variety of methods.

The great advantage of a boat for spinning is that the lure is fishing deep water for the maximum time possible. From the bank, the lure spends only a few seconds in the productive deep water before being

Spinners galore!

A range of effective perch spinners including the Abu Reflex **(1)** – the silver blade/red body is a particularly effective combo; the Mepps **(2)** in both small and large sizes; the ABU Droppen **(3);** the ABU Toby **(4);** and a couple of wire traces **(5),** which are essential in those waters which might hold pike (and most do).

Tip Slow down to catch more!

Tailor your retrieve to the hunting strategy of your quarry. Unlike pike, which burst upon their prey, perch harry small fish, chasing and plucking at their tails to disable them. A slower retrieve allows them to approach the lure in their usual way – that's why you may feel a number of plucks at the line before the spinner is finally taken.

Boat versus bank

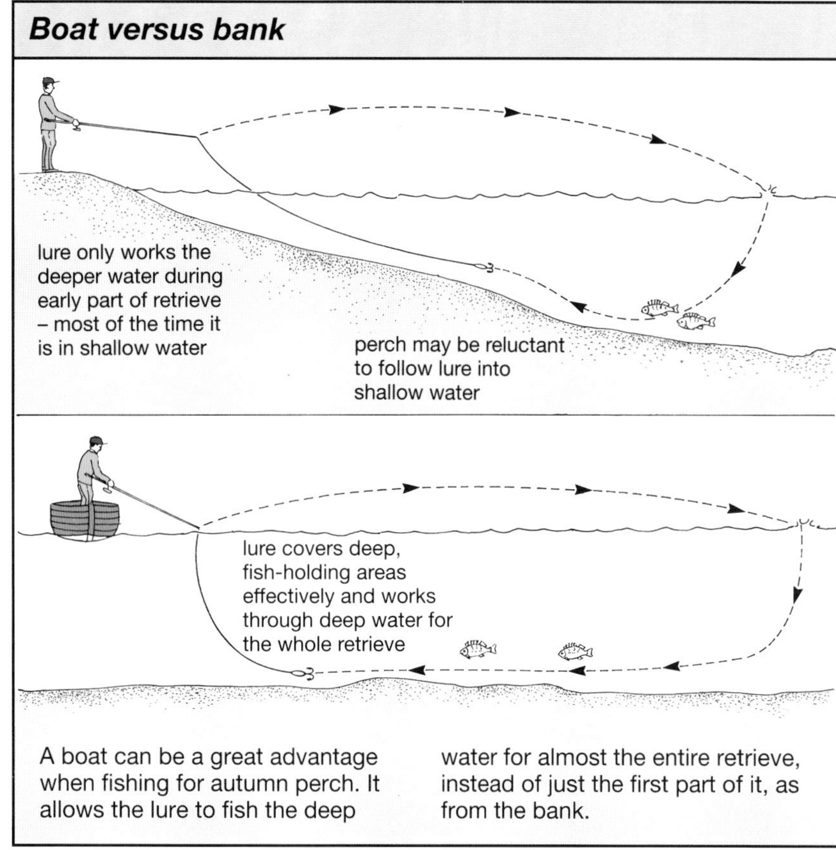

A boat can be a great advantage when fishing for autumn perch. It allows the lure to fish the deep water for almost the entire retrieve, instead of just the first part of it, as from the bank.

Big perch waters

Here are a few noted stillwater perch fisheries, all available on a day or season ticket basis.

- **Ardleigh Reservoir,** near Colchester, Essex. Day tickets for boat and bank from bailiff's hut from 1st October to end of February. Perch to over 3lb (1.4kg), mostly in deep water well out from bank.
- **Boyer Leisure Ltd.** owns a number of gravel pit fisheries in Middx/Bucks area. Day and season tickets and advice on the pits from: Boyer Leisure Ltd., Farlows Lake, Ford Lane, off Iver Lane, Bucks SL0 9LL.
- **Leisure Sport fisheries** owns many prime gravel pits all over Britain, some with huge perch. For details of the best waters write to: Leisure Sport Angling, Thorpe Park, Staines Road, Chertsey, Surrey.
- **Linear fisheries,** Newport Pagnell, Bucks. Series of 10 gravel pits ranging from 3-60 acres. Excellent perch fishing with fish over 3lb (1.4kg). For perch-related details write to: The Secretary, Linear House, 2 Northcroft, Shenley Lodge, Milton Keynes, Bucks. Tel 0908 607577.

▼ ***This beautiful perch was fooled by a Mepps spinner. It came from a water with no pike in it so the angler didn't use a wire trace, but if there's any doubt about that, don't take chances.***

wound back into the shallows. (This is clearly not a consideration when fishing for early season perch in the margins.)

It's well known that perch like moored boats, and a shoal which has been tempted into chasing spinners often stays near your boat once the fish have spotted it. Often you can take them from right under the boat as the day progresses.

If the boat also has a fish finder or echo sounder this can be an invaluable help in finding the deepest water. Remember, though, to wear a life jacket at all times, no matter how calm it seems. Dressed in heavy winter clothing, an angler falling into ice-cold water can easily drown, no matter how strong a swimmer he is.

Dennis Flack on the Little Ouse

Suffolk farmer Dennis Flack has caught over 30 dace of 1lb (0.45kg) or more from the Little Ouse. The river produced the British record dace in 1960 but has twice since been nearly wiped out by pollution.

► *Dennis Flack is known for his tally of specimen dace from the Little Ouse but he still has some way to go to equal the fine record of his late friend and mentor Billy Clarke, who caught over 40 dace of 1lb (0.45kg) or more from the same river!*

Spring is in the air as the season draws to a close on the banks of the Little Ouse at Brandon. The river is a touch higher and faster than usual following a day or two of rain, but still runs clear and steady through the dark, sandy soil.

10:30AM Brandon Stanch

Dennis reckons there's a bit too much extra water to fish immediately below the stanch, or floodgate. His friend Mark Stamp obviously had the same thought when he arrived earlier, as he has set up stall a fair way downstream. Dennis shoulders his tackle and heads off along the bank to see how he's getting on.

Local anglers have been catching dace to 12oz (340g) from this stretch recently and when Mark had a look yesterday evening he saw several good fish topping. So far this morning, however, he has been struggling, only taking the odd small dace on waggler-fished maggot. At his invitation, Dennis drops in a couple of swims below..

▼ *Tackling up by the side of the Little Ouse at Brandon in Suffolk. Don't let the old willow fishing basket fool you. As Dennis says, it's the angler that catches the fish, not his tackle.*

Dennis's baits and float

Dennis's favourite baits for Little Ouse dace are red-maggot casters and red and pink maggots, with bronzes as a standby.

Using a short, insert waggler and leaving a 2.5cm (1in) gap between the locking shot gives the cleanest strike, Dennis finds.

How to get there

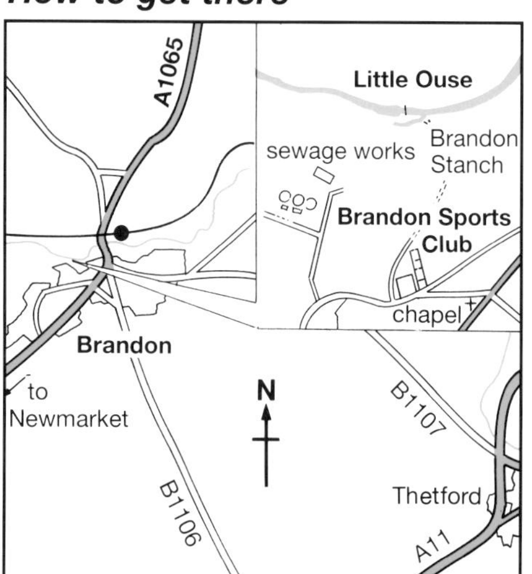

Brandon is on the A1065 in Suffolk. Brandon Stanch is within walking distance of the station. To get to the stanch, turn off the A1065 by the chapel and look for Brandon Sports Club on the right hand side. Turn into the club grounds and follow the track right down to the river. There is plenty of room for parking alongside the stanch.

▲ Dennis began well below Brandon Stanch but couldn't locate any dace early on. Finding the fish is half the battle.

Farm pond record

Dennis is an experienced match and pike angler as well as big dace hunter. He also holds the British silver bream record – with a 15oz (425g) specimen caught in 1988 from a pond on his Lakenheath farm!

11:00AM Why the waggler?

The river here looks ideal for the stick float today yet Dennis, like Mark, opts to trot it with a waggler. Why?

Dennis explains that the bottom is very weedy, making false bites hard to avoid. It's difficult to tell false bites from real ones, so you have to strike at everything. Because the water is shallow, repeated striking with a stick float causes so much commotion that the dace drop farther and farther downstream until eventually you lose them altogether.

Striking with a waggler causes less disturbance. To ensure a cleaner strike still, Dennis uses a short, insert waggler –

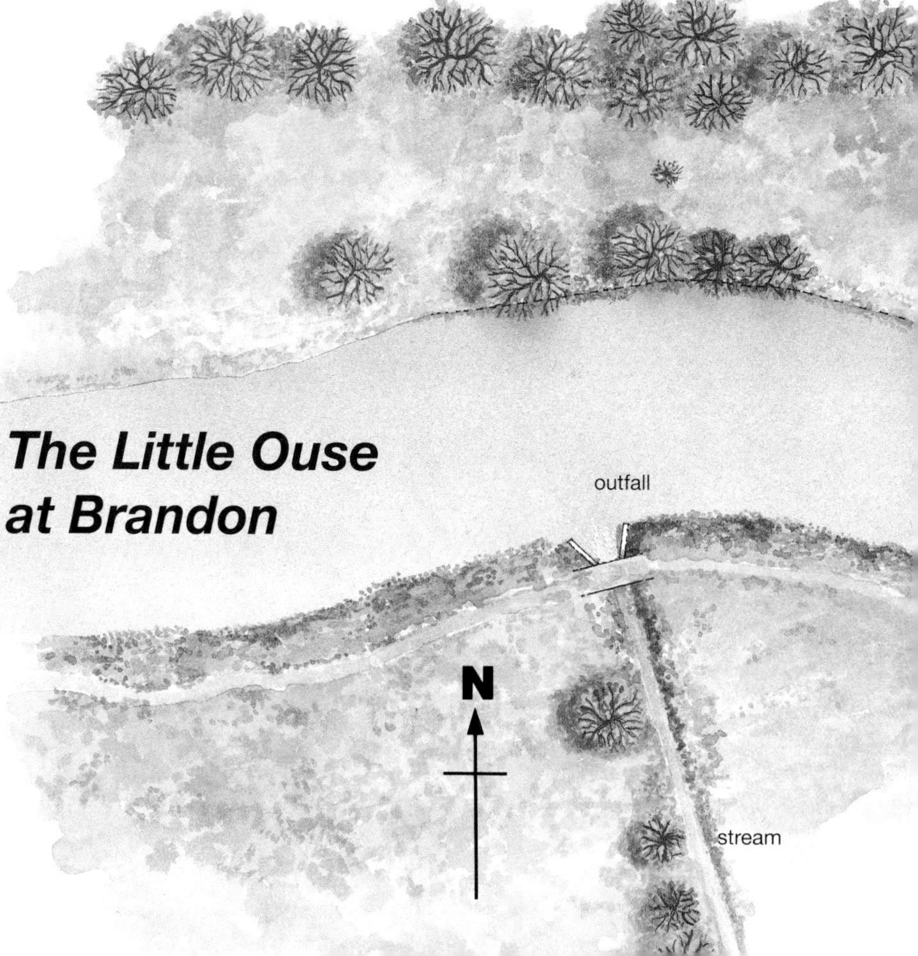

slightly undershotted to stop it dragging under too easily – and leaves a 2.5cm (1in) gap between the locking shot.

When the water is clear, as it is today, he believes that a colourless, transparent plastic waggler is less likely to be seen by the fish. He likes colourless, transparent line for the same reason.

11:15AM Red-maggot casters

Over the years Dennis has found that Little Ouse dace definitely prefer reddish baits. White, yellow and bronze maggots do catch of course – indeed, Dennis has brought along a pint of bronzes today, just in case – but not as well as red and pink maggots.

Casters can be an excellent bait too. They don't always work but when they do you tend to get the better fish. Dennis reckons that just as red maggots work better than white maggots, so casters turned from red maggots work better, being redder, than casters turned from white maggots.

11:20AM A clean run through

Dennis puts a few handfuls of casters and maggots in his pocket, picks up his rod and wades out a few feet. This is in contrast to Mark, who is sitting on his box on the bank. But Mark is on the outside of a slight bend where the main flow and deepest water are close in, almost under his rod tip. Where Dennis is fishing, the main flow and deepest water are past the middle. Standing in the water is therefore essential for full tackle control.

The average depth in the main flow on

▲ *In the morning, Dennis moved swims several times in an attempt to locate a shoal of feeding dace. There's no point in flogging away at a barren swim, wasting time and bait.*

"If you're going to catch a 1lb dace then you've got to catch a female. I doubt if there's a single male 1lb dace in any river the length of the country, let alone in the Little Ouse."

Fishery facts

Fishing is free on the Brandon side of the Little Ouse below Brandon Stanch. All you need is an Anglian rod licence. There is free fishing on a number of stretches of the river, plus quite a lot of club and day ticket water.

For details, contact: Rod 'n' Line, 15 White Hart Street, Thetford, Norfolk, IT24 1AA (Tel 0842 764825).

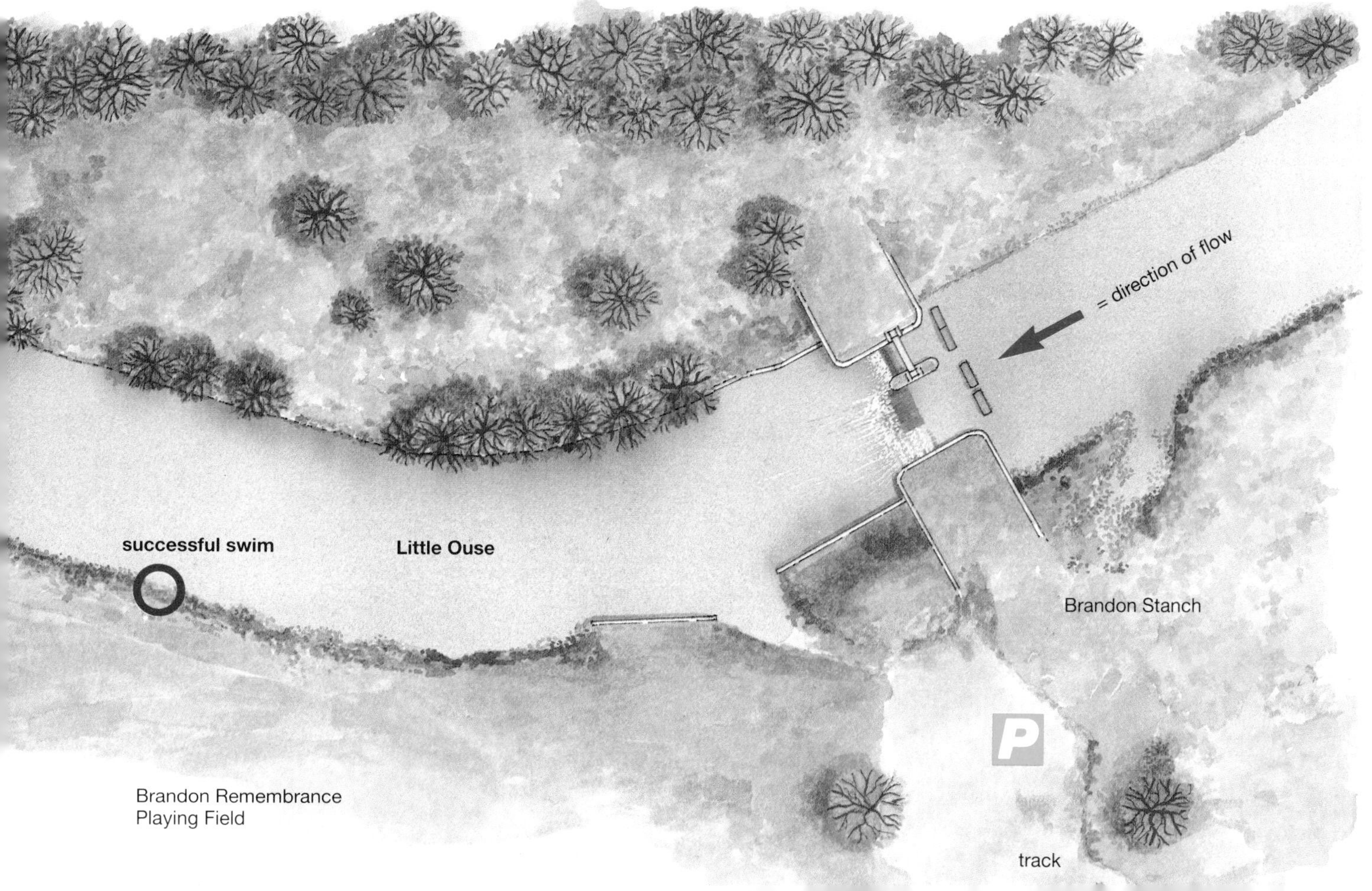

= direction of flow

successful swim

Little Ouse

Brandon Stanch

P

Brandon Remembrance
Playing Field

track

Dennis's waggler rig

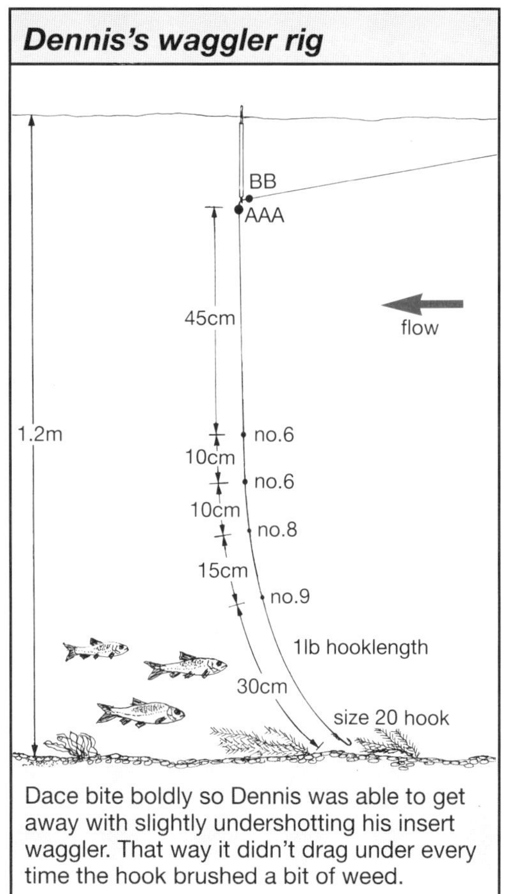

Dace bite boldly so Dennis was able to get away with slightly undershotting his insert waggler. That way it didn't drag under every time the hook brushed a bit of weed.

▲ ***In the afternoon Dennis located a shoal of dace in a swim below the stanch.***

The Little Ouse at Brandon marks the county boundary, so you could say that Dennis was standing in Suffolk but actually fishing in Norfolk!

▼ ***Rainy dace – once Dennis found the fish there was no holding him back and dace after dace fell to his rod. Here he has turned to face upstream as he swings in another small but plump fish. Note the shallow water at the edge, which made him forgo the use of a keepnet for the sake of the fish.***

this stretch is about 1m (3ft). Dennis sets his float accordingly and has a few trial runs through. It goes down unimpeded on the first trot so he moves the float up the line a few centimetres each time until the bare hook catches the weed and drags the float under.

Having found the depth to be about 1.2m (4ft), he runs it through a few more times on different lines, looking for the cleanest run possible. It's no good picking a line at random only to find you're fishing where there's too much weed. Satisfied that he has found a relatively weed-free line, he starts fishing.

11:30AM No bites, no nothing

Each cast, Dennis feeds about half a dozen maggots and the same number of casters. The dace shoals aren't very big here and if you feed too heavily the fish miss a lot of the bait going past and end up chasing it downstream and out of the swim.

To begin with he throws the feed straight out in front of him. Once you start catching you can throw it in above or below you according to where you're getting your bites. The aim is to concentrate the shoal about 10m (11yd) downstream – any higher up the swim and you risk scaring them off, any lower down and you miss too many bites.

Starting with a caster on the hook, Dennis trots the float down about 10m (11yd), holding the rod high to keep as much line off the water as possible. Occasionally he checks the float's progress to lift the bait enticingly off the bottom.

Ten minutes and no bites later, he tries a red maggot on the hook and lets the float run down a few yards farther each time, exploring the tail of the swim. "Once you've found the dace you can bring them to you,

Big dace don't come easy

The Little Ouse doesn't give up its big dace readily. First you have got to find them – not easy in miles of water. Then you have got to catch them – and for every specimen there are thousands of small fish. "I wouldn't like to think how many hours you have to spend to get a 1lb (0.45kg) dace," says Dennis – and he has been fishing the river since he was a boy!

◀ *He stoops to conquer – among the run of small dace, Dennis hooked the occasional one that was just that bit too big to swing in.*

▲ *Little Ouse dace are of superior stock, according to Dennis. Who knows, so long as there is no more pollution, this fine young fish could grow up to be a record breaker?*

but you've got to find them first," he says. "You often have to move a few times before you locate them."

Half an hour goes by and still nothing. Dennis is running his float down fully 30m (33yd) now, but the swim is seemingly devoid of dace – of feeding dace, at any rate. Mark, meanwhile, is still getting the occasional small fish. It's time to move.

Dennis tries a swim a little farther downstream: nothing. He moves down even farther: still nothing. He tries back in his original swim: nothing again. Perhaps all the dace are in Mark's swim; he's certainly

Dace and the Little Ouse

The British record dace weighed 1lb 4¼oz (574g) and was caught from the Little Ouse in 1960. It takes at least 10 years for a dace to grow to 1lb (0.45kg), says Dennis. Unfortunately, the Little Ouse has suffered from two massive fish kills since 1960. The first was caused by sewage pollution following the expansion of Thetford in the 1960s. The river eventually recovered and in 1987 Dennis caught a magnificent dace weighing only ¼oz (7g) less than the British record. Then in 1989 came the second disaster, a huge pig slurry spill from which the river is still recovering.

Really big dace are invariably female and the biggest of all are fish that are just about to spawn. The best chance of locating and catching a specimen dace, therefore, is in the last two weeks of the season, when they gather in shallow runs to spawn.

▶ *Dennis with his record-nudging 1lb 4oz (567g) Little Ouse dace, caught in 1987.*

▲ ***Another dace for Dennis. Small dace twist this way and that in an effort to shake the hook, so always keep a tight line on them from the moment you strike until the moment they are in your hand or in the net.***

▲ ***Mark Stamp found the dace right from the start, stayed in the same swim all day and finished up with a similar bag of fish to Dennis. Deep water close in allowed him to use a keepnet.***
Mark calls Dennis The Dace King of the Little Ouse!

► ***This splendid specimen was the best dace of the day for Dennis and was the reward for sticking it out in the afternoon rain. Dace over ½lb (230g) are usually female but this one was male. Males develop rough skin when ready to spawn.***

catching with annoying regularity now! To make matters worse, it has turned chilly and started raining. But Dennis is no quitter and remains confident he'll pin down a few dace before the day is out.

1:55PM Dace located

Dennis moves up to a swim in the shallower, faster water below the stanch and after only a few runs down hits into a lively dace on a pink maggot. It's only a small fish, but it's perfectly formed and has the distinctive brilliant silver colouring of dace from clear rivers. Dace from murky rivers literally pale by comparison. He carefully unhooks it and slips it back – the margin here is too shallow to stake out a keepnet properly.

It isn't long before Dennis is getting a bite almost every cast. Flashing and splashing across the surface, dace after dace is plucked from the shoal.

Most of the fish are small males, according to Dennis. At this time of the year, when they're getting ready to spawn, you can tell the difference by how they feel to the touch. Males feel rough, like chainmail almost, while females feel smooth and silky.

He varies the bait to try to catch a bigger dace, but it makes no difference. Single red maggot, double red maggot, maggot and caster cocktail – whatever he tries, small dace to 6oz (170g) or so keep coming. He's sure there are bigger fish there – it's just a matter of persevering until one gets to the hookbait first.

4:00PM Grand fish

Sure enough, after he has been catching small dace steadily for nearly two hours, Dennis hooks into a much better one that fights doggedly in the current before coming to the net. Dark backed and metal sided, at over ½lb (230g) it's a grand fish by any standards.

No to tiny barbless hooks

Hooked dace bend their bodies like bananas and twist and turn across the current in a spirited effort to get free. Don't make it easy for them by using a hook smaller than a 20 or a hook with no barb, says Dennis.

Appointment with carp – fishing a tight schedule

You don't have to spend days bivvied up on the bank to catch carp, says Warwickshire farmer Brian Ingram. If you've only got a few hours to spare between milking and mucking out, you can score with short session methods.

Dedicated carp anglers tend to concentrate on sessions lasting a few days or so. This can be a productive and challenging way to fish, but what about anglers who just can't spare the time for long stints? What can they do to make the most of the occasional four or five available hours? A semi-stalking and opportunistic approach doesn't guarantee fish, but it can fine tune your angling efforts to increase your chances of results.

Tip Foliage flake

If you're fishing in a swim where there's a lot of weed or leaves, breadflake can be a deadly bait as it sinks slowly and tempts carp sucking in the surface scum.

▶ Approach quietly and you may find carp surface-feeding in the margins. A floater – perhaps a dog biscuit – may tempt them.

Choice of water

Select a water that is fairly local to you, ideally under 20 acres. It's a bonus if you know the water well, especially the resident carps' favoured areas.

For such short visits try to avoid fishing very difficult or large waters unless they are local, or you have spent many hours on them and feel confident of locating carp fairly quickly.

When to go

It's a good idea to fish at the quietest time. When it's quiet, carp venture into areas where they never go at busy times. Early morning in mid-week is usually an excellent time to find carp in the margins.

If you can only fish at the weekends, try to make it Sunday afternoon which is often quiet. Bear in mind however, that if the water is fished by several long-session anglers you might find it charged with uneaten baits and this can make fishing more difficult. Thursday evenings can be quiet when weekend anglers are at home preparing gear.

▼ Not a bird-watcher but a carp angler on the lookout for signs of carp. It can be useful to search for fish from a raised vantage point, but you should try to stay hidden as much as possible.

Tip Quiet dinner

Always pack boilies for your short session fishing – 50-100 baits are ample. There's no need to take more as you are unlikely to lay a table of bait and fish over it. The disturbance caused by baiting up scares your carp out of the swim and you haven't the time to stick around and wait for them to return and feed. The whole idea is to locate feeding carp and present a bait without spooking them.

◀ ***All the gear – a bait bag and small quantities of various baits, along with polarized specs, binoculars and a floppy hat to help spot feeding fish. You can carry bits and pieces of tackle in a small bag or even a multi-pocketed waistcoat. Carry your two ready-tackled rods (even three if allowed), brolly and landing net in a quiver.***

Tip Leave them be

Never bait up on top of feeding carp – they're already tucking in so why spook them? Most carp fishing is done at range, so a boilie in the margins may catch a fish unaware.

Locating fish

Finding carp is paramount with this style of fishing – you can't afford to wait until fish find your bait. If you know the carp's favoured areas and feeding times, you'll have some idea where to look for them.

Try to find out where carp have been caught or last seen by asking anglers on the bank. Be prepared to spend time roaming until you find evidence of carp – you haven't the time to fish blind. Climb trees and look for stained water or bubblers. If the lake has good bankside cover, search the quiet margins. The bank farthest from the car park is often a good bet. If there are localized concentrations of weed carp will not be far away.

Casting to feeding carp

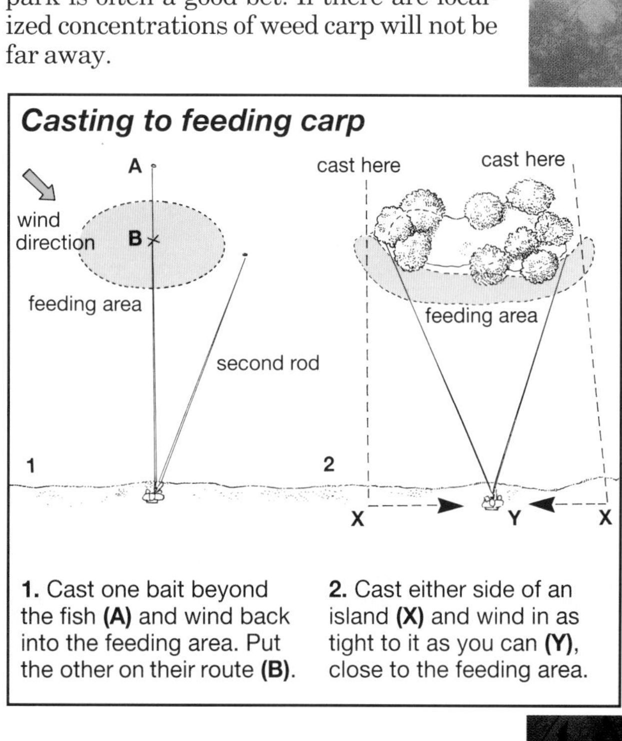

1. Cast one bait beyond the fish **(A)** and wind back into the feeding area. Put the other on their route **(B)**.

2. Cast either side of an island **(X)** and wind in as tight to it as you can **(Y)**, close to the feeding area.

▶ ***Quiet dawn on a lake – a superb setting for a carp session. Fish at quiet times or on lakes where there are few anglers about.***

▲ *Weeds, lily pads and overhanging trees are always worth a look. This quiet corner has all three carpy features. Vibrating lily pads may give away rooting carp below.*

Tackle and bait

This is a mobile type of fishing so keep your tackle to a minimum.

A small shoulder bag of the type used by trout anglers is handy. In it you can carry a small tackle box containing terminal tackle, a camera, binoculars, scales, a weigh sling, a pair of optonics, polarizing sunglasses, a catapult and a couple of pounds of floating dog biscuits.

In addition you need a rod bag. A quiver type sling is ideal for taking a landing net, rod rests, monkey climbers – and a lightweight nylon brolly. It also carries a couple of rods with the sections broken down but set up with reels and rigs ready to respond quickly should a chance unexpectedly present itself. Last but not least, carry an unhooking mat. It not only protects any carp you capture but doubles as a seat.

▼ *A 33lb (15kg) common carp is put back. You'd be pleased to catch a fish this size after a week on the bank, but there's no reason why you can't do it in a few hours.*

A five litre bucket with a lid is just the job for carrying your bait. Pack it with several small bait boxes containing boilies, a particle bait such as peanuts, a few lobworms, luncheon meat, bread and so on. The idea is to carry small amounts of several baits. Should you be lucky enough to get your unhooking mat wet with carp slime, the bucket can take over the seat duties.

Methods and tactics

Boilies fished on a bolt hair rig is the most popular combination for carp.

If a water receives plenty of boilies the resident carp come to regard them as a form of natural food. They may at the same time be wary if they've already been caught on them. Nevertheless, a bolt hair-rigged boilie on the bottom is the best method to adopt.

Imagine you have found carp bubbling 50m (55yd) out. Cast your boilie about 70m (77yd) out – beyond the feeding area. As soon as the lead hits the water click over the

An angler spots a carp patrolling the surface at dusk. Using the bush as cover, he prepares to present a floater.

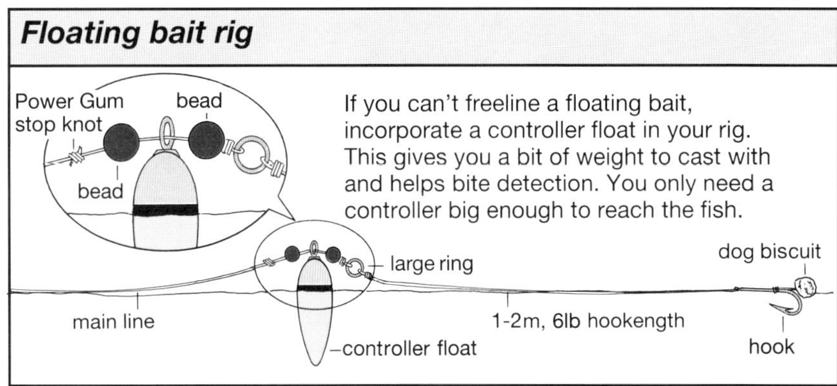

► ***It's a good job this short session angler only had a small fish to deal with – landing a big carp at this sort of angle could be tricky.***

bail arm and, holding the rod tip high, reel in quickly, drawing the tackle just under the surface towards the feeding area. As the lead and bait reach the action zone, stop reeling and let them sink to the bottom without causing a heavy splash. Repeat this process with the other rod but try with a different bait such as a worm.

You may prefer to cast the second bait to a spot where you think the fish are heading. By anticipating the carp's path you may even be able to feed a few loose baits without upsetting the fish.

Once the baits are out, put your rods with optonics in the rests and try not to recast. If the fish stay in the swim stick with it. But if they move off, or if you see a better possibility, move on. Use your judgement and assess your progress regularly.

If the fish are feeding tight to an island, cast either side of it or use the smallest lead that you can to reach the fish without spooking them.

▼ ***Roving short-session tactics accounted for this 20lb (9kg) capture. A boilie cast to it during a feeding binge did the trick.***

In the edge

Short session carp fishing really lends itself to margin fishing. With luck you'll be alone on the bank with no disturbance around. If undisturbed, carp explore the margins with confidence – giving you the opportunity to try rarely used methods.

Freelined breadflake is a deadly bait for carp patrolling the margins.

Freelined luncheon meat is also a prime catcher of patrolling carp. It tends to come off the hook during a cast so lower it into weedy areas at close range.

Dog biscuits are good as a floating bait cast to carp feeding on the surface. Loose feed a few at first to bring the carp on before offering a couple with a hook in.

A single boilie fished in the margins imitates a discarded bait and often picks up an unwary carp. Fish it on the bottom with a bolt hair rig, keeping the line slack.

Lobworms and brandlings are the best bait for catching carp that are bubbling.

These rarely used methods can be very effective but take a bit more effort than fishing a standard bolt rig, because you are fishing for bites. Hold the rod and watch the line closely, or, if the water is clear, watch the bait.

Graham Marsden goes a-chubbing

In the depths of December chub can play very hard to get, but once they get going the action is fast and furious. Graham Marsden pits his angling brain against Cheshire chub.

▼ *A cramped and inaccessible swim is often worth the extra effort – it may be very underfished. Here the banks are very steep, there isn't much room to fish and the trees on all sides hamper casting and striking – but the fish are feeding.*

Graham Marsden had decided to fish the Dane – a small, winding river in the Cheshire countryside. It's a good all-round fishery, known for decent chub and barbel. There are tree-lined, undercut banks, overhanging bushes – everything a fish could want. Much of it is shallow, but there are deep holes where big fish shelter in winter...

6:30AM Dream fish

On the bank it's a cold and nasty December pre-dawn, the birds aren't singing, and bed is calling. But it's no use, the chub are there to be caught, and you catch only imaginary fish in bed. The river is slightly low, but it's a only a week since the last flood and there's a touch of colour.

The Dane is a popular river, even midweek in winter like this Friday morning, but it's too early for all but the hardiest of anglers. So the river is Graham's for an hour or so of stalking. Because of this, and the slight hint of colour in the water, he decides to start by legering lobworm, looking for a fish from each likely swim.

6:40AM Chubby checker

Graham checks out a swim from behind some trees a few yards back from the water. "If a swim might produce, there's no point in telling the chub I'm after them." He likes what he sees and creeps forward, keeping below the level of the bank. That way there's no silhouette for the fish to spot.

It's still dark as he makes his first cast into a hole by an undercut bank, but even so, he keeps as still and hidden as he can. Never give a chub an even break.

The quivertip twitches. It's hard to see in the pre-dawn gloom, but when the tip

▲ *Apart from being a prolific angling writer, Graham Marsden is noted for his catches of big bream and most other coarse species. He loves those tricky fishing problems and uses match and specimen tactics to get among the fish – a day with him is bound to be informative.*

Tip Chub scarer

When stalking big fish in a small river you're likely to disturb the fish if you snag up in a swim. Move on to the next stretch of water and come back to it later.

◀ ***With little foliage to provide cover in winter, Graham keeps low and quiet.***

▼ ***Graham lands a small Dane chub of about 1lb (0.45kg), taken on a simple leger rig.***

moves again, he strikes. No fish results, but the twitches continue, despite the disturbance caused by striking. "It's a sure sign of small dace – but it's time to change swim anyway. The big chub won't feed after you've disturbed the swim."

Graham stops at an unusual swim. There's not much room at the bottom of a very steep bank, a tiny feeder stream enters the main river and there are trees all along the bank. "It's not the easiest swim to fish," says Graham, "and I don't often bother, but neither do other people so it's probably worth a go."

Graham casts slightly downstream into the crease. He's still being bothered by dace which are too small to swallow a size 8, but

How to get there

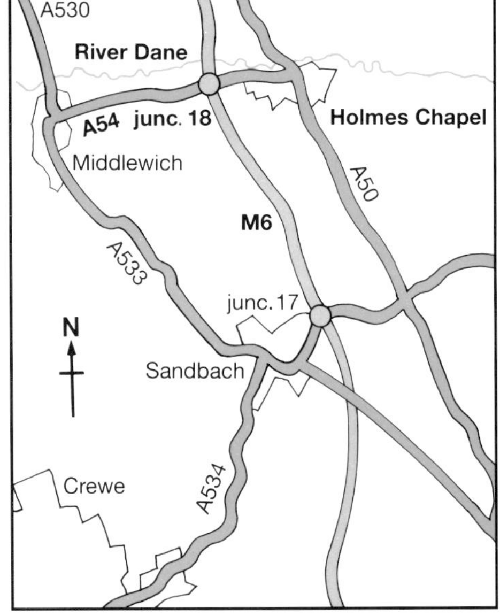

● **By car** Take the A54 towards Holmes Chapel from junction 18 of the M6. The first two turnings on the left are to Cotton Farm and Cotton Hall Farm where you buy day tickets.
● **By train** The nearest BR station is Holmes Chapel, on the Altrincham-Manchester line.

The Dane at Holmes Chapel

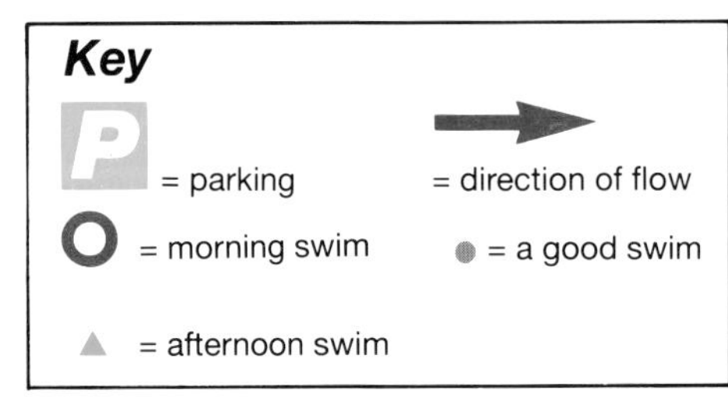

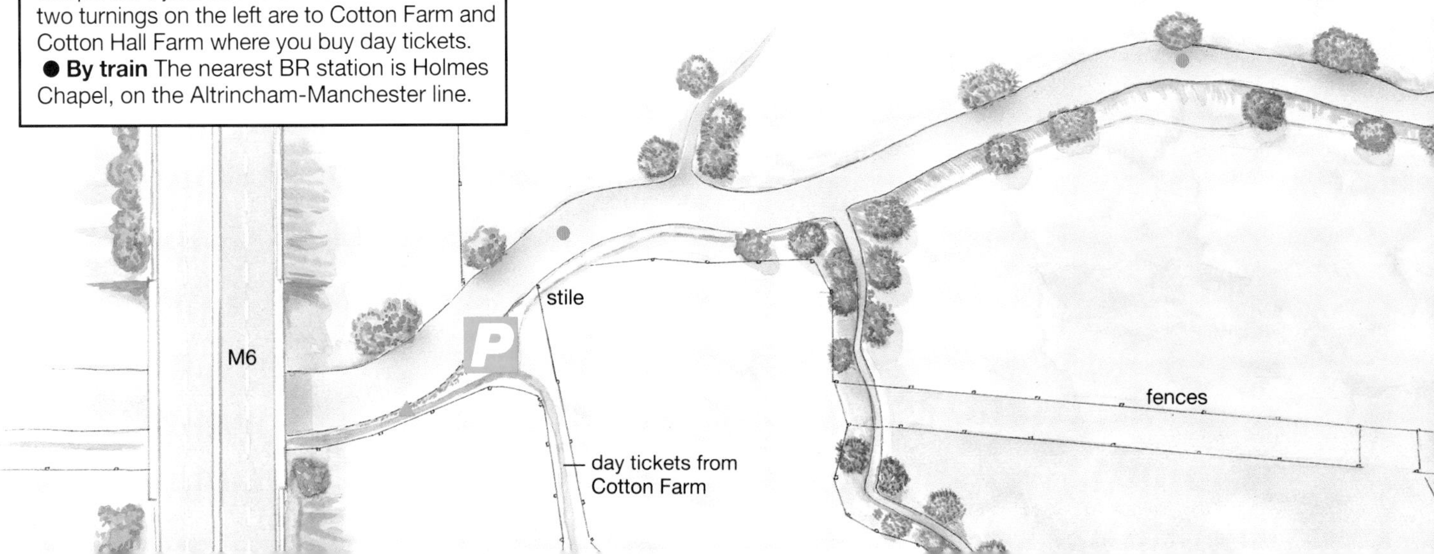

which continually nip the ends off the worm. Then without warning, a more pronounced bite, and, "I'm in." The first chub of the day – and it's early yet. It weighs about a pound (0.45kg) and is quickly returned – you can't use a keepnet when you're stalking – and Graham moves on.

At one of his more often-fished swims, Graham casts to a hole at the far bank. Every three or four biteless minutes he tries farther down, but when a small dace crams

◀ ***Keeping low to the skyline is essential if you want to surprise a big chub, as Graham here demonstrates. It may not be very comfortable, and casting may be awkward, but it's a great way to fish a small river if you want to explore its potential.***

▶ ***Legered lobworm can be a deadly bait, which accounts for specimens of many species. Today, unfortunately, only this small chub was interested.***

the hook into its tiny gob, he goes in search of a dace-free swim. Finally, near the end of the day-ticket stretch, he sees what he has been looking for...

7:30AM Chub city

The perfect swim – deeper water drifting gently up to a dam of debris, an eddy swirling around to the side and each end blocked by fallen trees – appears through the half light. "In good conditions I'd expect two or three big chub out of a swim like this. But they don't seem to want it today," Graham says, a little sadly.

Slowly the suspense builds. Graham casts as close to the raft of floating rubbish as he dares. No one breathes. Suddenly, there's a tap at the rod tip, and the mood collapses. More dace! The swim loses its magic and Graham seems resigned to taking dace.

Fishery facts

There are two day ticket stretches of the Dane, owned by Cotton Farm and Cotton Hall Farm. Buy your tickets on the way through them to the river.

The Dane rises and falls very rapidly, especially in winter, so check the levels on the day you want to fish it. The best times are often when the levels have dropped after a flood, leaving a tinge of colour, or the equivalent few hours as the waters are rising. If it's high, you're unlikely to catch.

" It's all about matching tactics to the day. If specimen techniques won't work, try the light line, match fishing approach – you must be flexible. "

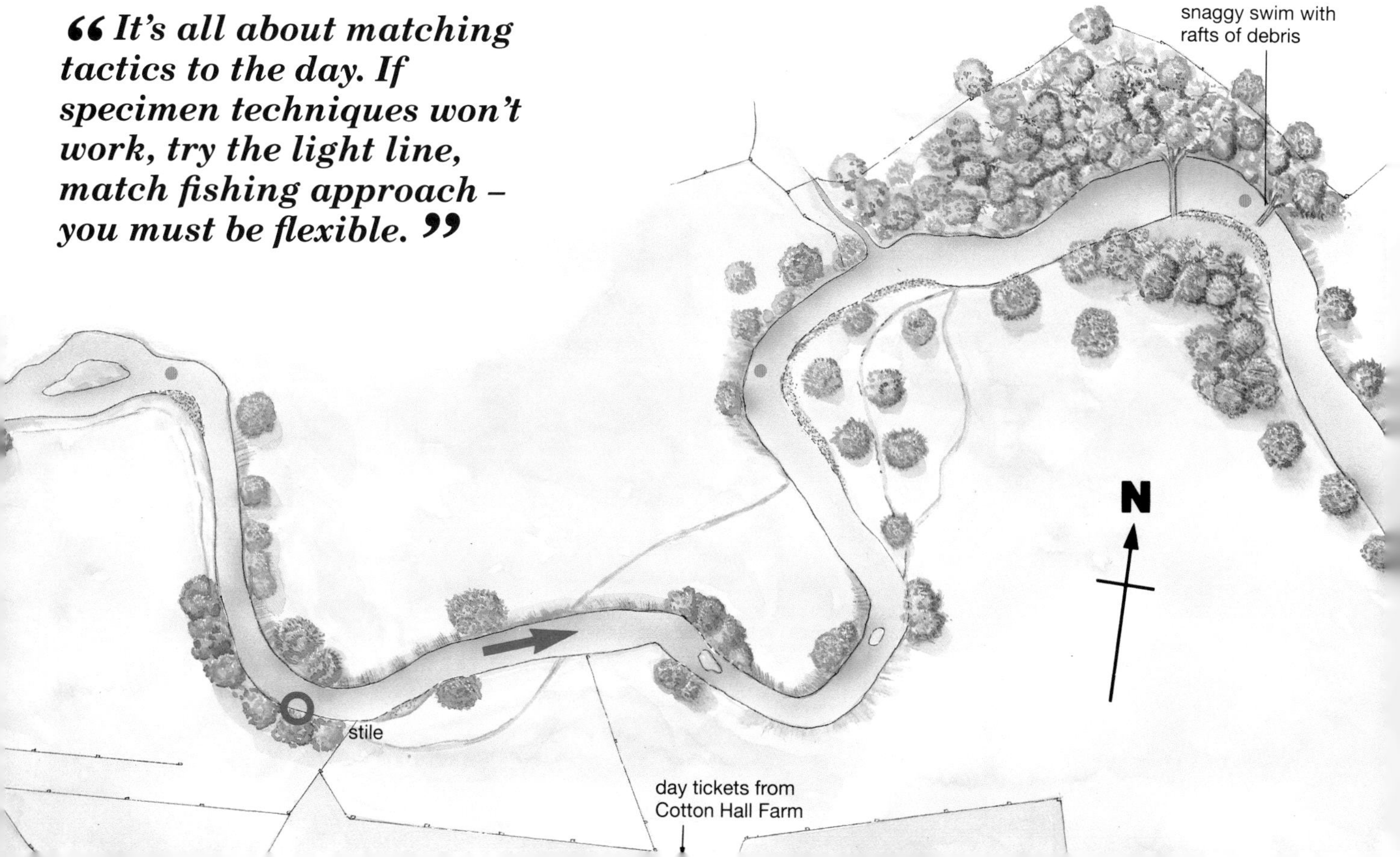

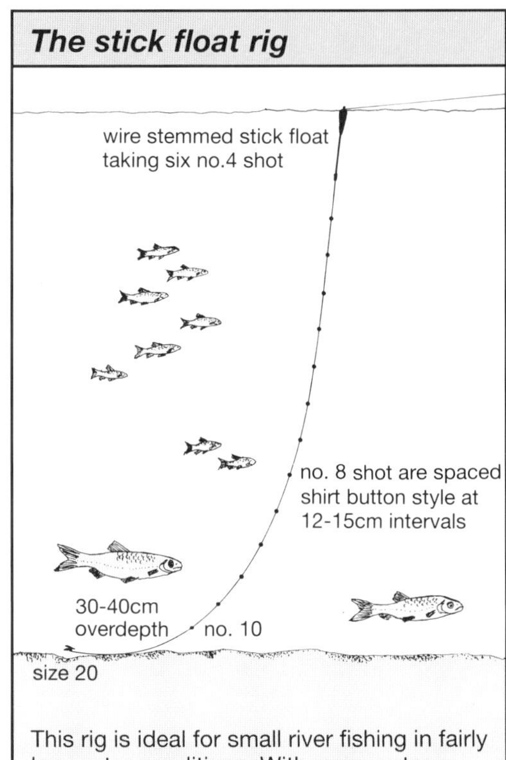

7:50AM Rethink

It's time to change tactics as the big fish techniques clearly aren't paying off. This river receives a lot of attention from pleasure anglers and practising matchmen so Graham decides to try the stick float with maggot hookbait. Fish can get very used to a regular free supply of maggot and caster, so they might just go for them when they won't take lobworm.

In the light of the early dawn, he can see that much of the colour has run off. Graham reckons this makes the fish even less likely to want a big bait, another reason for the change. It doesn't pay to carry too much gear when stalking, so it's back to the car for the float fishing tackle and keepnet.

Anglers have been arriving while Graham's been fishing, and all his favourite swims are full as he goes back for the other rod and his float gear. Returning upstream, of all the areas left available, only that tricky, rarely fished swim looks at all attractive, so Graham reluctantly sets up to fish it all over again.

▲ "You've got to keep a rhythm going. To cut down on feed, use less each time, don't feed less often." The throwing stick is a simple, one-handed operation.

8:15AM Match tactics

As Graham quietly sets up on a small patch of muddy ground, he feeds a couple of stickfuls of maggots. He's gone the whole hog, from specimen hunter to match angler, and he's using a wire-stemmed stick taking six no.6 shot, a 1½lb (0.7kg) hooklength and a fine wire, whisker barb size 20 hook.

He tosses the rig, with its cargo of double bronze maggot, out about one and a half rod lengths. Every time it nears the bottom end of the swim, he feeds about 15 maggots at the top end though he varies the amount according to how the fish are feeding.

Second run through, the float dips slightly. He strikes and he's into a decent

▶ There are loads of small dace like this in the Dane, which can be a problem if you're going for big chub, as they worry the bait.

The leger rig

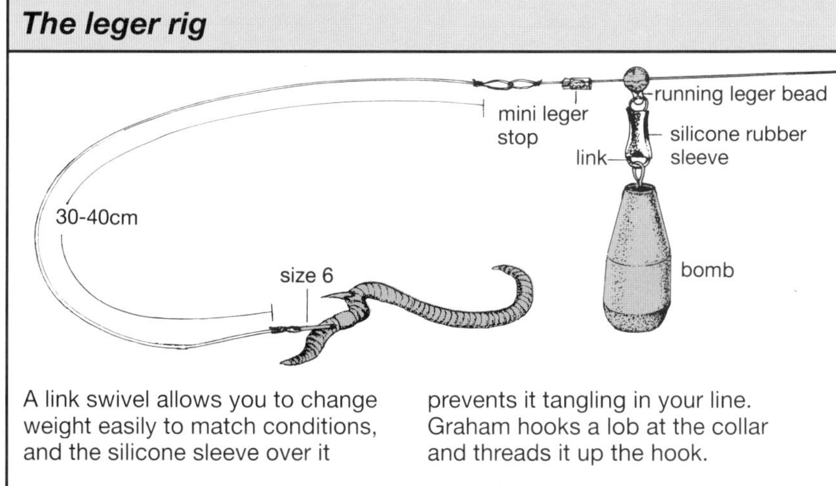

A link swivel allows you to change weight easily to match conditions, and the silicone sleeve over it prevents it tangling in your line. Graham hooks a lob at the collar and threads it up the hook.

dace of about ½lb (0.23kg), but he still isn't too hopeful of any chub. "If only I'd stopped at that big slow bend," he laments, "I'd have a sackful by now."

He trots the same line each time – the crease he was fishing with the leger – but in the light he can pick out some deeper water underneath. It's a sharp drop-off to about 1.8m (6ft) at 6m (20ft) out. This makes it doubly attractive to hungry fish.

8:25AM Lucky dip

Using the float has revealed another feature of the swim. The river bed rises slightly about 15m (50ft) downstream and to prevent the hook catching on the bottom (he's fishing slightly overdepth) Graham holds back so that the bait rides over the bump. Just as he does this for the fourth time, the float dips positively. Despite the trees which hinder striking, he makes contact with a much better fish.

On the lighter tackle he can't bully this fish into the net, and it's only his use of sidestrain that discourages it from seeking shelter in some exposed tree roots. There's not much room to run in this narrow river and for most of the tussle the fish bores, head down, into the deeper water. When it appears, Graham's well pleased with a chub of around 2 ½lb (1.1kg).

Next cast produces a roach of around 12oz (0.34kg) and then the swim comes alive. For the next hour or so, it's bites galore! The fish are really going for it, so he increases the feed. Most of the bites come at the same place – the bump where Graham has to hold back. As soon as the bait rises up in the current, the float dips.

▲ A nice chub makes a last ditch attempt to escape. This species fights very hard on light tackle.

► Treat all fish with care, especially when unhooking them, or they won't stay in good condition like this.

Maggot spin

Double maggot hooked 'head and tail' hang straighter and won't spin, twisting line, on the retrieve.

Tip Night chub

Chub are well-known evening feeders, especially when the water's clear, but they can also go wild at the other end of the day. In cold winter conditions, anything which helps with the catching of chub cannot be ignored.

Put a Betalight in a waggler adaptor whipped to the rod tip to show up bites at dawn and dusk.

◀A small dace comes to hand but there are some real whoppers in the Dane. Graham demonstrated this with a number of fish of about 10oz (0.28kg). Fish over 1lb (0.45kg) have been taken.

1:00PM "Waste of time..."

After lunch a swim right next to the motorway bridge becomes vacant when the angler fishing it gives up. He hasn't caught anything all day – "This swim's dead." Enter Graham Marsden, eyes aglow, brandishing float rod.

Within ten minutes he's taking dace, and some big specimens too – up to 10oz (0.28kg) – so the swim's not so dead after all. But there's no more chub to be had, even though he fishes through the dusk. As it begins to get dark, Graham packs up slowly – it's been a long day. The river waits peacefully for the dawn – and the beginning of the weekend hammering.

A check up on the other anglers who had fished the swims Graham wanted revealed one small barbel and one angler with two chub. Maybe the swim he chose wasn't so bad after all, or maybe he's just a very good angler who can adapt to suit the conditions.

10:00AM Happy dace

After two slightly larger chub and a smaller one, another roach of 12oz (0.34kg) and some nice dace up to 10oz (0.28kg), the bites become more finicky. Graham dots the float down further in an effort to make contact, but the bites he does connect with result in small dace.

On top of this, every time he feeds, these little fish are jumping out of the water – even though it's winter! The bait is also being taken on the drop under the rod tip by more of the tiny blighters. This leads to the inevitable conclusion that there aren't any big fish left here.

There is nowhere else he can go – every other half-decent swim is occupied, so he decides to leave this one alone for a bit.

10:30AM Pay-off

Half an hour later, Graham sends a couple of stickfuls of feed into the river, and follows it with the float down the crease. After two fruitless runs down, it disappears just as it reaches the shallower area. "I didn't even have to hold back for this one," says Graham bending into another good fish.

This one is content to sit in the main flow, and Graham doesn't have the line strength to budge it. For a few minutes it's stalemate, but finally the strain begins to tell on the fish and it moves downstream away from the irritating tugging at its mouth. The resistance doesn't last and Graham doesn't have too many more problems coaxing it into the net; indeed the chub seems glad of the rest. That really is it as far as fish from this swim are concerned, so Graham goes off to scout for another.

▶ The final net was over 18lb (8.2kg) of chub, roach and dace, most of it coming in the space of about two hours.

Peter Stone on the River Cherwell

River Cherwell chub grow large and fight hard. Peter Stone revisits some swims he last fished over ten years ago to see how they've changed.

◀ *Peter Stone chuckles at the thought of the chub he is going to tempt with this crusty bread. A renowned specimen hunter, Peter has been fooling big fish of all sorts for over forty years.*

As well as winkling out big chub from their lairs, he has fished for most coarse and sea species and loves catching big trout from fisheries.

▼ *First off, Peter sets up to fish a deep hole by a tree on the far bank, where he hopes the chub are waiting hungrily for his hookbait of crust...*

Mid February isn't exactly the most comfortable time of year to go fishing, particularly on a raw, blustery morning. But Peter Stone, respected specimen hunter and experienced all-round angler, is made of stern stuff, and if he says he'll catch winter chub from the Cherwell, then he will, come hell or high water.

After a few days of showers, the sun's making a brave attempt to beat the clouds but it looks as though it's going to be a pretty mixed up day. The rain means the river is up a touch on its usual winter level, but not enough to colour the water, and probably not enough to matter.

9:45AM *Well wrapped up*

It's certainly not a day for faint-hearts but Peter's well insulated against the cold and ready to go. Out comes a loaf of crusty white bread. "It's hard to beat crust for winter chub. Maggots are also good, because they use them in matches, so the chub are used to them. But with the water so clear I reckon we'll get 'em on crust."

Peter's rig is a simple link leger, with a piece of anti-tangle tubing on the link and a short (15cm/6in) hooklength of 5lb (2.3kg) double-strength line. He puts just enough swan shot on the link to hold bottom.

"If you stick a string of heavy shot on when you don't need to, you might put a

How to get there

- **By car** From Oxford take the Banbury Road (A4165) which becomes the A4260 after crossing the A40. Once through Kidlington, the Thrupp turning is on the right. Park by the canal. Cross the canal and Peter's swims are half a mile downstream.
- **By train** Oxford is the nearest BR station. Then take a Midland Red bus to the Thrupp turning or to Shipton-on-Cherwell.

River Cherwell
B4027
junction 9
M40
A4095
Woodstock
Thrupp
A34 (Bicester Road)
Kidlington
A4260
A44
River Ray
OXFORD
N
A34
A40

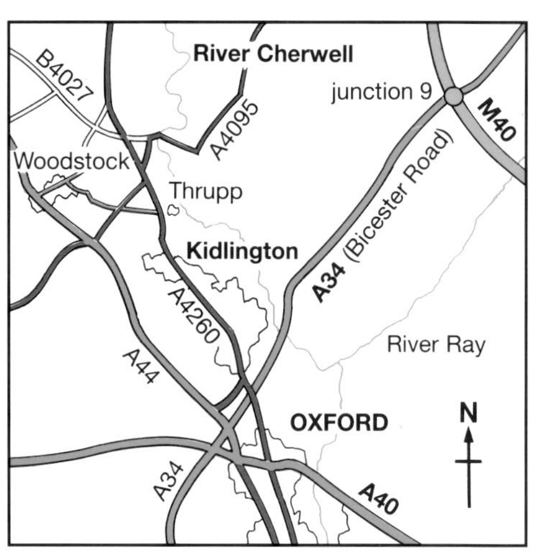

wily old chub off. I also like the bait to bump slowly around until it finds somewhere a little more sheltered – which is what the fish expect food to do, you see?"

Peter's using a quivertip rod with a ¾oz (21g) push-in quiver – ideal for legering rivers. At 11½ft (3.5m) long, it's useful for fishing the far bank. By holding the rod tip high, he can keep most of the line off the water and out of the main flow.

10:00AM Set up and fed

"I think I'll start here. My sources tell me that these two swims are the places they've been catching." He mixes up some extremely sloppy white crumb – it looks more like milk than feed – and squeezes it just hard enough to hold together to reach the far side of the river. He feeds a little upstream of his hookbait, so that both end up together on the river bed.

On days like this he feeds three handfuls every ten minutes or so, but if it's really cold, he cuts back on the feed.

"When I used to fish this stretch about twelve years back, it was full of four-pounders (1.8kg). But now the roach have come on, and I don't think we'll have much over 3lb (1.4kg) today, so that will have to be my target."

> ***"Don't be a one-fish angler. Try as many kinds of fishing as you can, stay flexible and you'll be a better angler for it."***

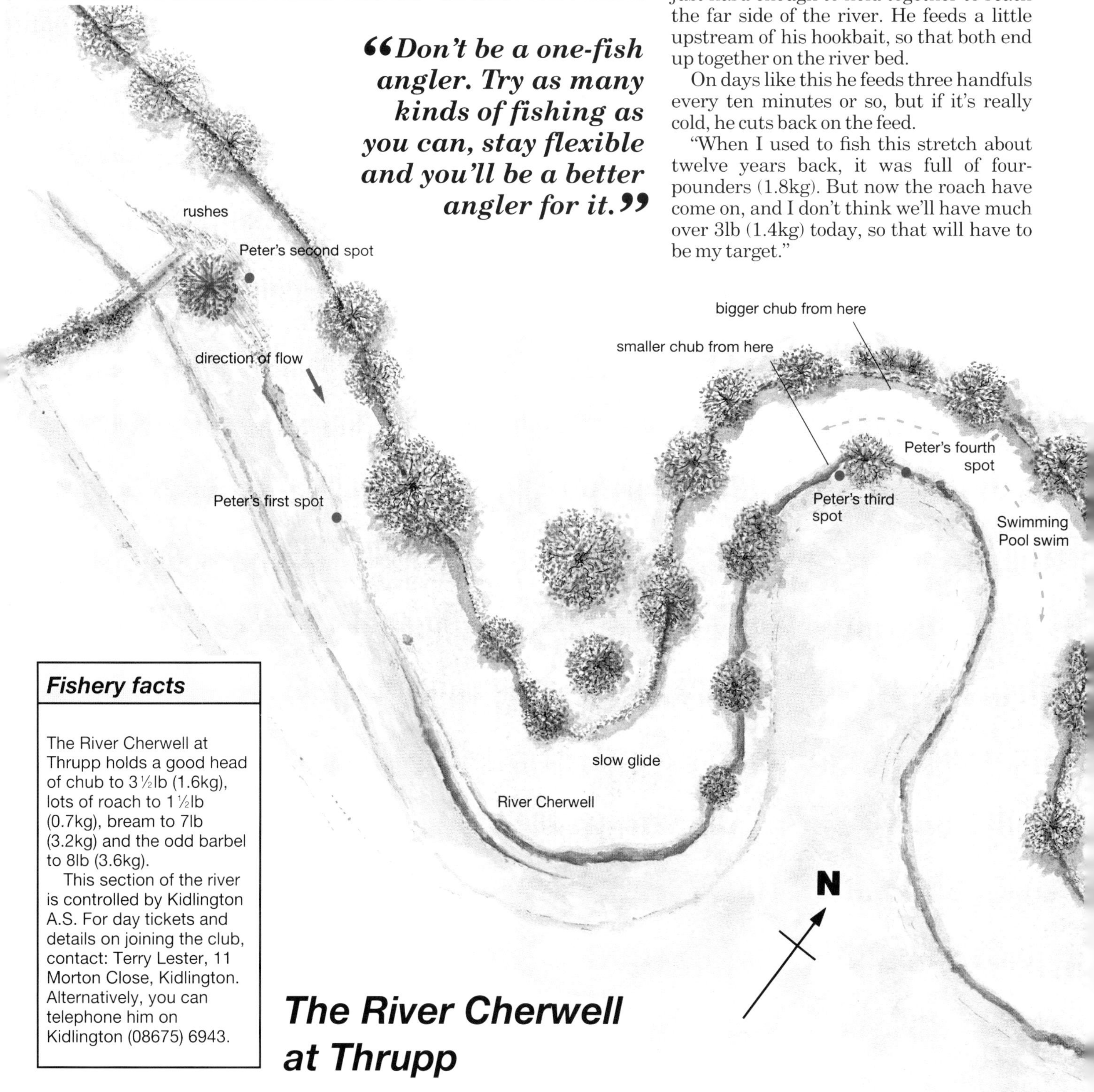

rushes
Peter's second spot
direction of flow
Peter's first spot
bigger chub from here
smaller chub from here
Peter's fourth spot
Peter's third spot
Swimming Pool swim
slow glide
River Cherwell
N

The River Cherwell at Thrupp

Fishery facts

The River Cherwell at Thrupp holds a good head of chub to 3½lb (1.6kg), lots of roach to 1½lb (0.7kg), bream to 7lb (3.2kg) and the odd barbel to 8lb (3.6kg).

This section of the river is controlled by Kidlington A.S. For day tickets and details on joining the club, contact: Terry Lester, 11 Morton Close, Kidlington. Alternatively, you can telephone him on Kidlington (08675) 6943.

He dips the crust to add casting weight and casts towards the white stain of groundbait drifting downstream by the far bank. His tip bounces around and a few seconds later he's bringing his gear back in. "I'll have to put another swan shot on, I think, if I want to hold bottom." Next cast, the bait slips into position in the current.

11:00AM Predictions

An hour later and Peter hasn't had a bite. "When I saw the river today, I thought I'd get two or three fish. I don't think that has changed. But I do think I shall have to try a different swim."

Peter moves upstream to fish under the bough of an overhanging tree. "When I used to fish here at this time of year, I caught a lot of fish in the Swimming Pool," he says, referring to a deep pool a short way downstream, not a top bathing spot. "But let's give these swims a proper try."

Three handfuls of sloppy crumb go into the far bank swim. The leger settles down and the line tightens in the flow, producing a nice curve in the quiver. Peter sits intent, holding the rod high, feeling the line and watching the tip with a beady eye. It's more work than putting the rod in rests, but it's the best way of keeping in touch with your bait and spotting slight indications.

Ten minutes pass, and Peter strikes to relieve the hook of its burden of crust – a curious chub investigating the crust might be more than a little surprised and put off to see it go whizzing past its nose as Peter retrieves. Besides, you never know... "I've had a few chub over the years from striking before the retrieve, and I never saw the slightest touch."

He hooks up another piece of crust and casts it back to the same place. A few fruitless casts later and lesser anglers might have stopped concentrating, but Peter's still intent on his quiver.

The tip yanks round and Peter strikes before he has time to say, "Now that was a proper bite," and "it's a good fish too." The rod bends and thumps as a chub's powerful

▲ Peter makes up a sloppy mix of crumb, though if the flow were faster he would make it stodgier to get through the current.

▼ After throwing in three handfuls of groundbait, Peter settles down and waits for his quivertip to pull round to a fish.

▲ After a biteless hour, Peter moves upstream to see if the elusive chub are sitting on the outside of the bend.

> **Tip Crust-phobia**
>
> Many anglers are afraid to fish bread because they think it falls off the hook. But this only happens when you use stale bread – the crust cracks and the flake is dry. Use only the freshest bread.

tail slaps the line – then straightens as the fish bumps off. "I don't believe it," says an amazed Peter. "I thought I had him good and proper."

But, as he explains, this is something that happens occasionally when you're fishing crust. With a fairly tough and bulky bait there's always a chance you won't hook them properly. Crust softens after a while in the water, so the problem is worst when you've just cast.

With the fish pricked and put down, he returns to his original swim, but the chub show no interest in either crust or his home-made cheese paste. Peter stands up and retrieves his tackle. "It looks like it's time to try the Swimming Pool then, doesn't it?"

NOON The Swimming Pool

The Swimming Pool is a lovely swim – a deep-water bend in the river, where the flow slows down, forming a big eddy on the inside of the bend. Peter fancies the eddy, where a bankside tree's roots make an ideal chub haunt, so he throws in a little crumb.

First off it's time to give the cheese paste another try. The rig's the same, though with a longer hooklength – about 30cm (12in). Peter drops the set-up into the edge of the eddy, and lets it find it's own stopping point on the gravel bottom.

Ten more minutes, and Peter changes back to crust. "In coloured water, cheese is often a killer, but when it's clear like today, I think crust usually does better."

Peter's rig for winter chub

15cm hooklength of 4lb b.s. (though it can be as short as 5cm when there is ice on the water)

small black swivel

black bead

small free-running black swivel

4lb main line

5cm length of thin silicone tubing to prevent tangles

size 8-10 medium wire hook

two swan shot

rough chunk of crust

push hook point into the crust, through the flake and back out of the crust so it ends up standing proud

leave some flake attached

A link leger is all you need to fish crust. Use a short hooklength as winter chub aren't inclined to chase a buoyant bait, such as crust, a long way off the bottom. With ice on the water, it should be only 5cm (2in) long. Cheese is not buoyant, so the hooklength can afford to be longer.

◀ ***Peter moves to the Swimming Pool swim and very soon his legered crust finds a hungry winter chub.***

▲ ***The duck is broken – after a brave, brief struggle the first chub gives in and submits to the net.***

Tip Slothful fish

Catching chub depends much more on water craft than on complicated rigs. Identify areas of cover in slower, deeper water, preferably with a gravel bottom. In winter, chub prefer to hang around such places where they don't have to expend as much energy as they do out in the main current.

▼ ***The first chub from the Swimming Pool swim is a 1½lb (0.7kg) fish which had holed up by some tree roots on the near bank.***

Sitting like a statue, Peter waits for a bite – fisherman at one with nature. This is the way he likes it. You've got to find the chub and then winkle them out with stealth and a well placed bait.

The quiver tip trembles and twitches. Peter strikes, but meets no resistance. "I think we've found them," he says. "But they're not being very definite." Next chuck he's proved right, as the pattern repeats itself. "I think I shall wait to see what they do with the bait this time."

The tip trembles and twitches. It twitches again, but Peter doesn't move. A second later, the fish gives a definite pull, with the tip moving about an inch (2.5cm). Peter strikes and the chub is on.

It bores for the sanctuary of the tree roots, and when it doesn't make it, it turns into the main current. But Peter's got the measure of it, and it isn't long before he steers a fine 1½lb (0.7kg) chub into the net.

"Well that's broken the duck. Let's get ourselves a big 'un now." A few photos and the chub is back in the water a couple of swims downstream, so it can't spook any other fish lurking in the same place.

12:30PM Shoaled up

Another piece of crust goes on, and Peter sits and waits for the next bite. He doesn't have to wait long. It follows exactly the same pattern – twitch, twitch, pull – and shortly after, a slightly larger 2lb (0.9kg) chub goes back downstream.

"Well I think we've got some smaller fish shoaled up in these roots. There may be a bigger one, but it's a real job getting through the littl'uns. I think I might try just under that bush over there."

The bush in question is on the far side of the pool in the main flow, and a lot more difficult to cast to. In goes the feed, then the crust hookbait. After a minute or so Peter retrieves his tackle. "I wasn't really happy with where I put that, and if you're not confident, you'd best do something so that you are." So saying he recasts slightly upstream of his position to the head of the deeper water.

That kind of accurate casting only comes with years of patient practice and quite a few brushes with branches, but it pays off now. The tip appears to do nothing but Peter strikes and bends into a fish. "I thought it was a bite, but I'm not sure how I knew. The tip almost moved..." Peter, who lives and dies by the maxim 'If in doubt, strike', proves his point. "It's a better fish too. It might even be the three I promised."

With the full force of the current to play with, the fish is not going to make life easy. Its first thought is to get under the bank, but it's never going to win that battle, so it settles instead for a rush downstream. Peter chuckles. "I'd be very surprised if this wasn't the one we were after. Very surprised indeed."

Out comes the net. In slides a tired chub, and Peter relaxes. On the bank he examines his prize. "Yes, this is what we've come for. I'd put this at about 3lb 4oz (1.5kg). Let's see, shall we?"

The scales are calibrated and Peter puts the fish in a wet sling. The needle wobbles and makes up its mind – 3lb 3oz (1.45kg). Not bad, not bad. "Twelve years ago that would have been an average fish. But these things come and go. There'll be fours in here again someday."

Peter fishes on, trying maggot and feeder, hoping for a big winter barbel, but only small perch and gudgeon oblige. An hour or so later, he decides to pack up, and who can blame him? He said he'd have two or three fish, topped by a three-pounder (1.4kg), and he has. The urge to prove himself right, and the creeping chill are incentive enough.

"You know, it's funny the way the Swimming Pool produced. I reckon that the water being just a shade up made all the fish drop back into the slower, deeper water. That's why there wasn't much in those first swims."

Whatever the reason, the River Cherwell has been kind. Okay, she hasn't yielded up one of her big winter barbel, or any of the fine roach. But we came for the chub, and Peter Stone and the Cherwell contrived to give them to us.

▲ After tempting another fish of 2lb (0.9kg) from the near bank, Peter casts under the bushes on the far bank – and it isn't long before he's into a good fish.

◄ ▼ With the fish landed, Peter weighs it (left). At 3lb 3oz (1.4kg) it's about the maximum size you might expect from this stretch of the Cherwell – so no wonder he looks pleased with it (below). The river used to hold bigger specimens, but recently the roach have increased in size and numbers, and have taken over from the chub.

Keeping a logbook

A detailed fishing diary helps improve your fishing and provides for hours of fireside reading pleasure, writes John Bailey.

Most top anglers keep logbooks to record their fishing adventures (their failures as well as their successes!). They know that taking the time and trouble to write up each trip improves their fishing by replacing reminiscence with fact. Logbooks are also great fun to read in years to come, sparking as they do so many memories.

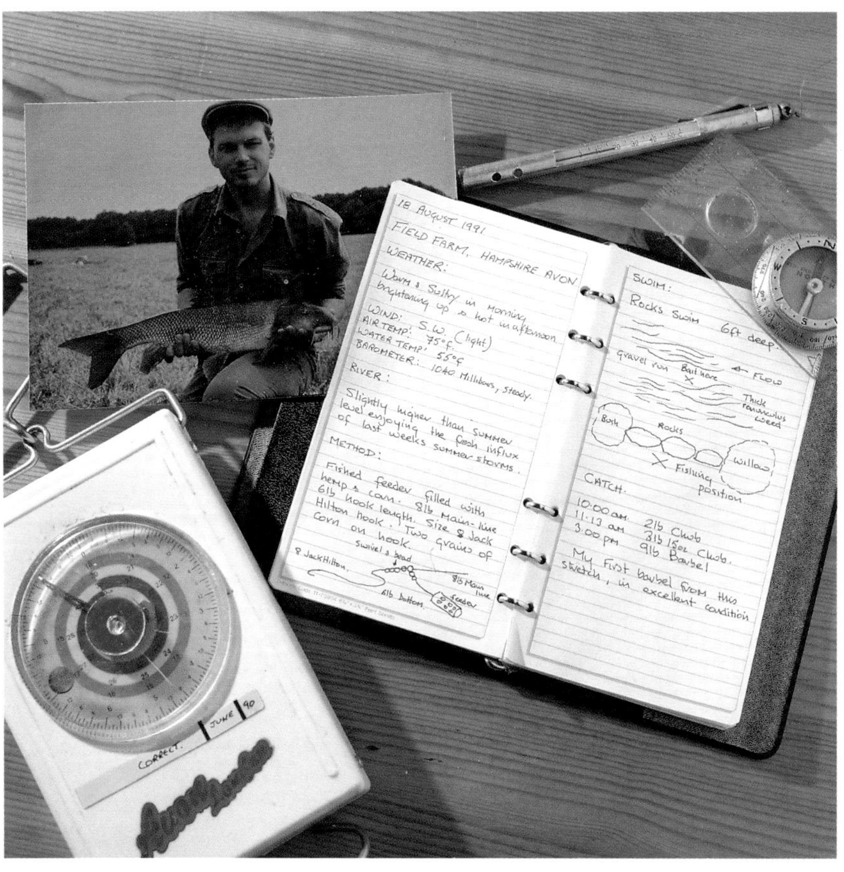

▲ *More than just a memory... Write up your fishing trips in a logbook, and in the future you will have great fun looking through it and recalling days both good and bad. The detailed information recorded is also an invaluable guide for your fishing.*

Scrapbook style

You can use any kind of notebook, but a very good one for the job is A4-size with nearly 200 ruled pages and a hard cover. It is long-lasting and has ample space to record a good number of sessions in great detail. It also has plenty of room for photographs, newspaper and magazine cuttings, letters, diagrams and so on.

The nitty-gritty

In your logbook you should record all the obvious facts: date and time you fished; venue; swim or swims fished; weather and water conditions; tackle, methods and baits used; and size and number of fish caught. Over a number of seasons you find that definite patterns do emerge.

Don't cut corners when recording these facts. Each one is an important piece in the overall puzzle and Sod's Law says that whatever you omit is bound to be crucial.

Bits and pieces

Useful items to take with you in your tackle box or bag are a thermometer, a compass and a photographer's light meter.

With a thermometer you can check water

◀ *When it's fine and you're out for a long session, why not take your logbook with you? You can then write up events (or the lack of them!) as they happen, and so record them as accurately as possible.*

Of course, if you're only out for an hour or two and the weather is atrocious, it's better to wait until you get back home.

The moon: sphere of influence

In the past few years," says John Bailey, "I have noted the phases of the moon in my logbooks.

"There is a strong belief among anglers on the Continent that the phases of the moon have a big influence on the feeding habits of fish, and my own logbooks are beginning to suggest that new and full moons are periods of peak potential for fishing."

▲▶ *Changes in water temperature can have a critical influence on whether fish feed, especially in winter.*

Basically, if the water is getting warmer, you can hope to catch – while if it's getting colder, you are likely to blank.

and air temperatures. Take regular readings so you can relate success or failure to rising or falling temperatures. Get a good quality thermometer – either an electronic one, or a glass one in a protective metal casing on a length of strong cord.

A compass lets you record wind direction accurately. Again, take regular readings so you can note any changes and relate them to fishing success or failure.

A light meter lets you check light values accurately. As with temperatures, slight changes can be critical to success. Be sure to point it at the same object each time.

A barometer is another useful item to have – at home, this time. Note the air pressure before you set out and when you get back. You can then relate your catches to high or low and falling or rising pressure.

Colour it out

You could just leave it at that, but you'll enjoy looking through your logbook so much more if you also note all the interesting, if not necessarily 'important', events of the day. Conversations on the bank, wildlife observed, amusing incidents – these are the kinds of things that bring a logbook to life and make it really enjoyable to read.

▼*A budding John Bailey does battle with a big eel on a fine summer's day. It's moments like this you'll enjoy reliving when browsing through your logbook in the close season... unless you don't make the effort to keep a logbook, of course!*

Index

Page numbers in *italics* refer to illustrations

ACKNOWLEDGEMENTS
Photographs: Stewart Allum 99(b); John Bailey 6, 10(c), 13(r); Bruno Broughton 92(b); Jon Culley 12(b); Eaglemoss (Eric Crichton) 119-124, 126(t), (Ian Christy) 55(t), (Ben Eveling) 82(t), (Adam Frost) 81(b), 82(b); (Peter Gathercole) 37-42; (Neil Holmes) 53(b), 70(b), 83-88, 93-98, 103-108, (Bob James) 63-68; (Dennis Linley) 17-22, 113-118, (Patrick Llewelyn-Davies) 79, 101, (Bill Meadows) 73-78, (Mike Millman) 24(b), 25, (Martin Norris) 35(l), (Steve Tanner) 10(t,b), 11, 12(t), (Gordon Thompson) 57-62, (Stuart Windsor) 27-32, 45(t), 46(t), 47-52, 71(t); Jim Gibbinson 69, 70(t), 71(b); Len Gurd 3; Trevor Housby 91, 99(t); Bob James 23(t); Dennis Linley 46(b), 53(t); Graham Marsden 15(t), 16(b), 36(tl), 80, 81(t), 100; Mike Millman 112(t); Natural Science 13(bl), 16(t), 102, 110(b), 111(t,bl), 126(b); Andy Orme 55(b); Kevin Smith 13(tl), 23(b), 24(t), 33, 36(tr), 44, 45(b), 109(r), 110(t), 111(br), 112(b), 125; John Watson 15(b), 26(b), 72, 89(r), 90(t), 92(t); Ken Whitehead 26(t); John Wilson 9, 14, 34, 35(r), 36(b), 43, 54, 56, 89(l), 90(b), 109(l).

Illustrations: Peter Bull 48-49, 84-85; Robert Cook 28-29; Frazer Hudson 120; John Ridyard 94-95; Ann Winterbotham 38-39, 64-65, 75, 88, 104-105, 114-115.